W9-CLY-436

DIS̶C̶A̶R̶D̶

STRAIGHTS

А 31,85

Straights

DISCARDED

Heterosexuality in Post-Closeted Culture

James Joseph Dean

NEW YORK UNIVERSITY PRESS

New York and London

Shelton State Libraries
Shelton State Community College

NEW YORK UNIVERSITY PRESS
New York and London
www.nyupress.org

© 2014 by New York University
All rights reserved

References to Internet websites (URLs) were accurate at the time of writing.
Neither the author nor New York University Press is responsible for URLs that
may have expired or changed since the manuscript was prepared.

Library of Congress Cataloging-in-Publication Data

Dean, James Joseph.
Straights : heterosexuality in post-closeted culture / James Joseph Dean.
pages cm
Includes bibliographical references and index.
ISBN 978-0-8147-6275-2 (hardback) — ISBN 978-0-8147-6459-6 (pb)
1. Heterosexuality—United States. 2. Sexual orientation—United States. 3. Sex—United
States. I. Title.
HQ72.8.D43 2014
306.76—dc23
                                    2014006073

New York University Press books are printed on acid-free paper,
and their binding materials are chosen for strength and durability.
We strive to use environmentally responsible suppliers and materials
to the greatest extent possible in publishing our books.

Manufactured in the United States of America
10 9 8 7 6 5 4 3 2 1

Also available as an ebook

To my mother, father, and brother,
with love and in acknowledgment of our bonds

CONTENTS

ACKNOWLEDGMENTS

First of all, I thank Steve Seidman for being a great intellectual role model. I am grateful for finding such an amazing teacher whom I also call my friend. I thank my mother, Rita Ramirez, for listening to my ideas and for her intellect and belief in me, my father, John, for his passion, directness, and ability as a coach to be heard across a court to play defense, and my brother, Gene, for our shared friendship and mutual admiration.

I am lucky to say that I'm blessed by the richness of my friendships, and for that I have many people to acknowledge. For their friendship, aid in my growth, or advice regarding this study, I thank the following: Dalia Abdel-Hady, the late Chet Meeks, Jennifer Gunsaullus, Amy Lutz, Marcia Hernandez, Mounah Abdel Samad, Shawn Flanigan, Kristin Stainbrook, C. J. Pascoe, Tariq Islam, Sarah Sobieraj, Heather Laube, Evan Cooper, Harry Pearce, Deirdre Oakley, Elena Vesselinov, Gayle Sulik, Jannette Swanson, Edelmira Reynoso, Karen Tejada, and Juan Esteva.

Other friends who maintained my spirits include Lance Elhers, Craig Persiko, Bob Barkowski, Regina Keenan, Huey Merchant, Ynolde Smith, Paul Ciavardoni, Andy Ruby, Kevin Dowd, Belinda DeLeon, Sandra Lutz, Thao Tran, Kimberly Schaffer, and Mark Thompson. My gratitude also goes to Kathy Vila for returning to me things that I had lost and for her wisdom over the years.

I need to express my appreciation to other scholars who guided me at the start. I thank Glenna Spitze for reading multiple drafts of my work over the years. Her insight, kindness, and intellectual support have been part of my good fortune, first in having her on my committee, and then in continuing our relationship into my professional life. Chris Bose's support, close reading of my work, and consideration were greatly appreciated. And I thank Ron Jacobs for his empathetic advice and support, and for being a true believer and model of a dynamic sociology.

Many other scholars and friends have read my work and were incredibly generous with their time and insight. I thank Leila Rupp for her extensive comments and sage advice in revising my historical chapter. I am very much grateful to Nancy Fischer for her keen insight and rigorous feedback on my work. I especially thank Andy Roth for reading my work and providing penetrating analyses of it. It was always a pleasure to read Andy's reviews, which were teeming with insight and critical support. Josh Gamson provided early feedback on a rough draft of the material on straight men. Thanks, Josh, for pointing me in the right direction. I thank Eric Anderson for his reading of my later article on straight men. As the culture editor of *Sociology Compass*, Arlene Stein asked me to publish from this project. Thank you, Arlene. I thank Linda Nicholson for giving me advice, recommending readings, and connecting me to Andrea Friedman. Andrea Friedman deserves special recognition for helping me find my way through the historiographical research on heterosexual women. I am grateful for that amazing bibliography. I thank Hui-shen Tsao for her help with the demographic data and information. Finally, I thank Erik Balsley for reading and commenting on my work as well as for creating a map and graphs for this book.

I am pleased to thank my editor, Ilene Kalish, for her support of the book from the beginning and her editorial eye toward revising it at the end. I appreciate the assistance of Caelyn Cobb at New York University Press in getting the book together. Thanks, Caelyn. The production process was expeditiously handled by the managing editor, Dorothea S. Halliday. Thanks, Dorothea. And I thank Rosalie Morales Kearns for her excellent copyediting of the manuscript. My gratitude also goes to the anonymous reviewers whose detailed evaluations helped me to improve the project and make this a better book.

Others who helped me bring my work to appreciative audiences include Amy Lutz and the Department of Sociology at Syracuse University as well as Nan Alamilla Boyd and the Queer Studies Lecture Series at Sonoma State University (SSU). Additionally, I thank Peter Nardi for inviting me to talk about my work at Pitzer College, the audience at the University of the Pacific, particularly Marcia Hernandez, and the audience of students, staff, and faculty at Pittsburg State University, particularly David Adams.

Colleagues who provided an encouraging environment for my work at Sonoma State University include Kathy Charmaz and the Faculty Writing Group she leads at SSU, Melinda Milligan, Robert McNamara, Peter Phillips, Sheila Katz, Cindy Stearns, Myrna Goodman, Heather Smith, Richard Senghas, Matthew Paloucci Callahan, Laura Nauman, Diana Grant, Jean Wasp, and Elaine Wellin. I single out Dean Elaine Leeder for her annual summer grant and the Brown Bag Lunch Series in the School of Social Sciences, both of which nourished my work over the years. And I am pleased to acknowledge Paula Hammett and her bibliographic assistance.

I owe a debt of gratitude to my past employers at Policy Research Associates, especially Pam Robbins, and the staff at Outreach and Education in the Department of Health, especially Faith Schottenfeld, the late Charlene Spaminato, and Shannon Ryan. In addition, I thank Vanessa Franklin for her assistance.

Shannon Wiseman, Tate Brown, and Nick Ramirez provided excellent research assistance. I warmly thank Nicole Bettencourt for preparing a draft of the bibliography and a draft of the index. And I appreciate Cary Escovedo's hard work in completing the index and checking the bibliographic references. Thanks, Cary.

Portions of chapters 1 and 3 appeared in a journal article published in the *Sociological Quarterly* 54 (Fall 2013). I am grateful to the publishers and editors of the journal for their permission to draw on this previously published material.

Lastly, I am grateful to the men and women who shared their experiences and stories with me during the interview process. Final responsibility for this work is my own.

Introduction

My white straight younger brother, Gene, graduated from college and started living with a black gay male friend after graduation.[1] His friend was dark-skinned with dreadlocks, and had a jovial but conventionally masculine demeanor that most people, including my mother, took to be indicative of a straight identity. However, one day when I was on the phone with my mother, she expressed her surprise after Gene informed her that his roommate was gay. She had never before questioned his roommate's sexuality and assumed he was straight upon meeting him. I think the discovery that my straight brother was living with a gay roommate also made her worry—was her only other son "turning" gay? I think that my mother, like a lot of people, was surprised to learn that a masculine black male was gay; equally surprising was that he was living with a straight male.

This book is about straight individuals like my brother and mother. It is about how straight individuals like my brother let others know they're straight even though they might have close gay friends. And it is about how race and gender shape and change the meaning of being straight (and nonstraight) for black and white men and women today.[2]

Of course, not every straight guy would be willing to live with an openly gay male. And many straight men and women are still homophobic. America today, however, is not the America of 1980 (the year my brother was born). Between then and now, significant changes have occurred in the status of gay and lesbian lives, from the increasing enfranchisement of gay and lesbian legal rights on local, state, and federal levels to the unprecedented proliferation of lesbian, gay, bisexual, transgender, and queer (LGBTQ) images in popular culture. Heterosexuality itself has also changed significantly over the last three decades. Although straight identities are still normative, and the norm of heterosexuality remains structurally dominant in every institution— from the family and mass media to religion and the government—sexualities scholars nonetheless highlight the increasing visibility and growing inclusivity, although uneven and unequal, of gays and lesbians in everyday life and across the nation's major social institutions.

In post-closeted cultural contexts, straights can neither assume the invisibility of gays and lesbians, nor count on others to always assume their heterosexuality. In this context, straights also cannot assume that other straights are homophobic or intolerant of gays and lesbians. That is, gay and lesbian tolerance and acceptance are conditioned by the development and increasing growth of straights' antihomophobic practices.

Although I use my study to map a continuum of homophobic and antihomophobic practices, I claim that a post-closeted cultural dynamic, which I define as the presence of openly gay and lesbian individuals and representations of them, is increasingly common in core areas of social life. Utilizing candid in-depth interviews with sixty black and white straight men and women, I argue that a post-closeted cultural dynamic in the United States is shaping and changing black and white straight men's and women's identities, the normative status of heterosexuality, and homophobic practices today.

Consequently, I explore how straights fashion boundaries between heterosexuality and homosexuality in order to create and secure a privileged straight identity. Straight identities are socially constructed processes that each individual accomplishes through negotiating a diverse array of everyday social situations. For example, straight individuals might talk about individual men or women they find attractive. They might display pictures of their spouse and children on their desks at work; or they might wear wedding rings to signal their marital status, which, until the 2003 Massachusetts State Supreme Court case legalizing same-sex marriages, would have been a civil right reserved only for straights.

Sociologically, straight identity practices are significant to the extent that core parts of an individual's social life—work, family, and friendships—are organized by this master identity category. I argue that straight masculinities and straight femininities are always and already refracted through a racial lens. We need to talk about the racial shaping of straight masculinities and femininities through sexual and gender identity practices, on one hand, and through practices of homophobic (and antihomophobic) social distance and exclusion that straights draw (or don't draw) between themselves and gays and lesbians, on the other. In short, I examine the social construction of black and white straight masculinities and femininities in the context of the rise of a post-closeted culture.

To understand the overall historical developments and social shifts in straight identities, I draw on two types of data. First, I analyze the historical research on the establishment of straight identities over the course of the late nineteenth and twentieth centuries. Historians have documented how sexual identities became increasingly distinct from gender identities in America over the course of the twentieth century, but they have also observed the centrality of gender dynamics in the establishment of sexualities. Using this historical research, I sketch the social and historical conditions that gave rise to the Stonewall generation of out gay men and lesbians in the late 1960s and 1970s. This historical framework provides the basis for my understanding of the current period in heterosexual and homosexual relations and the beginning of the development of a post-closeted culture. Second, and more importantly, I have spoken to black and white straight men and women about their everyday sense of themselves as straight, asking them to define what their straight identities meant to them. Through a semistructured, in-depth interview schedule, I examined the following four key facets of straight identities in a post-closeted culture: (1) descriptions and stories of the everyday enactment of straight identity practices; (2) the relationship of their racial and gendered identities to their straight identity practices; (3) their thoughts on out and visible lesbian and gay people in their lives and in popular culture; and (4) changes and shifts in homophobic and antihomophobic practices during their lifetime. During the interviews, I used the terms "gay" and "homosexual" interchangeably as well as "heterosexual" and "straight" interchangeably, and I have maintained that usage throughout this book as well.

I used a series of open-ended questions to address these four facets in the interviews. The first explored the socially constructed character of straight identities. I asked questions to gauge how the interviewee decided whether someone he or she interacted with was straight or gay, and what kinds of social cues the interviewee used to let others know his or her sexual identity. The next series of questions focused on how gender and race shaped straight identities. For example, I asked what kinds of sexual stereotypes black straight men and women have experienced in interacting with others. The third series looked at how the straight respondent has reacted to gays and lesbians coming out to him or her, and how he or she has responded to gay visibility in popular culture. The fourth series delved into how the individual perceived homophobic and antihomophobic practices in everyday life.

Although my small sample is not a cross-section of straight Americans, it includes straight men and women from diverse racial, class, occupational, and religious backgrounds. And as sociologists who make interviewing methods central to their empirical work note, in-depth interviews are good for capturing the breadth of identities and the range of an identity's social practices (Lamont 2000). Still, this study is based on a non-random sample and is limited by its lack of generalizability beyond the reported interviews (Burawoy et al. 1991; Charmaz 2007). Although these interviews emphasize conceptual themes over representativeness, I situate these themes within the quantitative social science research that examines trends of growing homosexual tolerance and acceptance and the broader social changes in gender arrangements, family pathways, and economic structures of the last half of the twentieth century and the first decades of the twenty-first century (e.g., Laumann et al. 1994; Loftus 2001).

The straight individuals I interviewed shared a general set of understandings about their straight identities, so that toward the end of my research, I could often anticipate what they were going to say before they actually said it. This indicated that I had captured central themes in the social construction of black and white straight masculinities and femininities (Glaser and Strauss 1967; Charmaz 2007). Finally, the historical research I analyzed and the interview narratives I collected overlapped in their themes and patterns, indicating a good fit between my sociological study and the historiographical work.

Defining the Concept of a Post-Closeted Culture

The sociological value of the concept of a post-closeted culture needs to be understood in relation to the term that it seeks to qualify and bracket:

the closet. This notion, if it is to have more than rhetorical value, refers to a specific social-historical condition in which a regime of compulsory heterosexuality imposed patterns of passing and a double life upon the vast majority of individuals for whom same-sex desire was salient. Under conditions of the closet, same-sex desire was rendered a core, primary social identity of an oppressed minority, while other-sex desire assumed the taken-for-granted normative status of the vast majority of Americans. The rise of the closet as a national formation is often dated to the 1930s, and it continued to develop over the 1940s and 1950s (Chauncey 1994, 2004; D'Emilio 1983; Eskridge 1999; Faderman 1991; Seidman 2002). Ironically, scholars argue that the conditions of compulsory heterosexuality and the closet also gave birth to a collective, political gay and lesbian movement (Adam 1995; D'Emilio 1983; Epstein 1999; Faderman 1991). During the 1950s, the first homosexual or homophile organizations developed in some major urban centers in America. These organizations sought to "purify" the homosexual self by projecting an emphatic sense as a normal and highly conventional American (Adam 1995; D'Emilio 1983; Epstein 1999; Faderman 1991). In subsequent decades, state-sanctioned homosexual repression, along with medical and popular cultural politics, enforced compulsory heterosexuality and the closet, while also enforcing rigidly conventional masculine and feminine identities (Adam 1995; Bérubé 1990; Chauncey 1994; Eskridge 1999; Ehrenreich 1983; Faderman 1991; Rich [1980] 1993).

Following historians who argue that the decades from the 1960s to the 1990s witnessed the dismantling of the closet and many of the discriminatory measures put in place during the three previous decades (Chauncey 2004, 2008; D'Emilio 1983, 2002; D'Emilio and Freedman 2012), I suggest that there is a plausible case to be made for the declining significance of the closet in American life since at least the mid-1990s. To be sure, this declining significance is more evident in urban spaces and urbane circles, in the professions and in bureaucratic, globally oriented institutions, in formal public cultures, in some regions of the United States more than others, and so on (Barton 2012; Eskridge 1999; Gamson 2002; Ghaziani 2011; Raeburn 2004; Seidman 2002; Stein 2010; Walters 2001; Weeks 2007). Still, the notion of a post-closeted cultural dynamic aims to capture real shifts in American sexual and gender patterns, such as the institutional incorporation and cultural legitimation of "normalized" gay men and lesbians and their expanded latitude in negotiating desire, gender, and identity. Normalization suggests an ambiguous process. On the one hand, it refers to the acquisition of a moral status as a person or ordinary human deserving of respect, rights, and integration. On the other hand, it reserves this moral status only for individuals who display decidedly culturally specific traits and behaviors such as gender normativity, economic individualism, a couple-centered, family-oriented intimacy, and conventional attitudes more generally.

I believe that the concept of a post-closeted culture is useful in exploring changes in sexual identities and relationships both between and among gay and straight Americans. Two historical periods stand out in the rise of a post-closeted dynamic as a national formation. First, the Stonewall riots of 1969 signal the rise of the politics of coming out of the closet and the development of large, visible gay and lesbian communities and institutions throughout the country (Armstrong 2002; Chauncey 2004; Epstein 1999). For example, in chronicling gay and lesbian movements in the United States at this time, historians have found a rapid proliferation of gay organizations, such as newspapers, crisis hotlines, and social clubs, which increased from just fifty in 1969 to more than a thousand in 1973 (Epstein 1999). The normalization of homosexuality and Americans' liberalization toward homosexuals are then social-historical developments conditioned by the subcultural growth signaled by the Stonewall riots of 1969 and the newly minted gay and lesbian politics of coming out to straight society, not just to other gays (D'Emilio 1983; Epstein 1999).

Second, the mid-1990s represent a period of newfound mass media visibility and significant social and political gains, from the development and spread of domestic partner benefits and antidiscrimination laws to significant attitudinal shifts among Americans toward tolerance and acceptance of gays as never seen before (Loftus 2001; Hicks and Lee 2006). Polling data confirm that the liberalizing of attitudes toward gays and lesbians is a clear trend among Americans over the last four decades. For instance, as shown in figure I.1, in 1999, 50 percent of Americans stated that lesbian and gay relationships between consenting adults should be legal, and by 2013 the percentage of support had increased by 14 percent to 64 percent (Gallup 1977–2013).[3]

Similarly, as shown in figure I.2, when Americans were asked whether lesbians' and gay men's marriages "should or should not be recognized by the law as valid," 27 percent of Americans supported same-sex marital rights in 1996. By 2013, support for same-sex marriages rose to 54 percent, the highest it has been in recent time, showing that a small majority of Americans now embrace the recognition of gay marital rights (Gallup 1996–2013). It is clear from the polling data that Americans in general have become increasingly supportive of lesbians' and gays' legal rights since the mid- to late 1990s.

Do you think gay or lesbian relations between consenting adults should or should not be legal?

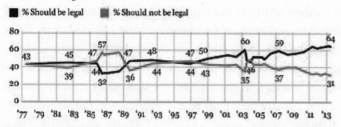

1977–2008 wording: Do you think homosexual relations between consenting adults should or should not be legal?

Figure I.1. Source: Gallup polling data, 1977–2008. Copyright © 2013 Gallup, Inc. All rights reserved. The content is used with permission; however, Gallup retains all rights of republication.

Do you think marriages between same-sex couples should or should not be recognized by the law as valid, with the same rights as traditional marriages?

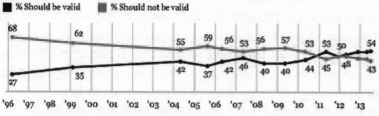

Note: Trend shown for polls in which same-sex marriage question followed questions on gay/lesbian rights and relations

1996–2005 wording: "Do you think marriages between homosexuals . . ."

Figure I.2. Source: Gallup polling data, 1996–2005. Copyright © 2013 Gallup, Inc. All rights reserved. The content is used with permission; however, Gallup retains all rights of republication.

Economic and Other Broad Social
Changes in American Society

Alongside the rise of a post-closeted culture, we have seen broad changes in American society over the course of the last several decades, including the reorganization of the economy, the development of second-wave feminism, and the accompanying transformation of gender relations and women's social statuses, as well as dramatic changes in family life. Scholars now talk of living in a postmodern society, where economics, gender, and family relations are flexible and performative, involving a diversity of pathways and arrangements (Butler 1990; Castells 1996; Gerson 2010; Harvey 1990; Stacey 1996, 1998).

Before the industrial revolution in America, the economic existence of most men and women was based on the private family farm. With the rise of the industrial factory in the nineteenth century, the number of individuals working in agriculture dramatically declined while the number of workers in manufacturing industries rose in almost direct proportion. Mostly men worked in factories, and they were increasingly paid a "breadwinner" wage to support a wife and family. These male factory workers replaced the family farmers of the past who owned their own land and required the collective work of a wife and on average six to eight children to maintain it (Eitzen, Zinn, and Smith 2012; Hochschild and Machung [1989] 2012, 237).

By 1950, manufacturing jobs as a proportion of total private-sector jobs were 35 percent of the economy. Today, however, manufacturing employment constitutes less than 13 percent of the total jobs in the United States. Over roughly the last forty years, a postindustrial economy, based in new technologies (computers and electronic devices, the Internet, fiber optics, biotechnology, and cellular telephony) and knowledge (witnessed by the growing necessity and value of undergraduate and graduate credentials), along with an increasingly large service sector to attend to these new and old professions (e.g., teachers, doctors, and lawyers), has replaced the older manufacturing-based economy (Bourdieu 1984; Eitzen, Zinn, and Smith 2012, 186).

Women have been and are still at the center of the changes in the economy and society's shift from an industrial to a postindustrial organization. Since the 1950s women have been increasingly likely to work outside the home, but significant increases in the number of college-educated women and the rise of second-wave feminism in the 1960s and 1970s made this trend permanent, and women's participation in the workforce surged to new levels in the following decades (Nicholson 1986, 2008). For example, in 1950, 30 percent of women were in the workforce. By 2011, 59 percent of women were engaged in paid work (Hochschild and Machung [1989] 2012, 2). However, the service sector jobs of many women, such as administrative positions, health aide roles, and day care staff, pay less but are more reliable forms of employment than those of their "male" blue-collar job counterparts (Eitzen, Zinn, and Smith 2012, 187; Hochschild and Machung [1989] 2012, 265).

Women's working has been a major shift in the postindustrial economy, but it has just as greatly changed the pathways and arrangements of family life. As more women started to work, they became less dependent on men's "breadwinner" wage in marriages. Moreover, if these women found themselves unhappy in their marriages, they could divorce, as their paid work conditioned their ability to support themselves and their children without their husbands' income. The family sociologist Andrew Cherlin (2009) notes that between 1960 and 1980, the divorce rate doubled. Over the last several decades, divorce rates have ranged between 40 and 50 percent. Still, even in this era of divorce, marriage rates remain high, with almost 90 percent of Americans projected to marry at some point (Cherlin 2009, 7, 4).

While marriage has declined as the predominant family arrangement, cohabitation has grown, and it was the "major source of change in living arrangements in the 1980s and 1990s" (Cherlin 2009, 98). Cohabitation in America, though, leads to either a marriage or a breakup. Unlike cohabitation in many European countries, cohabitation in the United States is not a patterned stepping-stone to a long-term relationship outside the institution of marriage. Although young Americans are still more likely to cohabit, cohabiting couples range from the college-educated to those without high school diplomas to couples living with and without children (Cherlin 2009).

Heterosexual men's roles as husbands and fathers have also nominally changed due to heterosexual women's economic advancements and the attendant demands by their wives that the men do more at home (Ridgeway 2011). Studies show that fathers are now more involved with their children, but mothers still "spend about twice as many hours caring for children as men do," and although women do less housework than in past generations, they still do "twice the housework that men do" (Ridgeway 2011, 128).

Non–college-educated heterosexual men, though, face tougher economic and marital predicaments. These working-class men are hard-pressed to find jobs and potential wives in the current economy. Jobs as welders, machinists, or auto assembly linemen—highly desirable "male" blue-collar jobs—have been adversely impacted by offshoring, automation, and the Great Recession of 2008, making these jobs less reliable sources for long-term employment (Hochschild and Machung [1989] 2012, 265). On the marital front, then, as steady employment remains a mainstay of desirability for marriage, working-class men make less attractive marital partners, and cohabitation thus becomes a more likely prospect for anxious straight couples worried about financial stability. "A cohabiting relationship may be all a young man with a low-paying or temporary job can aspire to, or all that he can find a partner to agree to," notes Cherlin (2009, 98).

In this context of the decline of lifetime marriages and persistently high divorce rates, along with the increasing "preference" for cohabitation among straight men and women, it is important to remember that medical scientific developments (e.g., the birth control pill, in vitro fertilization, alternative insemination, and other pharmaceutical drugs like the "morning after" pill) in relation to the promulgation of the socio-legal concept of the right to privacy made it possible for women to separate and unlink their gender identities from their sex lives, marriages, and childbearing choices. For example, before the rise of the birth control pill in 1960, women who became pregnant generally ended up marrying the father of their child (Cherlin 2009, 185–86). However, as an individualistic culture of sex as a private matter developed in American culture, and with the backing of three watershed US Supreme Court cases on reproductive rights and sexual intimacy, rights to privacy as both the right "to be let alone" and the right to "decisional privacy" over one's personal and intimate identity and life choices are now protected (Cohen 2002, 25–26).

The first ruling occurred in 1965. In *Griswold v. Connecticut*, the US Supreme Court struck down state laws that criminalized the use of contraceptives by married couples, recognizing married couples' right to privacy in reproductive matters and, by extension, legitimizing non-procreative sex among them. In 1972, it extended this privacy protection to unmarried couples in *Eisenstadt v. Baird*. Then, in 1973, in *Roe v. Wade*, the Court ruled that abortion is constitutionally protected as part of a woman's fundamental "right to privacy" over decisions regarding her personal bodily integrity (Cohen 2002). These Supreme Court decisions, along with the availability of the pill, made women's socio-legal equality possible, conditioning women's ability to claim equality in their private lives as sexual partners and in their public lives as workers who now controlled their reproductive sexuality. In sum, American society no longer legally sanctioned reproductive sexuality and monogamous heterosexual marriages as vested state interests. Rather, the state now emphasized the sexual autonomy of the individual, and the law provided protections regarding sexual intimacy as part of the right to privacy.

This line of legal rulings, moreover, bore directly on sexuality as a form of personal liberty protected under privacy rights, and it shielded consensual adult sexual relationships from state interference. Lesbians and gay men were still outsiders to citizenship rights at this point, but gay rights lawyers and movement leaders saw an avenue to the legal enfranchisement of lesbians and gay men. The sociologist Steven Seidman (2002) observes, "Appealing to a constitutional right to privacy and equal treatment, state laws that criminalized sodomy were challenged. By 1983, twenty-five states had decriminalized consensual sodomy" (176).

Although the US Supreme Court upheld state sodomy laws as constitutional in 1986 with its *Bowers v. Hardwick* decision, viewing sodomy laws as rightly part of a "millennial of moral teaching," and thus dealing a huge blow to the gay rights movement of the time (Chauncey 2008, 27), the legal scholar William Eskridge (1999) makes the case that by 1981 states and cities throughout the country had put in place laws that protected lesbians and gay men from discrimination and violence as well as recognized gay couples and families through domestic partnerships and second parent adoptions. Eskridge argues that by the 1980s legal protections could be said to have afforded a "post-closeted regime where openly gay people could participate in the public culture"

(124). In 2003, the US Supreme Court overturned its 1986 *Bowers v. Hardwick* ruling. In *Lawrence v. Texas*, the Court made all remaining sodomy laws unconstitutional and extended the right to privacy and equal protection to gay individuals. Finally, in 2013, the Court ruled in *United States v. Windsor* that Congress's 1996 Defense of Marriage Act (DOMA), which denied federal benefits to same-sex couples who were married under state law, was unconstitutional. Extending the Equal Protection Clause of the Constitution's Fourteenth Amendment to lesbian and gay marriages, the justices noted that when states have recognized same-sex marriages, they have "conferred upon them a dignity and status of immense import" (Cole 2013, 28–29).

Returning to the concept of a post-closeted culture, then, this discussion of the rise of this dynamic of visibility and integration is meant to take stock of the considerable changes in the social status of gay men and lesbians in America. In a historically unprecedented manner, many gay men and lesbians live openly and are increasingly integrated into relationships with friends, family members, and coworkers. As a corollary development, straights are increasingly in contact with openly gay and lesbian friends, family members, and coworkers as well. Furthermore, this concept points to indications that no longer is the social isolation of closeted gays nor hard forms of straight homophobia necessarily the defining conditions of gay and straight life. While hard practices of homophobic discrimination, derision, and violence, although uneven across diverse populations and geographies, have weakened or declined, soft forms of homophobia or risk avoidance have replaced them (Yoshino 2006). Soft homophobia is established through two main social practices. First, straights deploy hyperconventional or hegemonic gender identity practices to perform and secure unimpeachable straight masculine and feminine identities. Second, straights variably construct strongly aversive, weak, or blurred boundaries of social distance from gay and lesbian individuals, symbols, and social spaces to signal, maintain, and enforce a clear straight masculine or feminine identity status.[4] In short, at the micro level, straight privilege and normativity continue to operate while the avoidance of publicly blatant homophobic and heterosexist acts variably increases. Indeed, as sexual desire is somewhat less fraught these days, gender seems to have stepped forward as the site of struggle around the dominance of normative heterosexuality, while the boundaries between heterosexuals and homosexuals are saturated with gender politics.

The notions of the closet and post-closetedness are not immune to enormous variations reflecting varied social locations. Just as the closet is experienced in varied class-, gender-, and race-specific ways, the same is true of its weakening (Barton 2012; Gamson 1998; Gray 2009; Moore 2011; Ghaziani 2011; Seidman 2002; Stein 2010). In short, there are multiple experiences of a post-closeted cultural dynamic. The concept of a post-closeted culture should be understood as a social-historical pattern and trend in American society, but one that exists alongside other mixed and complicated patterns, including, sadly, a normative system of heterosexuality that is still compulsory in many towns, regions, institutions, and cultural practices.

Through my interviews with straight men and women, I explore how a post-closeted culture is shaping and altering the identities of black and white straight men and women. Holding in mind the changing character of straight identities, I examine the attending shifts and changes in normative heterosexuality and practices of homophobia and antihomophobia. I document how a post-closeted culture is making straight identities more deliberate and conscious and changing the interactions, and in some cases the relationships, straight people have with lesbian and gay male acquaintances, friends, kin, and fellow workers. With the decline of compulsory heterosexuality and the rise of pro-gay values, straight men's and women's interactions with gay men and lesbians are shifting and are now more varied, numerous, and complicated in post-closeted contexts. Today nonheterosexuals have more options regarding the association of sexual desire, behavior, and identity; and straights are often more deliberate, reflective, and defensive about establishing a heterosexual identity.

Methodology: Method, Data, and Research Site

Data for this research are based on sixty in-depth interviews with individuals who self-identify as black or white straight men or women. The interviews lasted from 1.5 to 2.5 hours on average. I conducted the interviews from 2004 to 2005 in "Orangetown," a city in the northeastern

United States. It is important to note that this region of the country is found to report less restrictive attitudes toward homosexuality than other regions like the South (Barton 2012; Hicks and Lee 2006). As is the standard practice to protect the real identities of one's respondents and their exact geographical location, all respondents' names, along with the city and names of the places mentioned in this book, have been changed in order to maintain confidentiality.[5]

Orangetown is part of a large tri-city metropolitan area with a population of over 800,000. Overall, it is a mixed working-class/middle-class city. In 2005 there were around 78,000 people living in Orangetown. The racial composition of the city was 60 percent white and 33 percent black (US Census Bureau 2005). The median household income from 2007 to 2011 was $38,394, more than $10,000 below the national average. Similarly, about 25 percent of Orangetown residents lived below the poverty line, almost double the national average of 14.3 percent. These differences are reflective of the large black population that makes up the city, which is much higher than the national average of 13.1 percent but is typical of northeastern cities that saw net black in-migration over the course of the twentieth century. For instance, the median household income for whites in Orangetown was $41,863; in contrast, for blacks it was $26,303. These differences persist across rates of college attendance, owner-occupied housing, and other economic characteristics (US Census Bureau 2010).

There were practical and sociohistorical reasons for choosing to study the racial shaping of straight identities by interviewing black and white individuals. The practical reason had to do with the racial demographics of the region where I was able to access respondents for the study. This region's racial demographics lent itself to comparing blacks and whites, as there were few Asian Americans or Latinos in the population as a whole. The sociohistorical rationale supported the practical one. Historically, black and white divisions in the northeastern and southern states of the United States have been and continue to be among the most pressing racial divisions and issues facing the nation (Collins 2004; Oliver and Shapiro 2006). Furthermore, the dynamics of racial formation in the United States often use a black and white dichotomy in categorizing other racial groups; for instance, Latino and Asian American individuals are, depending on factors such as skin color and social class status, viewed as more racially like "whites" than "blacks" (Alba 1999).

In 2000, 1,806 same-sex couples reported living in the metropolitan area that includes Orangetown; their numbers grew to 2,978 by 2010. For comparison, 8,902 same-sex couples reported living in San Francisco in 2000, and that number rose to 10,461 by 2010 (US Census Bureau 2000, 2010). At the time of my interviews, only Massachusetts had passed legislation making marriage legal for lesbians and gays.

The research design purposefully sampled for race and gender to analytically compare them along the axis of heterosexuality. Still, these case studies of straight identities are based on a nonrandom, snowball sample and are limited by their lack of generalizability beyond the reported interviews (Burawoy et al. 1991). As qualitative interviews emphasize conceptual points over quantifiable data, I developed categories, such as homophobic or antihomophobic, through identifying the range of a phenomenon and focusing on individuals or groups where these social processes and phenomena are salient. Specifically, I used social distance theory in order to capture a diverse range of straight men's and women's accounts of their straight sexualities as well as their homophobic and antihomophobic stances. The subjects in this study ranged from those who have daily interaction with Orangetown's active and "out" lesbian and gay community (since they lived, worked, or socialized in mixed gay/straight neighborhoods) to those who had little daily interaction with gay and lesbian persons or the LGBTQ community. I initially contacted persons who worked at local establishments in Orangetown, such as gyms, bars, restaurants, K-12 schools, and colleges. As race was a key part of the research design, I sought out black organizations in the community and on college campuses, conducting initial interviews with their members.

The neighborhood in figure I.3 labeled "Center City" was the location of the five mostly gay male bars in Orangetown. In addition to these primarily gay establishments, there was a cluster of bars, restaurants, and shops patronized by mixed crowds of straight and lesbian and gay people along the main streets of this commercial and residential neighborhood. Although this concentration of gay life is nowhere near as dense as San Francisco's Castro District or New York's Chelsea neighborhood, it was a clearly demarcated geographical area that all of my straight respondents knew of as Orangetown's "gay" neighborhood. Many had patronized the various establishments at some point, or regularly socialized there, with some respondents calling the neighborhood home as they rented apartments or owned homes in the area. The two mainly black neighborhoods were in close proximity, and I have labeled them "North Town" and "South Village." I interviewed straight respondents who lived or worked in all three of these neighborhoods, among other neighborhoods in and outside the city limits of Orangetown as well (see figure I.3).

Based on the snowball sampling technique, I obtained my sample through the social networks of my respondents while also employing purposeful sampling to capture a wide range of straight identity practices. For example, I interviewed straight men and women who worked with a number of gay men or lesbians in their workplace, such as an HIV/AIDS drop-in center or restaurants and bars with large gay clienteles. Further, this strategy dovetails with my argument that social interaction with gays and lesbians creates a stronger sense of straight identity, constituting the practices through which straights understand themselves, sexual others, and the larger social world.

I initially contacted respondents through my own personal contacts or those of colleagues and friends. For example, I worked out at a local gym in Orangetown and I was acquainted with several black and white straight men and women who used the facilities there. I asked these respondents whether they would be willing to be interviewed, and if so, I then asked them to refer me to others who would be willing to be respondents. I tried to sample a range of workplaces from educational settings and government employment to manual labor job sites and nonprofit organizations, some of which focused on providing HIV and AIDS services to this metropolitan area in general and its African American community in particular. My general aim was to capture as diverse a range of straight identities as possible given the constraints of time, money, and location.

The interviews were typically conducted in person and at a place convenient to the interviewee, such as their workplace, my workplace, or their home or mine. Some interviews were done over the phone for the convenience of the interviewee and also to avoid having the interviewee react to my identity as a gay male. The interviews were recorded

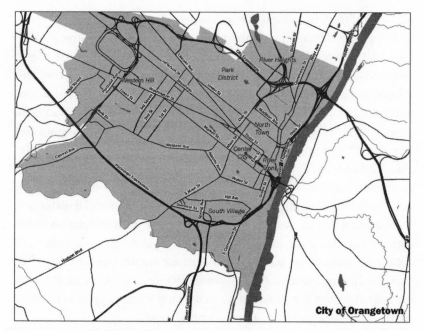

Figure I.3. Map of Orangetown.

and transcribed by me or by a trained research assistant to protect the identity of the respondent. Analysis involved transcribing and coding the interview data into over thirty-five thematic memos (Charmaz 2007). Themes were dictated by the concepts that emerged as I coded the data. A conceptual map was developed from these concepts, showing how the concepts related to one another.

Regarding the demographics, I refer the reader to tables A.1 and A.2 in the appendix, but I will also describe characteristics of the sample here. The black male respondents' ages range from twenty-one to fifty-six, while the white male respondents' ages range from twenty-two to fifty-six. Eight of the black men are single; four are divorced; three are married. Ten of the white men are single; four are married; and one is divorced and single. One-third of the white men come from a working-class background, just over half from a middle-class background, and the remaining from the upper class, while three-fifths of the black straight men identified as having a working poor or working-class background and the other two-fifths as middle-class. However, the majority of the white and black male respondents have a college degree, and higher educational attainment has been found to positively influence attitudes toward homosexuality (Loftus 2001). Black men's modal religious affiliation was Protestant, ranging from Assembly of God and Baptist to Episcopalian and Pentecostal; other religious identifications among them included Catholic, Masonic Order, Muslim, Christian, atheist, or no affiliation. White men's modal religious affiliation was no religious affiliation; they were also agnostic, Greek Orthodox, Presbyterian, Catholic, and Jewish. Table A.1 provides the aforementioned information on each male respondent, including his educational attainment, occupational status, and position on the continuum of social distance.

The black female respondents' ages range from nineteen to sixty-eight, while the white female respondents' ages range from twenty to sixty-one. Among the black women, ten are single; three are married; two are divorced and single. Five of the white women are single; four are married; four are divorced and currently single; two are currently married but divorced from a previous marriage.

Over half of the black women come from a working-class and the rest from middle-class backgrounds. Just under half of the white women come from working-class backgrounds and the other just under a half from middle-class ones, with one from the upper class. Like the men, the majority of the white and black female respondents have a college degree, and they also most likely have more accepting attitudes toward gays and lesbians partly due to their higher educational attainment. Black women's modal religious affiliation was Protestant, composed of denominations such as Baptist, Episcopalian, and Methodist; others were nonreligious, spiritual, Catholic, and Christian. The modal religious affiliation for white female respondents was Catholic and no affiliation; others were spiritual, Jewish, Methodist, and Episcopalian. Table A.2 provides the aforementioned information on each female respondent, including her educational attainment, occupational status, and position on the continuum.

Overview of the Book

Chapter 1 draws on research in sexualities, gender, and race studies to explore the multiple patterns of black and white straight masculinities and femininities. First, I define the concept of heterosexual identities and theoretically situate my study within a Foucauldian and Butlerian framework. Further, I go on to make the case for the rise of a post-closeted culture as a growing pattern in American society by examining some of the sociological literature on gay and lesbian life. Situating the study within the new sociology of critical heterosexual studies, I start from the standpoint that heterosexualities are multiple, variable, and not reducible in any simple way to the norm of heterosexuality or heterosexism. I therefore question studies of masculinity that conflate heterosexual masculinity as automatically entailing homophobic stances, and I develop theories to sketch the multiplicity of straight femininities. Drawing on race theorizing, I argue for the need to make clear the racially specific meanings of heterosexuality by analyzing how race (whiteness and blackness) refracts and alters the meanings of straight identity through white privilege and black racial stigma.

Analyzing the historical rise of heterosexual identities in the United States, chapter 2 synthesizes the extant historical research on heterosexualities in order to show the origins of straight supremacy. Prior to the twentieth century, heterosexual identities were submerged within the gender identities of "normal" men and women and can be said to not exist as we know them today. The establishment of heterosexual identity is a twentieth-century phenomenon and is the result of the human sciences' discursive construction and discovery of the homosexual as a species or human type (Foucault 1978; Katz 1996). With the pathologizing of the homosexual, the heterosexual was born as his or her opposite. The heterosexual came to define and embody psychological health, social normality, and the ideals of good citizenship.

Drawing on the interview data with black and white straight men, in chapter 3, I explore shifts in the role of homophobia in the construction of straight masculinities. Using a continuum to map a variety of heterosexual masculinities, I chart a range of identity practices from homophobic heterosexual masculinities to antihomophobic ones. The chapter shows that straight men who construct homophobic practices that define homosexuality as socially inferior to heterosexuality establish strongly aversive boundaries of social distance from gay individuals, spaces, and symbols in order to project an unpolluted straight masculinity. Then, I use the analytical continuum to map a range of antihomophobic practices by straight men, moving from men who establish weak normative boundaries of social distance to those who blur them. These straight men's pro-gay stances trade on the prestige of being tolerant of gays, with black men's antihomophobias drawing on their experiences with racism.

Chapter 4 continues the discussion started in the previous chapter but presents case studies of straight femininities. Aspects of the lives of straight women are sketched with the purpose of illustrating a series of positions on a continuum. This continuum, like that in the last chapter, uses the homophobic and antihomophobic practices that straight women draw on in establishing boundaries of social distance from lesbian and gay individuals, identity symbols, and social spaces as the basis of its organization. I show how race shapes and frames black and white straight women's homophobic and antihomophobic stances. The analysis divides straight femininities into three sections, exploring homophobic straight femininities, which are often based in Christian religious beliefs that condemn homosexuality; straight femininities that contest compulsory heterosexuality and aim to be gay-affirmative; and an activist-like group of straight women who blur boundaries between lesbian and straight identity statuses through their acts of sexual intimacy with other women and who refuse to claim straight status and privilege at times. These straight women actively aim to transform the homophobic stances of other straight individuals and challenge sexual and gender norms, static conceptions of sexual identities, and the institutional formations that enforce straight supremacy.

Revisiting select respondents from chapters 3 and 4, in chapter 5 I highlight queered and nonnormative heterosexualities among the black and white straight men and women. Bringing a queer studies perspective to bear on the narratives of the straight interviewees, I analyze the nonnormative practices of some straight men by focusing on the emergence of metrosexual identifications among them. Metrosexual men negotiate gay identity codes while identifying as straight and antihomophobic. Queered straight identifications, in contrast, are a development exclusively found among the women in my sample. These women told me about their sexual experiences with other women, which ranged from same-sex desires and fantasies to sexual encounters with bisexual women, lesbians, and other straight women as well. Queered straight identifications show us the limit of binary thinking in that it misses the complexity of sexual identifications in post-closeted contexts, where some women define themselves as straight but have same-sex desires and experiences that complicate simple binary understandings of people as either heterosexual or homosexual.

In the concluding chapter, I reflect on the theories and patterns discussed in the previous chapters by arguing that a post-closeted cultural dynamic has refashioned sexual identity practices, normative heterosexuality, and homophobias. I also explore the limits of the concept of a post-closeted dynamic by acknowledging that it better captures the micro-sociological phenomena taking place than the structural dynamics that persist in many social institutions, regions, and places. Lastly, I summarize the analytical continuum that documents straight identity practices and the way race shapes each respondent's position on it. Table 6.2 in this chapter details the continuum and summarizes the main points of the book.

1

Thinking Straight

Gender, Race, and (Anti)homophobias

When I started graduate school in 1997, I moved from Southern California to upstate New York. In order to keep up with current events, I subscribed to the *New York Times*. That same year, I started to follow the *Times*'s coverage of a court case in Vermont, where three same-sex couples filed lawsuits arguing that the state discriminated against them by not offering them the same rights as heterosexual married couples. The case proved disappointing. In 1999, the Vermont State Supreme Court ruled that it was unconstitutional to deny the same benefits of marriage to lesbian and gay couples, but the state's legislature had accorded gay couples these benefits through "civil unions." The second-class status of "civil unions" asserted a clear heteronormative message: same-sex relationships are inferior and unequal to straight relationships.

Between news reports of Vermont's decision in 1999 and the Massachusetts Supreme Court's decision in 2003, which made Massachusetts the first state to grant lesbian and gay couples the right to marry, I noticed that in September 2002 the *New York Times* started to include celebrations of same-sex couples' commitment ceremonies in its Sunday Styles section. As a result of the inclusion of lesbian and gay couples, the heading in the Sunday Styles section changed from "Weddings" to "Weddings/Celebrations." In this small but significant inclusionary change by this prestigious newspaper, regarded as the national keeper of the public record, I witnessed a newfound respect for lesbian and gay life and our relationships as deserving of the same recognition as straight couples' marriages. Although the *New York Times*'s inclusion did not translate in a direct way into same-sex couples' right to marry, it contributed to the trend of a post-closeted culture of open lesbian and gay couples as well as the social integration and cultural normalization of gay couples as equal to their straight counterparts.[1]

I start with these stories to call attention to the unique focus of this study. Reversing the focus on how lesbian women's and gay men's coming-out stories affect and change straight men and women and the larger American society, I ask, instead, how straight men's and women's attitudes and actions accommodate, resist, or paradoxically support gay equality yet remain homophobic in post-closeted contexts. How do straight men and women construct, maintain, and alter their identity practices due to the cultural presence of out lesbian women and gay men? American society today is experiencing an unprecedented proliferation of lesbian and gay representations in the mass media and popular culture. These remarkable changes in the cultural sphere are a product of the significant political victories of LGBTQ movements for a range of rights, policy inclusions, and recognitions over the last four decades. With this context in mind, I analyze how a post-closeted cultural dynamic shapes the meanings of heterosexuality, affects the performances of straight identity, and conditions the development of softer forms of homophobia, along with consciously pro-queer alliances on the part of straight men and women.

Further, this book analyzes the way gender (masculinities and femininities) and race (blackness and whiteness) shape and change the meaning of straight identities. Through in-depth interviews with a diverse range of straight individuals, I illustrate that there are a dizzying array of patterns of straight sexual identities in American society today. To understand the diversity of these constructions of racial straight masculinities and femininities, this book draws on research in sexualities studies, gender studies, and race studies to empirically explore the multiple patterns and dynamics of straight identity performances.

In this chapter I discuss the current research on heterosexualities by first defining the concept of heterosexual identities and situating my study within a Foucauldian and Butlerian theoretical framework. I then make the case for the rise of a post-closeted culture as a pattern in American society by examining some of the sociological literature on the status of gay and lesbian life. Keeping in mind the insight that heterosexualities are multiple, I problematize gender studies for conflating straight masculinity with homophobic practices and chart a multiplicity of straight femininities, from emphasized femininity to female masculinity. I argue for the need to understand how whiteness and sexual normativity are coupled in relation to blackness and hypersexuality in constructions of straight sexualities.

Defining Heterosexualities, Normalizing Power, and Performative Identities

Heterosexual identities need to be situated within the context of the rise of an out and visible lesbian, gay, and queer culture. The concept of a heterosexual identity aims to capture both one's sense of self and the group that one identifies with on its basis. In its simplest form, a heterosexual identity is constructed by individuals taking on the attribution heterosexual or straight themselves.

More broadly, heterosexualities are configurations of practice and discourse that refer to the identity category heterosexuals and generally, but not necessarily, align with sexual behaviors and desires orientated to the other—as opposed to the same—gender. That is, an individual may claim a heterosexual identity but engage in same-sex behaviors and experience same-sex desires at various points in his or her lifetime. The fluidity and situational character of sexualities mean that individual factors (e.g., a person-based definition of sexual desire), social contexts (e.g., college life, a prison term, employment in the porn industry), and historical events (e.g., second-wave feminism) shape and are shaped by heterosexualities in particular and sexualities in general.

My study of heterosexualities, though, is less about sexual behaviors and desires and more about the identity practices or the words and deeds that straights use in social interactions and situations to project themselves as straight. For example, the traditional practice of wearing a wedding band, claiming a marital status as a husband or wife, and simply expressing sexual or romantic interest in the other gender are acts meant to indicate a straight status.

Significantly, straight identities are established through social norms that make up our society's social structures and organizations, such as government bureaucracies, economic systems, and legal orders. These social structures, along with our social institutions, such as marriage, the family, schools and colleges, corporations, political parties, and the armed forces, create both individual and institutional privileges (unearned advantages, resources, and rights given without any effort on an individual's part) that favor straight persons, relations, marriages, and families over nonstraight ones. This creates what is referred to as heteronormativity (the privileging of heterosexuality as normal, natural, and right over homosexuality) in daily life and social institutional settings.

Living in a heteronormative society, heterosexual individuals are accorded heterosexual privilege. This privilege is often invisible. It is enacted by the view that heterosexuality is "normal," social-psychologically healthy, and complex, as well as through entitlements to "first-class" citizenship. The institutional legitimation of heterosexual identities is the linchpin of its hierarchical dominance over homosexualities. For example, heterosexual families are automatically viewed as better, healthier, and more "normal" than lesbian and gay families. Children are also thought to be best parented by a heterosexual mother and father (see, however, Stacey and Biblarz 2001; and Biblarz and Stacey 2010, who refute these notions).

Heterosexual identity, though, varies in strength for individuals: some individuals realize that heterosexual is merely an ascriptive category that one falls into, while others have a strong investment in the identity in their daily interactions. Paradoxically, individuals with normative identities (e.g., heterosexuals, whites, men) often experience the sense that they lack an identity since they serve as the standard by which others (e.g., nonheterosexuals, nonwhites, women) are measured and marked by their difference (Connell 1995; Perry 2002; Richardson 1996).

The invisible and compulsory nature of straight identities is not just due to their assumed normal or "majority" status. Straight identities, like sexual identities in general, are always and already constructed in part through gender norms and identities. This is because gender is a routine, methodical, and recurring accomplishment of daily life, and it is central to being viewed as an intelligible human being (West and Zimmerman 1987; Glick and Fiske 1999). Thus, gender norms and conventional displays construct and reinforce straight identity statuses, and heteronormativity affirms sex and gender binary conceptions of male/female, masculine/feminine, and man/woman as opposite but complementary pairings, although lesbians and gay men are increasingly embodying traditional gender norms and presentations while straights are taking on nontraditional gender conventions, complicating the use of gender displays as clear indicators of sexual identities. While a gendered social order enforces the construction of men's and women's gender identities as binary and supposedly "natural," complementary opposites, heteronormativity establishes, sustains, and bolsters a gender order where men and women are meant only for each other. This ideological construction naturalizes straight sexual relations, reproduction, and identities as outside social norms and historical time.

In postmodern societies, however, power is neither simply group-based (e.g., heterosexuals over homosexuals) nor only the effect of macro-social structures (e.g., economics or the state) on a population. Although this form of juridical power, defined by the sociologist Max Weber as "the chance of a man or of a number of men to realize their own will in a communal action, even against the resistance of others who are participating in the action" (1946, 180), still operates in societies today, it fails to conceptualize the more refined, slippery, and invisible techniques through which power circulates as part of the micro-processes of identity formations.

Following the French social theorist Michel Foucault (1978), I understand the micro–power politics of social identities as constructed through norms, practices, discourses, and institutions that escape the machinations of any one group of people. Micro–power processes are normalizing and coextensive with social identity formation. Historicizing Foucault, though, is important, as the macro form of juridical power that structured the existence of homosexual lives in a top-down way was predominant from the 1930s to the 1960s (see chapter 2 for the historiographical research and my argument on the rise and fall of the closet). This top-down or macro conception of power is historicized by the concept of the closet. The closet was a macro-power formation based in state practices of prejudice and discrimination that oppressed homosexual people and life. Through its administrate and legal powers, public policies, and police force, the closet as a state formation imposed a double life on homosexual persons. For lesbians and gay men, the closet meant a double life: confining one's homosexual self-presentation to a private sphere of homosexual friends and intimates while simultaneously passing as heterosexual in public in order to live a socioeconomically viable existence.

The effect of the repressive closet was not to eliminate homosexuals but to contain, circumscribe, and overwhelmingly stigmatize their existence. It formed a homosexual self based on anxieties of exposure, shame, and self-loathing. Ironically, this repressive power of containment and stigmatization led to the development of gay social worlds that would grow into powerful social movements that "reversed" the discourse of their stigmatization into a politics and discourse of rights, recognition, and visibility, aiming to rectify the wrongful prejudice, discrimination, and legal disenfranchisement they experienced. Symbolically, the Stonewall riots of 1969 signal the historical triumph of homosexuals as they reversed the discourse of stigma, pathology, and oppression used to repress them and turned it back on heterosexual society and its state-sanctioned institutions of control. As Foucault expressed it in an often-quoted passage,

> There is no question that the appearance in nineteenth-century psychiatry, jurisprudence, and literature of a whole series of discourses on the species and subspecies of homosexuality, inversion, pederasty, and "psychic hermaphrodism" made possible a strong advance of social controls into this area of "perversity"; but it also made possible the formation of a "reverse" discourse: homosexuality began to speak in its own behalf, to demand that its legitimacy or "naturality" be acknowledged, often in the same vocabulary, using the same categories by which it was medically disqualified. (1978, 101)

For Foucault, however, this reverse discourse that explains the normalization of homosexuality does not mean unregulated freedom, total liberation, or the disappearance of social forces that shape, circumscribe, and control sexuality. Rather, as repressive juridical power recedes, normalizing forces adjust, shift, and expand. Normalizing power builds on the sociohistorical conditions it inherits. In a post-Stonewall context, this means the further entrenchment of the view that sexuality is an essential, core part of one's self-identity. Sexual desire and identity are consolidated into the master categories of a binary divide: homosexuality and heterosexuality. Sexual desire is now seen as organizing not only one's choice of a partner but a wide range of aspects unrelated to sexual desire, ranging from one's personality and taste in cultural products like clothing styles and grooming habits to leisure activities and occupational pursuits. This logic of sexual desire and identity views homosexuality and heterosexuality as mutually exclusive and internally coherent categories. As a result, other axes of social difference and identity, such as race, class, gender, age, nationality, and immigration status are at times sidelined and minimized when the shared experience of being homosexual or heterosexual is emphasized.

Following Foucault, the philosopher Judith Butler (1990, 1992, 2004) argues that the notion of identity as the container of liberation is a ruse of normalizing power. She argues that power is coextensive with an individual's subjectivity and identity formation. In her cautious theory of performative identities, Butler argues that identity performances are recurring and accomplished processes of daily life but are also deeply constructed by the effects of male domination and heteronormativity. In *Gender Trouble: Feminism and the Subversion of Identity*, Butler (1990) contends that

> [t]he repetition of heterosexual constructs within sexual cultures both gay and straight may well be the inevitable site of the denaturalization and mobilization of gender categories. The replication of heterosexual constructs in non-heterosexual frames brings into relief the utterly constructed status of the so-called heterosexual original. Thus, gay is to straight *not* as copy is to original, but, rather, as copy is to copy. The parodic repetition of "the original" . . . reveals the original to be nothing other than a parody of the *idea* of the natural and the original. (31; italics in original)

In other words, straight identities are not the basis of gay identities or related to gay identities as an original is to a copy. Rather, as all identities are parodic performances, all identities are copies of copies. The parodic repetitious nature of straight identities (and this applies to identities more broadly) reveals them to be compulsory performances of norms (or copies of norms) that are enacted on bodies, bodies that are interpreted for sexuality, gender, and sex from a heteronormative principle of social organization.

In sum, Butler's performative theory argues for seeing identities as the "stylized repetition of acts . . . [that constitute] sustained social performances" and that come into being through the very acts of the performance (1990, 140–41). Recent criticisms of Butler, however, contend that her performative theory underemphasizes the contextual and relational dimensions of identity performances. In her book *Illicit Flirtations: Labor, Migration, and Sex Trafficking in Tokyo*, Rhacel Parreñas (2011) analyzes the gender performances of Filipina transgender women hostesses to show that their performances as women require recognition by their Japanese male customers or other transgender men.

> For transgender hostesses . . . the performance of gender, in this case of femininity, in itself does not constitute their identity of being "like women." Instead, it is the acknowledgement of these performances, their recognition, and validation with masculine gestures that would constitute their feminine identity. My insistence on situating gender in a social context forces us to expand Judith Butler's assertion that gender's performance and reiteration of such a performance would on their own constitute the notion of a stable gender identity. (208)

Similarly, the sociologist Jane Ward (2010), examining the gender labor of queer femmes in recognizing, validating, and thus helping to enact the masculine performances of their romantic female-to-male (FtM) transmale partners, emphasizes how queer femmes do the labor of being "the girl" in the relationship. A queer femme ends up engaging in conscious acts of "forgetting" the transmale partner's girlhood past in order to establish his masculine performance as legible, authentic, and real.

Parreñas and Ward, then, allow us to reexamine straight men's identity performances as based on their relational recognition by straight (or lesbian) women's feminine gestures or the feminine gestures of transwomen and feminine gay and straight men, along with the shared recognition and validation of their straight masculinity performances they receive from other masculine men (or women), straight or gay. Similarly, straight women's performances of straight femininity are corroborated and confirmed through the masculine gestures of men, straight and gay, as well as the mutually approving feminine gestures of straight and lesbian women, on one hand, or the masculine enactments of butch lesbians and transmen, on the other.

In this book, I examine how straight men and women talk about acts of gender and sexuality to establish their own identity performances as well as those of lesbians and gay men. One way straight individuals reinforce their sexual-gender privilege is to view lesbians and gay men as failed women and men, whereas, in contrast, antihomophobic straight individuals often refuse to use traditional gender acts as signs of heterosexuality, viewing gays and lesbians as diverse in their embodiment of both normative and nonnormative gender performances. These straight men and women validate a wider range of gender expressions as masculine and feminine in their efforts to be gay-friendly and pro-queer.

The Implications of Queer Theory and the New Sociology of Heterosexualities

In thinking about the social construction of straight identities, Foucault, Butler, and other queer theorists (Fuss 1991; Sedgwick 1990; Seidman 1997; Somerville 2000; Warner 1993, 1999) have brought into analytical view the importance of shifting the study of sexuality "from explaining the modern homosexual to questions of the operation of the hetero/homosexual binary, from an exclusive preoccupation with homosexuality to a focus on heterosexuality as a social and political organizing principle, and from a politics of minority interest to a politics of knowledge and difference" (Seidman 1996, 9). Queer theory, then, makes clear the importance of focusing on the social construction of heterosexualities as not simply behaviors but as a set of identity practices in relation to nonheterosexualities. It is important to understand heterosexual identities as not only multiple and variable, but also irreducible to the social system that enforces the norm of heterosexuality across society (Corber and Valocchi 2003; Martin 2009). In other words, heterosexual identities should not be conflated with a singular, unitary set of identity practices, nor should they be viewed as automatically constitutive of normative heterosexuality's institutional dominance. Rather, through solidarity and alliance with LGBTQ persons and issues, heterosexuals can challenge homophobia, refuse heterosexual privilege, and promote respect, recognition, and rights for LGBTQ identities and lives.

Sociological analysis of heterosexuality is a recent development. Thinking of heterosexualities as hegemonic, current scholarship shows how sexuality shapes the identities of straight individuals to be normative, neutral, and taken-for-granted practices in everyday life and institutional settings. These studies examine how straights fashion boundaries between heterosexuality and homosexuality in order to create and secure a privileged straight identity. Heterosexual identities are in positions of privilege and structural advantage. One main way privilege works is for heterosexuals to view their identities as neither identities nor forms of privilege. Since heterosexuals are able to take for granted their unacknowledged privilege, heterosexual rituals, social norms, and other behaviors go unseen as mechanisms through which heterosexual identity is made dominant in daily and institutional life. Straight identity practices are sociologically significant to the extent that core parts of an individual's social life—work, family, and friendships—are organized by this identity category.

The sociology of heterosexualities exposes the identity work of heterosexual privilege, analyzing its accomplished and routinized roles in rituals and institutions. Among the first sociologists to study heterosexuality as part of social arrangements and cultural discourses that enforce compulsory heterosexuality among both women and men are Chrys Ingraham (1999, 2005) and Amy Best (2000).

In *White Weddings: Romancing Heterosexuality in Popular Culture*, Ingraham (1999) argues that weddings and marriages show that heterosexuality is a ritualized cultural practice that creates rules for behavior. Wedding and marriage rituals privilege heterosexuals in both economic terms (e.g., taxation, health care, and housing benefits) and cultural ones (e.g., by reinforcing normative heterosexuality as the standard for legitimate cultural and sexual relations). They are sites where the "heterosexual imaginary," a "way of thinking which conceals the operation of heterosexuality in structuring gender (across race, class, and sexuality) and closes off any critical analysis of heterosexuality as an organizing institution," operates par excellence (Ingraham 1999, 16). Further, dominant class and race relations are reproduced through the "recession-proof" wedding industry, which relies on these ideological forces to maintain its multibillion-dollar annual profits, and the institution of marriage reinforces racial hierarchies, as white Americans have better life chances of marrying than their black counterparts (Ingraham 1999, 27–31).

Similarly, Amy Best (2000), in *Prom Night: Youth, Schools, and Popular Culture*, shows how the prom is a high-status event encouraging youth to practice a ritual that fashions masculine and feminine selves through scripts of romance, dating, and public recognition of the heterosexual couple as the idealized form for social and sexual relations. The prom, in other words, acts as a ritual that is practice for one's ostensibly inevitable heterosexual marriage and wedding.

Psychoanalytic sociologists argue that dominant masculinities are based on heterosexuality as the assumed, compulsory object-choice desire of masculine men (Benjamin 1998; Chodorow 1978, 1999; Martin 1996; Stein 2005). Straight masculine selves are characterized by defensive ego boundaries, a defining of self in opposition to others, and an antagonism toward femininity due to separation dynamics from mothers, who are assumed to be the primary parent in a child's life. Object relations theory maintains that masculinity often acts as the bridge between gender practices defined as active and aggressive, and a heterosexuality that is by definition male-dominant and active (Chodorow 1998). The social psychology of masculinity is centrally formed by suppressing, splitting off from, or disidentifying with femininity. The sociologist and psychoanalyst Nancy Chodorow argues that heterosexual men's homophobia partly centers on "men not being men and women not being with men" (1998, 4). By this she means that homosexual male identities often serve as the unconscious and preconscious container for heterosexual men's homophobic anxiety of a man being perceived as feminine and passive, as this is the overriding stereotype of gay masculinities, whereas lesbians, especially lesbian couples, create an anxiety of women who do not need or want men sexually.

Psychoanalytic theories of the formation of girls' identities in childhood also help to explain some of the persisting patterns sociologists

document among straight women. In contrast to straight masculine selves, straight femininities are often defined by relational selves.
Assuming, again, that mothers act as the primary parent, these sociologists and psychologists argue that girls internalize their mothers'
emotional and relational dynamics early on in life. This internalization conditions in broad ways the formation of feminine selves that are
generally less defensive, are more porous in their establishment of ego
boundaries, and use merging with others to connect and create relationships (Chodorow 1978, 1999; Corbett 2009; Gilligan [1982] 1993).
For example, these social-psychological patterns can be seen in straight
women's more emotionally elaborate and physically tactile displays of
affection with female friends, while men's friendships with other men
neither embrace this kind of tactility nor view displays of affection as
common or acceptable (Felmlee 1999).

The sociology of heterosexualities and psychoanalytic sociology perspectives provide insight into the reproduction of normative heterosexuality and the social construction of heterosexual masculinities and
femininities. They do not, however, provide an empirical account of the
social processes involved in the daily accomplishment of straight identities. In other words, how do straight men and women project their
sexual-gender identities in social interactions and everyday life? What
words and deeds do they use to let others know they're straight?

Examining the changing status of heterosexuality in post-closeted
contexts, Steven Seidman (2002), in *Beyond the Closet: The Social
Transformation of Gay and Lesbian Life*, explores how young heterosexuals, born between 1970 and 1980, are contending with the
increased visibility of gays in the 1990s. He argues that gay visibility
is making young heterosexuals more self-conscious of their own heterosexualities. Social interaction with gay individuals, he finds, erodes
the presumption of heterosexuality for them. The entrenchment of
the heterosexual/homosexual definition as a central cultural binary in
America implants homosexual suspicion as one of the effects of gay
visibility (Anderson 2009; Sedgwick 1990). The notion of homosexual
suspicion means that individuals are not automatically presumed to
be heterosexual and, as a consequence, some straight men and women
now purposefully flag their straight identity in everyday life (Seidman
2002, 119).

While some straights are made self-conscious and anxious about their heterosexuality, others take this new social context as an opportunity to participate in anti-labeling practice by not claiming a public identity as heterosexual. Although Seidman's work suggests important themes, it does not examine how race and gender shape the meanings and enactments of straight identities. By focusing on young adults, he also does not capture a range of straight identities across age groups and life course situations.

Gay and Lesbian Identities and the Rise of a Post-Closeted Culture

Over the last third of the twentieth century and beginning decades of the twenty-first century, Americans have seen the decline of virulent stereotypes of lesbian and gay images and the rise of their visibility and more positive depictions in popular media forms—from Hollywood and art house movies to television sitcoms and news reports to mainstream newspaper and magazine stories (Chasin 2000; Gamson 2002; Russo 1987). In order to make clear the social changes that I include in the concept of a post-closeted culture, I explore some of the sociological literature that supports the claim that a post-closeted cultural dynamic credibly captures key changes in the status of gay and lesbian life in the United States.

In *All the Rage: The Story of Gay Visibility in America*, the sociologist Suzanna Walters (2001) argues that the new gay visibility of the 1990s must be understood as situated within the context of capitalist commercialism and mainstream straight culture's new interest in gay life. For her, TV programming represents the most illustrative case in the shift from invisibility to unprecedented visibility in 1990s popular culture. Sketching a brief history of television representations, Walters observes that the first depictions of gay characters on TV appeared in the 1970s, but that these characters were almost uniformly portrayed as "closeted" and self-loathing. By the 1980s, however, there were recurring gay characters on a number of shows, thus creating the conditions for the dramatic increase in the number as well as more complicated, positive portrayals of gay characters in the 1990s. Sitcoms in the 1990s like *Roseanne* paved the way for later ones that would feature the first lesbian or gay lead character (e.g., *Ellen* and *Will & Grace*). While Walters primarily focuses on the cultural sphere of mass media, the sociologist Steven Seidman (2002), in *Beyond the Closet*, finds that gay and lesbian normalization and integration form a pattern across America, from everyday social life to shifts in sexual laws and institutional policies. This pattern of normalization dramatizes the decline of compulsory heterosexuality but not the end of the institutional enforcement of heterosexuality.

Seidman finds that by the mid-1990s, many of the gays and lesbians he interviewed were no longer "making life-shaping decisions to avoid exposure or suspicion. They may still conceal their sexuality from some people or in some situations and they may still struggle with shame and fear" (2002, 63), but this struggle does not define their lives, force them to go back into the closet, or create the need for a double life. This new personal latitude extends to negotiating the meaning of same-sex desire and gender practices. As heterosexuality is less compulsory, there is a new flexibility to stake out the meanings and arrangement of sexuality, gender, and identity. Interestingly, the lesbian and gay community, now largely one oriented to rights, identity normalization, and social incorporation, is a key social force enforcing a unitary sexual identity and, at times, a binary gender normativity (Duggan 2003; Ward 2008b; Warner 1999).

While Walters and Seidman provide broad-scale sketches of the shifts in heteronormativity and the social and cultural status of gays and lesbians, the sociologist Joshua Gamson (1998), in his book *Freaks Talk Back*, presents a fine-grained analysis of how TV talk shows predate the newfound public visibility of gays. Before primetime TV's normalized presentations of gay characters and plots, talk shows already regularly included LGBTQ persons and their issues by the late 1970s and early 1980s. This is roughly a decade earlier than the gay visibility witnessed in fictional and nonfictional TV genres of the 1990s. Unlike sitcoms and news programs, the talk show genre—from early shows like *Donahue* and *The Oprah Winfrey Show* to later 1990s newcomers like *The Jerry Springer Show* and *Jenny Jones*—allowed and continues to allow LGBTQ individuals to exercise a voice and degree of agency absent from other TV genres. Talk shows exhibit, exploit, but nonetheless portray the rarely seen racial (nonwhite) and class (non–middle-class) diversities of the LGBTQ community. Although not without their contradictions and sometimes uncomfortable politics, TV talk shows carve out public space for diverse representations of LGBTQ people. Overall, Gamson argues that the public visibility procured by LGBTQ people on talk shows is part of the larger political battle being fought in American culture and society.

While Gamson's rich study of gay visibility shows its effects on talk shows, the sociologist Wayne Brekhus (2003), in *Peacocks, Chameleons, Centaurs: Gay Suburbia and the Grammar of Social Identity*, takes us into what in most people's minds epitomizes middle America—suburbia—except his focus is on the suburban gay male. Illustrating the more deliberate approach to identity characteristic of a post-closeted condition, Brekhus finds that many suburban gay men reject a core, primary gay identity, and instead view being gay as one of many identities.

Brekhus delineates two types of suburban gay men. "Chameleons" view gay identity as a compartmentalized social status that is situationally specific. In their everyday suburban lives, they are assumed to be and pass as straight, but when they travel to gay spaces they experience being gay as their primary, core identity. In contrast, "centaurs" prefer to integrate being gay into everyday life, but don't allow their gay identity to overshadow their other identities as, say, a corporate employee, a masculine man, or a homeowner. The phenomenon of gay suburbanites speaks to the larger trends of gays' integration and normalization into mainstream America. However, the relationship between gay normalization and social developments, such as suburban gay men or a lesbian TV lead character like *Ellen*, needs to be historically and socially situated within the larger patterns and changes in the social organization of sexualities in America.

If lesbians and gay men lead lives beyond the closet and media culture embraces a range, although uneven and unequal, of LGBTQ representations, then how do straight individuals respond to and negotiate these new post-closeted cultural dynamics and contexts? My findings document a continuum to map a range of social identity practices through which straights enact their straight masculine and feminine identities. The continuum captures the multiplicity of practices and stances that straights use, from homophobic defensive ones to nonhomophobic and

antihomophobic ones. In the next section, I turn to gender and race theorizing to examine the intersections between practices of straight masculinities and femininities, and to explore how the categories of blackness and
whiteness refract these sexual-gender identity practices and discourses.

Bringing in Gender, Race, and (Anti)homophobias
Straight Masculinities

Sexuality and gender scholars argue that heterosexuality is central to
the construction of dominant masculinities and the ability to claim
power, status, and authority over others (Connell 1987; Kimmel 2005;
Pascoe 2007). Raewyn Connell developed the concept of hegemonic
masculinity to theorize the superordinate form of masculinity that all
men must negotiate in enacting their gender practices (1987, 1995). In
theorizing hegemonic masculinity, masculinity scholars (Carrigan,
Connell, and Lee 2002; Whitehead and Barrett 2001) conceptualize
masculinity as multiple and hierarchical. For instance, the masculine
practices of straight men of color as well as straight working-class
men are marginalized for their less valued racial and class statuses,
respectively, but valued for their performances of gender and sexual
normativity. Further, the subordination of women and the repudia-
tion of practices associated with femininity continue to be central to
conceptions of hegemonic masculinity (Connell and Messerschmidt
2005; Schippers 2007). Straight men similarly invoke homophobic
practices to subordinate gay masculinities as effeminate (Hennen
2008).

The concept of hegemonic masculinity captures the structural relationship between heterosexuality as dominant and the accompanying
homophobic practices that subordinate homosexuality. Although this
concept is useful in orientating the study of dominant and subordinate
masculinities, we lack empirical studies of how straight masculinities employ homophobic practices in *everyday life* to project a straight
masculinity and marginalize homosexual masculinities, as many studies of straight boys' homophobia are based on analyses of the *institutional context of schools* (e.g., Epstein and Johnson 1998; Mac an Ghaill
1994; Nayak and Kehily 1997; Pascoe 2007). The concept, however, does
provide a continuum for grading masculinities from hegemonic to

counterhegemonic within a male-dominant, normatively heterosexual society.

Debate persists on the relational links between practices of heterosexual masculinities and homophobia. The sociologist Michael Kimmel (2005, 2008) argues that the projection of masculine identity in general is based on homophobia: "homophobia, men's fear of other men, is the animating condition of the dominant definition of [heterosexual] masculinity in America, [and] the reigning definition of masculinity is a defensive effort to prevent being emasculated" (2005, 39). Following Kimmel, then, we should think of homophobia as a gender strategy for performing one's heterosexual masculinity. A gender strategy is defined by the actions one takes to negotiate the cultural norms of gender, given the current ideological conditions one faces (Hamilton 2007; Hochschild and Machung [1989] 2012). In this view, homophobia can be understood as both a gender *and* sexual identity strategy that solves the problem of identifying oneself as both normatively masculine and heterosexual by deriding gay men.

A problem with this conception of homophobia is that it connects masculinity to the social construction of heterosexuality so tightly that the two concepts collapse into one another, with masculinity serving as a proxy for heterosexuality. This theoretical conflation is understandable: in practice, many heterosexual men invoke this exact strategy in performing heterosexual masculinities. That is, straight men often aim to be conventionally, even exaggeratedly, masculine in their identity performances as a way to project a straight status.

Although men's performances of conventionally masculine identities often connote heterosexuality, they do not necessitate practices of homophobia. Heterosexual masculinities can be antihomophobic, even when they rely on conventional masculine practices to project a heterosexual identity. While Connell's (1987, 1995) theory of hegemonic masculinity and Kimmel's (2005, 2008) conceptualization of masculinity as homophobia captured a sociohistorically dominant and contemporarily persistent pattern, increasing lesbian and gay visibility and tolerance of homosexuality by Americans indicate an uncoupling of some heterosexual masculinities from hegemonic homophobic forms (Hicks and Lee 2006; Loftus 2001).

In their reformulation of hegemonic masculinity, Connell and Messerschmidt (2005) state that "the conceptualization of hegemonic

masculinity should explicitly acknowledge the possibility of democratizing gender relations, of abolishing power differentials, not just of
reproducing hierarchy" (83). Nonetheless, the concept has been used to
study the structural relations of dominant and subordinate masculinities, not democratizing or inclusive ones (Schrock and Schwalbe 2009).

Recent scholarship has started to explore the antihomophobic practices of high school boys (McCormack 2011; McCormack and Anderson 2010) and college men. For example, Anderson (2005) finds that
white college heterosexual male cheerleaders often become less homophobic when they befriend gay men on their teams. He also observes
gay-friendly attitudes among a college fraternity that recruits gay members (2009). Anderson's work shows that in some contexts the theory
of hegemonic masculinity does not capture all masculine dynamics in
play among straight men (2009). Rather, his studies document a new
pattern among white college men that shows they are increasingly prac-
ticing "inclusive" masculinities, which embrace antihomophobic attitudes due to decreases in cultural homophobia.

Straight masculinities, then, do not necessarily rely on homophobia
for their establishment (McCormack 2011; McCormack and Anderson 2010). That is, one can identify as straight without being homophobic. In following Arlene Stein's (2005) argument for understanding homophobias as plural, where she documents that homophobias
are culturally malleable and may target gender-normative gays, as
opposed to gender-nonconforming ones, I suggest that we approach
understanding *antihomophobic* practices as plural and constitutive in
the establishment of some straight masculinities (and femininities). By
antihomophobia, I mean practices that aim to counter prejudice and
discrimination against gays and lesbians as well as practices that may
expose, and sometimes renounce, straight status and privilege. Antihomophobic practices on the part of straight men (and women) indicate a decline in cultural homophobia and are a way that some straight
men may gain prestige by expressing support for lesbians and gay men
and thus enhance their masculine standing. By analyzing the complicated ways race shapes and reshapes expressions of straight masculinities and men's attendant practices of antihomophobia (and homophobia), I contribute to the empirical scholarship in gender and sexualities
studies.

Straight Femininities

The concept of straight femininities has not been explicitly theorized, but in mapping the multiplicity of femininities, gender theorists have developed concepts that are useful for analyzing the dynamics of straight women's feminine identity practices. The concepts of emphasized femininity and female masculinity capture two poles of women's gendered practices, with emphasized femininity naming the hegemonic location of feminine identity practices and female masculinity describing one form of nonnormative femininities.

Emphasized femininity is Connell's concept for practices of normative femininity that are compliant with hegemonic masculinity (1987). According to Connell, emphasized femininity entails "the display of sociability rather than technical competence, fragility in mating scenes, compliance with men's desire for titillation and ego-stroking in office relationships, acceptance of marriage and childcare as a response to labor-market discrimination against women" (1987, 187). Emphasized feminine practices, however, do not exercise dominance over other femininities as much as they try to marginalize them (Schippers 2007).

At the other end of the spectrum is what the cultural studies scholar Judith Halberstam (1998) calls female masculinity. Female masculinity is her term for the masculine practices of female bodies, sometimes lesbian, sometimes heterosexual, but always a masculinity practice without men and male bodies. Although Halberstam focuses on queer female masculinity, she highlights the importance of masculinity practices for women in general: "many women, not only inverts and lesbians, over time may have cultivated masculine body aesthetics in order to work, play, compete, or simply survive. The masculine heterosexual woman need not be viewed as a lesbian in denial; she may merely be a woman who rejects the strictures of femininity" (1998, 57–58). Beyond masculine body aesthetics, masculine practices like authority, power, and educational capital are used by women in general to gain status, respect, and recognition from others in everyday life and in social institutions, but most saliently in the bureaucratic workplace (Bourdieu 2001; Hays 1996). In their reformulation of the concept of hegemonic masculinity, Connell and Messerschmidt (2005) note that women draw on traditional masculine strategies to claim status and gain recognition:

"bourgeois women may appropriate aspects of hegemonic masculinity in constructing corporate or professional careers" (847). However, I do not limit this appropriation of masculine practice to just the workplace; rather, I think of it as key to institutional spheres from school and sports to the family and the workplace as well.

New work in the sociology of straight femininities has documented how straight women in college avoid and stigmatize lesbian students in order to maintain an unpolluted straight femininity (Hamilton 2007). Here, straight women use boundaries of social distance from lesbians in order to enact a soft form of homophobia, as opposed to developing a discourse of the "dyke," which would be analogous to Pascoe's "fag" discourse that high school boys use with other boys in disciplining each other's masculinity displays. Other studies document that straight girls use makeup to project an immodest and lustful straight femininity in schools that have strict rules regarding it (Epstein and Johnson 1998) and that in workplace settings women wear makeup to perform a legible straight feminine status, as women who don't wear it are often labeled lesbian or possibly nonheterosexual due to appearance norms in work environments (Dellinger and Williams 1997).

Regarding the construction of straight women as good mothers and mothering as central to children's adoption of heterosexual identities, the sociologist Karin Martin (2009) shows that the strength of heteronormativity is in its ability to have most heterosexual mothers assume that their young children will grow up to be heterosexual. Heterosexual mothers socialize their children into heterosexual identity paths by conceiving of love, romantic relationships, and marriage in strictly straight terms. As Martin explains, "mothers are constituted by the very heteronormative context that they then reconstruct for their children. As transmitters of cultural norms about heterosexuality, mothers are simultaneously constrained by what it means to be a good mother and the many dimensions on which mothers are judged for their mothering" (2009, 192–93). Consequently, I suggest that motherhood acts as an impetus for many straight women to reinvest in their own straight identity status as well as to be invested in maintaining their families, marriages, and children's future romantic relationships as strictly straight as well. Straight women's constructions of themselves as ideologically "good" mothers, then, may be a key link to identifications and contexts that condition straight women's homophobic acts and desire to privilege straight identities over nonstraight ones.

Blackness/Whiteness, Religion, and Homophobias

Straight identity practices are always already constructed through race and a society's historical racial formations (Omi and Winant 1994; Ferguson 2004; Moore 2011). Scholars who focus on black sexualities (Clatterburgh 1997; Collins [1990] 2000, 2004; hooks 2004; West 1993) argue that racial and racist discourses tend to construct blackness as exaggeratedly sexual while leaving whiteness unmarked and associated with sexual normativity (Ward 2008c). In other words, these discourses construct black heterosexualities as hypersexual, whereas white heterosexualities are marked as neither hypersexual nor abnormally asexual but rather as normal, ideal, and neutral.

Whiteness, as the privileged racial identity, also bestows advantage by invisibly constructing whites as lacking a racial identity and therefore reinforcing the ideology of white men and women as "individuals," not members of a privileged racial group marked with the social status and prestige of normality. In contrast, blacks in discourses of race in American contexts are viewed not as lone "individuals" but members of a clear racial group, situated within a variety of stereotypes, stereotypes that frame their sexualities.

To theorize whiteness and its relation to heterosexualities is to analyze how normative identity categories intersect in everyday life and in social structural formations (Corrado 2010; Frankenberg 1993; Hughey 2012; Twine and Gallagher 2008). It is to argue that whiteness is a sociohistorical construction and a category that has changed through the incorporation of the wave of European immigrants from 1890 to the 1920s, for instance (Roediger 2005). Even today the question of who is included and who is excluded from the category of white continues to change. For example, examining census data, sociologists note the demographic inclusion of the children of interracial couples with white fathers but nonwhite mothers; these interracial couples tend to report their children as white on their census forms (Waters 2002). Even Latinos, if they are light-skinned, as well as Asian Americans and multiracial individuals, are increasingly being seen as racially "white," although "culturally" different. Blacks and blackness continue to symbolically and socially define the racial other in US racial identity politics (see Warren and Twine 1997).

Regarding the link between homophobic practices and black identities, blacks have been documented to be on average more disapproving of homosexuality than whites (Braumbaugh, Nock, and White 2008; Lewis 2003; Moore 2010a). In comparison to other racial groups, blacks are the most likely (88 percent) to claim formal religious affiliations (Pew 2008), and 85 percent of blacks define religion as very important in their lives, compared to 58 percent of whites (Pew 2008). Adding to the strength of their religiosity, blacks tend to belong to more conservative Protestant denominations, which have evangelical views that are more strongly condemning of homosexuality than liberal Protestant faiths (Laumann et al. 1994). These studies suggest that racial differences in disapproval of homosexuality can be accounted for by blacks' higher rates of religiosity and the importance of the black church (Schulte and Battle 2004), as well as by their lower levels of education, combined with blacks' lack of racial and oftentimes class privilege as well (Collins 2004; Froyum 2007). However, as Moore (2010a) explains, "blacks of the same religion and with similar levels of education as whites were still more likely to express negative attitudes towards homosexuality" (317), indicating the difficulty of disentangling race, religion, and other factors in explaining homophobic attitudes among blacks.

Despite this body of research, in public opinion polls, blacks are more supportive than whites of civil rights for gays, although blacks still express more moral disapproval of homosexuality (Lewis 2003; Yang 1999). My findings simultaneously build upon and challenge these accounts of the connections among straight sexualities, race, religion, and practices of homophobia and antihomophobia. I analyze the way race subtly and complexly shapes straight men's and women's reported homophobic and antihomophobic practices.

However, in *Pray the Gay Away: The Extraordinary Lives of Bible Belt Gays*, the sociologist Bernadette Barton (2012) shows that white evangelical heterosexuals in Bible Belt states enact strong homophobic practices, from the extreme belief in being able to exorcise homosexuality out of gay individuals through the "laying on of hands" to a toxic Christian religiosity that rejects openly gay family members, friends, and neighbors. Of course, here, whiteness, religion, and region become the key categories for understanding the salience of a closeted pattern of existence. Although polls confirm the commonsense beliefs that regions like the Northeast, West Coast, and upper Midwest tend to be more pro-gay than the southern states of the Bible Belt, it is important to recognize that college towns and cities in the South, places like Austin, New Orleans, and Atlanta, are cities of tolerance and acceptance with elaborate lesbian and gay communities, indicating that a post-closeted dynamic is present within even strongly antigay regions of the country (Barton 2012; Chauncey 2004; Gray 2009).

2

From "Normal" to Heterosexual

The Historical Making of Heterosexualities

Images of heterosexual identity invoke well-worn associations of a nuclear family, or a married straight couple, or, to use the current lingo, the casual sex "hookups" of college students and other nonmonogamous straight men and women. These images, though, are not natural results emanating from biological male and female differences, nor are they socially random. Rather, they are socially constructed. That they are not natural phenomena is demonstrated not only by their variance across time and place but also by their ever-changing social status, identity conception, and historical arrangement. Further, these variations are largely explained by the shifts and changes in sociohistorical constructions of heterosexualities and their boundary relations with homosexualities since the late nineteenth century. These shifts and changes were both systematic and shaped by the culture and principles of social organization of the society to which they belonged. And these changes helped to construct part of the realm of sexual life as we know it today.

It is useful to think of another society or a different historical period than our own to get a concrete sense of how varied sexualities can be and to relativize our own culture's organization of homo/heterosexualities. The anthropologist Gilbert Herdt's (1981) famous study *Guardians of the Flutes* examines the Sambia of Papua New Guinea, who combine rituals of homosexual and heterosexual behaviors in transitioning boys into manhood. In their movement toward adult relations with women and with the aim of reproducing their tribe's existence through having children of their own, all Sambian boys engage in ritualized homosexual behavior, where they suck and ingest the semen of an older adult tribesman. This cultural ritual is based on the belief that boys do not produce masculine fluid (semen) on their own. And in order to become big, strong, and virile men, they must practice this ritual of same-sex fellatio in order to store up and obtain the masculine fluid that will allow them to later impregnate women. This is an example of a different culture's organization of acts of homosexual and heterosexual behavior that is distinct from our own.

Closer to home, we need only turn to nineteenth-century Victorian America to find a historical time period with a qualitatively different organization of the meanings of sex and love among women and men. Victorian Americans did not view sex as an expression of love, nor did they conceive of love as expressed through acts of sex. This changed only in the twentieth century, when a cultural shift that sexualized love and eroticized sex took place. At this time, the rise of the new norm of romantic love was accompanied by notions of companionate dating and marriage (D'Emilio and Freedman 2012; Seidman 1991). In contrast to our notion of romantic love, during the nineteenth century, Victorian Americans defined love as a spiritual feeling, and sex was aimed at primarily procreative purposes within the institution of marriage, although there were degrees of eroticism and intimacy between couples, and the institution of prostitution flourished beside the institution of marriage (D'Emilio and Freedman 2012; Lystra 1989). In part, Victorian women's statuses were attached to their association with the higher purpose of love as spirituality, whereas men's sexualities were viewed as animalistic and thus lowly and instinctual, needing to be tamed by women's higher nature and spiritual love. The fact that we no longer view women and men nor sex and love as polar opposites is an example of our own historical present's different organization of heterosexual sex and love.

Heterosexual/homosexual desires, behaviors, and identities have a complex relation to one another, the society in which they are configured, and the historical period in which they gain meaning and help constitute how one experiences social life. In this chapter, I sketch the changing historical character of heterosexual masculinities[1] and heterosexual femininities in America since the late nineteenth century. Analytically, I focus on historiographical studies that explicitly analyze heterosexualities and their shaping of black and white men's and women's experiences.[2] Much of the historical research in gender and race scholarship does not account for the development of heterosexual identities. Rather, lesbian, gay, and feminist scholars have been pioneers in studying the sociohistorical construction of heterosexualities in their efforts to study and document lesbian and gay life, although new historical research shows an attentiveness to analyzing sexualities that was absent in prior research.

In her virtuosic statement *Epistemology of the Closet*, the late literary theorist Eve Sedgwick (1990) captures the defining move of sexualities scholars and queer theorists to study sexualities as a general principle of social organization in American society. Sedgwick argues that "many nodes of the thought and knowledge in twentieth-century Western culture as a whole are structured—indeed, fractured—by a chronic, now endemic crisis of homo/heterosexual definition" (1). This analytical move by queer theorists shifted sexualities scholarship from explaining the modern homosexual to analyzing the power relations of the homo/heterosexual definition. Queer theorists changed the discussion from being exclusively focused on homosexualities to more broadly focusing on sexualities, thus including heterosexualities, as a general principle of social knowledge, social difference, and identity formations. This move is central to my project of turning the lens back on heterosexuals and making their identities and privileges subject to social and historical analysis (Butler 1992; Fuss 1991; Katz 1996; Seidman 1996; Somerville 2000; Warner 1993).

Moreover, the extant historical scholarship on heterosexualities demonstrates that its formation is inextricably tied to the construction of homosexualities over the late nineteenth and twentieth centuries. The development of heterosexual identities over time consolidated a sexual hierarchy, distinct from but often reinforcing of gender, racial, and class hierarchies, that constructed heterosexualities as natural, the internalization of psychological health, and the normative ideal of one's personal and public self (D'Emilio and Freedman 2012). Central to this sexual hierarchy and its enforcement of normative heterosexuality is the establishment of homosexualities as a polluting social force that stigmatizes nonheterosexual behaviors, styles, and relations. While the development of the homo/heterosexual definition sought to distinguish sexuality from gender, the rise of sexuality as a distinct domain of humanity paradoxically reinforced the importance of gender identity politics by connecting heterosexual normativity to the embodiment of gender normativity. These normative relations are the hallmark of the false dichotomies that designate masculine men and feminine women as performing ostensibly heterosexual identities and feminine men and masculine women as performing supposedly homosexual ones.

Since the construction of heterosexual men's and women's identities occurred partly as a result of the rise of homosexual identities, heterosexual men's privilege and identity are based on the pollution of homosexual masculinities as womanlike, sexually licentious, and an inversion of the traditional social roles ascribed to men, such as father, husband, and protector. Similarly, heterosexual women's privilege and identity use polluting images of lesbians, who are portrayed as pathologically manlike, sexually aggressive, and inverting the traditional social roles of women as mothers, wives, and those who need to be protected.

Gender has always been a fundamental organizing principle in the social and historical constructions of heterosexual and homosexual identity formations in America. Heterosexuals define themselves as heterosexual by disidentifying with homosexuals of their same gender. For instance, heterosexual men are not like homosexual men, who desire men, but rather are men who desire women exclusively, and it is their heterosexuality that ostensibly and fundamentally alters the meaning of their masculinities. This point is historically evidenced by the emergence of homosexual male subcultures before lesbian ones, and consequently the prior development of conscious heterosexual identities among men before women (Chauncey 1994; Faderman 1991). The later development of lesbian and heterosexual femininities is related to women's subordination under patriarchal institutions, where women were economically and socially dependent upon fathers, husbands, and men more broadly for their welfare. And, as I document in this chapter, a gendered social organization has been central to the organization of sexual behaviors and identities among and between heterosexual and homosexual men and women. Further, a gendered ordering of sexual identities continues to this day, where a gendered set of codes circulates among straight and gay Americans as an informal system of symbols that are viewed as proxies for heterosexual and homosexual identities. These gender codes, though, are problematic proxies for sexual identities in a society where a diversity of gender displays is common among gay and straight individuals alike.

The hierarchical boundaries between heterosexualities and homosexualities were also central to reinforcing a racial hierarchy that marked black sexualities as pathological and abnormal in comparison to white sexualities, which went unmarked but served as the embodiment of health, normality, and beauty (D'Emilio and Freedman 2012). The concept of respectability is key to understanding how black women in particular aimed to counteract the pathologizing of their sexualities, wanting to project themselves as decent and good, sexually and otherwise, to white society as well as to one another (Higginbotham 1993; Hine 1989; Mitchell 2004; Summers 2004; Wolcott 2001).

This chapter introduces and integrates the historical scholarship on the rise of heterosexual masculinities and heterosexual femininities in the United States from the 1890s to the 1990s. First, I examine when the terms "heterosexual" and "homosexual" were invented and started to be diffused into American culture. Before the creation of a sexual system of identity, individuals were defined by a gendered social order, where marriage, reproduction, and laws against nonprocreative sexual behaviors governed the relations between men and women, men and men, and men and animals. Using the concepts of the changing definition of heterosexualities and the rise and fall of the closet to organize my analysis, and to advance my argument of the importance of understanding post-closeted dynamics in America today, I synthesize the historiographical work on the rise of the homo/heterosexual definition among men and women.

In the first historical period, from 1890 to the 1930s, which I refer to as "the birth of heterosexuality and the pre-closet period," I show that a gendered organization still predominated but that a visible homosexual male subculture existed in major American cities, where homosexual men socialized and had sex with "normal" men, the historical predecessors of "heterosexual" men. Since the colonial era, female sexuality had been defined by women's reproductive capacity in the family; this had changed by the 1880s, when "romantic friendships" between women, previously viewed as a common part of women's affectionate attachments, were now regarded with suspicion as possibly "perverted" and lesbian.

In addition, historians document the elaboration of a new culture of sexual liberalism, also referred to as the first sexual revolution, in the 1920s across America. Sexual liberalism promoted a new awareness of sexual agency, independence, and self-discovery among women. Following this, from the 1930s to the 1960s, was the period I refer to as "heterosexual hegemony and the rise of the closet." In my discussion of this period, I delineate the formation and hardening of boundaries between heterosexuals and homosexuals, with the state's repression of everyday homosexual life and its implementation of laws and policies that singled out homosexuals for discrimination. By this time, and in contrast to the previous period, heterosexual identities are defined through the exclusion of all same-sex contact. Furthermore, I describe how the increasing development of nonprocreative heterosexual masculinities and femininities led to the end of this limited sexual freedom referred to as sexual liberalism, as sexual liberalism emphasized marriage as the predominant arrangement for heterosexual relations throughout most of the twentieth century. In the chapter's final section, "Challenges to Heterosexual Hegemony and the Decline of the Closet, 1960s–1990s," I show how the Stonewall generation changed what it meant to be gay and lesbian by refashioning identity politics. Before Stonewall, homosexuals generally came out only to other homosexuals. After Stonewall, the social and political act of coming out was revolutionized and redefined by LGBT persons, so that now it meant coming out to heterosexuals and challenging the closet's repression of sexual and gender difference. These changes brought about newfound freedoms for LGBT persons while challenging heterosexual Americans' homophobia, heterosexism, and gender normativity in profound and unprecedented ways.

This sociohistorical chapter demonstrates that sexual desires, behaviors, and identities are deeply constructed by a society's social categories, norms, and discourses. I show that the formation of sexuality as an independent principle of social organization is interlocked with American society's gendered, racial, and social class formations. To imagine a different, more democratic sexual order, we need to look to the past for answers to why and how society is the way it is presently. A post-closeted culture of LGBT individuals is a clear pattern and trend in the contemporary United States, and this cultural force is reshaping and changing straight Americans' identities and their interactional practices with nonheterosexuals. In the following empirical chapters I analyze straight Americans' identity conceptions and their social interactions with LGBT individuals, and sociologically account for how the rise of a post-closeted culture is transforming straight sexualities today. In this chapter, I utilize the invention of heterosexualities and the rise and fall of the closet as the analytical frames for understanding the shifts in the definition of homo/heterosexual identities during this hundred-year period from 1890 to 1990.

Before Heterosexuality

Historians argue that from the colonial era to the late nineteenth century in America, same-sex sexuality was viewed as only a *behavior*, not yet an *identity* of a subcultural group. From 1600 to the late 1800s, homosexuality was prohibited through sodomy laws, which were aimed not at homosexual individuals but at nonprocreative, nonmarital sexual *behaviors* more broadly. It was only during the late nineteenth and early twentieth centuries that prohibitions against sodomy were regularly enforced, and now against a subcultural group of people thought to embody homosexual *identities*. Thus, the distinction between homosexual (and heterosexual) *behavior* and *identity* is crucial for understanding the development of the homosexual/heterosexual categories and later social relations.

In his book *The Invention of Heterosexuality*, the historian Jonathan Ned Katz (1996) argues that in the early part of the Victorian era, from about 1820 to 1860, neither the notion of heterosexual *behavior* nor the notion of *identity* existed in America. Rather, the social organization of sexual behaviors and intercourse was based on notions of a true manhood, a true womanhood, and a spiritual love. A major concern for Americans was whether sexual relations took place within or outside marriage (Seidman 1991). Socially sanctioned sexual relations were to occur between married persons and to be aimed at procreation. Marriage was the sacrosanct cornerstone of Victorian life, and a proper womanhood, manhood, and progeny—not an erotic heterosexual love based on pleasure or carnal desire—were organized through this institution. While nonprocreative sex, as well as sex outside marriage, was culturally maligned, prostitution was a growing phenomenon in American cities due to the double standards that allowed men to seek sexual release with sex workers, who unburdened wives from husbands' stronger sexual appetites (D'Emilio and Freedman 2012, 140). Overall, though, sex was generally conceived of as an instinct aimed at reproduction, not the basis of an identity, and marriage was the container of socially appropriate sexual reproductive behavior and central in establishing Victorian men's and women's gender roles, social honor, and respectability.

In fact, the terms "homosexual" and "heterosexual" were invented in 1868, according to the *Oxford English Dictionary Supplement* (Katz 1996, 10). The "terms heterosexual and homosexual apparently came into common use only in the first quarter of this [twentieth] century and before that time, if words are clues to concepts, people did not conceive of a social universe polarized into heteros and homos," Katz notes (1996, 10). One of the great ironies of these modern terms is that Karl-Maria Kertbeny, a German law reformer, coined the term "homosexual" in his effort to amend sodomy laws in Germany at the time, but not to stigmatize homosexuals. This progressive reformer used the word "heterosexual" in 1880 in his public defense of homosexuality, naming a heterosexual individual's sexual sense of himself as a way to promote tolerance of homosexuals (Ghaziani 2010; Katz 1996).

However, the formation of the idea of homosexuality came before heterosexuality, as European sexologists, physicians, and other scientists provided the first medical interpretations of homosexuality as a form of pathology in the 1860s. Over time, they sought to distinguish homosexuality and homosexuals from a changing group that was called "normal," "unafflicted," and "heterosexual" (Terry 1999).

Heterosexual identity, then, is a modern invention of the late nineteenth century, and it is not reducible to the reproduction of the human species; nor is *heterosexual identity* simply an extension of one's sexed body, whether understood as based in genitalia, chromosomes, or hormonal differences between males and females. *Heterosexual identity* is also not one's gender identity. That is, embodying gender-conventional behaviors or being viewed as a "masculine" man or a "feminine" woman does not make one heterosexual. Rather, this is a culturally dominant ideology that falsely equates the embodiment of gender-traditional displays with heterosexuality. And, finally, *heterosexual identity* is not reducible to sexual intercourse between a man and a woman, as sexual *behaviors* do not necessarily include the adoption of an *identity*.

The notion of a sexual *identity* was new to American culture in the nineteenth century, when people understood themselves through a gender principle of social organization, primarily arranged through the institutions of marriage and family. A sexual *identity* was a new form of selfhood, where erotic life became a defining part of one's self and a new form of difference distinguishing one from others (Duggan 2000). *Heterosexual identity* names an individual's sense of self and the collective grouping he or she identifies with on its basis. The sociological construction of *heterosexual identities* developed through their relationship to homosexual identities. Paradoxically, heterosexuality was and is defined against homosexuality. But by being defined against homosexuality, heterosexuality is at the same time dependent upon the existence of homosexuality for its meaning (Fuss 1991). The birth of the heterosexual/homosexual binary in Western culture, then, became imbricated with other key categories of modern Western culture, such as disclosure/secrecy, public/private, masculine/feminine, majority/minority, and natural/artificial (Sedgwick 1990).

The rise of *heterosexual identities* among women did not occur until the twentieth century. Before that, late nineteenth-century Victorian white women understood their sense of self through the construction of a "true womanhood." Marriage was the foundation of white middle-class women's lives and was based on the notion of a "true love" between man and woman. For example, Katz explains, "special purity claimed for this era's true women referred not to asexuality but to middle-class women's better control than men over their carnal impulses. . . . True love was a hierarchical system, topped by an intense spiritual feeling powerful enough to justify marriage, reproduction, and an otherwise unhallowed sensuality" (1996, 44). The historical construction of white Victorian women often presents an image of them as angelic creatures whose identities are based on a spiritual love, and Victorian men as aggressive and sexually voracious "beasts" who had to exercise gentlemanly restraint at home in their roles as husbands. However, recent historical accounts have modified this image of Victorian men and women as totally unromantic in their marriages and relations. The historian Karen Lystra (1989) finds that Victorian men and women embraced romantic notions in their letters to one another, especially during courtship. Still, neither married Victorians nor their unmarried counterparts considered themselves heterosexual or homosexual at this time.

Between 1860 and 1890, however, a shift occurred. During this period the concepts of heterosexuality and homosexuality emerged as part of the knowledge domains of sexology, psychoanalysis, and medical science (e.g., psychiatry), as well as legal, media, and other cultural domains. These new knowledge domains delegitimized and aimed to replace religious views, which had been culturally dominant and had defined sexual behaviors as sinful or not (Weeks 1977). Heterosexual sexual *behaviors*, however, that were not aimed at procreation were still seen as deviant, but now alongside a deviant, nonprocreative homosexuality. Heterosexual sexual *behaviors'* legitimacy still rested on a procreative justification, and so heterosexual sexual *behaviors* that were lustful and nonprocreative in aim were seen as pathological just like homosexual sodomy (Katz 1996). For example, the first usage of the word "heterosexuality" in an American medical article occurred in 1892. In this article, Dr. James G. Kiernan defined pathological heterosexuality as sexual desire not oriented toward reproduction, viewing a focus on sexual pleasure as deviant. This definition of heterosexuality lasted until the 1920s in American middle-class culture.

A key figure at this point is Sigmund Freud ([1922] 1949, 1962), the father of psychoanalysis. Freud's theory of sexuality establishes sexual object choice (the person one desires) as an integral development of the human self, and his theory informs the foundational approaches taken by medical psychiatry, psychology, and psychoanalysis in conceptualizing sexualities. By the early part of the twentieth century, Freud, as well as other sex researchers, who are referred to as sexologists, such as the British researcher Havelock Ellis and the Austro-German researcher Richard von Krafft-Ebing, made opposite-sex object choice the organizing principle of a healthy social-psychological sexual identity, and same-sex object choice a psychic disease.[3] At this time heterosexuality lost its negative connotations, and began to be seen as the embodiment of psychological health, while homosexuality became its unhealthy complement.

The importance of Freud and the shift he represents in medical science, the social sciences, and American culture more broadly is in defining heterosexuality as an acquired social-psychological *identity*, not simply as a desire or behavior oriented toward procreation. In contrast to earlier definitions that defined the heterosexual sexual instinct's aim as solely toward procreation, Freud argues that procreation is a secondary development in the pursuit of happiness. He states that pleasure is the main purpose of a human being's mental apparatus. Thus a person's sexual "instinct" can be directed toward pleasure, self-expression, love, or procreation. The Foucauldian (1978) argument is instructive here: Freud makes the heterosexual sexual instinct into a feeling (or a psychology of selfhood) and therefore a central part of one's self-understanding, not reducible to acts of procreation. Heterosexual and homosexual categories are no longer descriptions of only sexual *behaviors*; rather, they are now social *identities* imbued with psychological notions of healthiness or unhealthiness and social statuses of normalcy or deviancy.

The Birth of Heterosexuality and the Pre-Closet Period, 1890–1930s

A major misconception of the history of sexuality in America is that heterosexual domination is assumed to have created a closeted existence for homosexuals since the colonial era or before. This was not the case. As we have seen, first the terms "heterosexual" and "homosexual" had to be invented by medical-scientific experts whose discourses were disseminated into American culture, and then put into practice by men and women in everyday social life. Before the development of the heterosexual/homosexual system of sexual identity that we know, a gender system of social organization overlaid same-sex and other-sex behaviors. From roughly 1890 to 1930, "normal" men and fairies, who were womanlike men who had sex with men, were defined by a gendered sense of self. That is, "normal" men were allowed to have sex with other men, as long as they maintained both a traditional masculine display and the dominant penetrator role in anal sex. Likewise, men who made same-sex sexualities central to their lives were expected to display feminine manners and assumed to take on the role of the penetrated. For women, same-sex intimacies were permitted under the respected institution of women's "romantic friendships" with one another. Whether genital sexual relations took place between "romantic friends" remains a matter of historical dispute, yet these female same-sex love relationships were fundamental to the proto-lesbian identities and subcultures that would emerge in the twentieth century. The sexualization of women as lesbian or heterosexual in the 1920s and 1930s set the frame for the homo/heterosexual definition among women later in the century. In sum, at this historical juncture, sexuality—heterosexuality and homosexuality—as a distinct axis of identity was still submerged within the gender roles, arrangements, and institutions of the period.

Historically, heterosexual men's identities must be understood in relation to homosexual men's; likewise, women's heterosexual and homosexual identities must be understood in relation to one another. This claim is supported by the historical scholarship that documents clear and salient gender differences in the emergence of homosexualities; and this difference is related to the later development of lesbian identities and subcultures in the United States in comparison to nineteenth-century gay male subcultures present earlier in cities like New York, Chicago, and San Francisco. Women throughout the nineteenth century lacked access to both wage-earning jobs and public spaces where they could form same-sex subcultures parallel to those among men (Boyd 2003; Chauncey 1994; Faderman 1991; Heap 2009; Stryker and Van Buskirk 1996). Furthermore, the prominence of "romantic friendships" among women has made distinguishing women's affectionate companionship from sexual, specifically genital, relations a historically complicated issue, as "romantic friendships" ran the gamut from friendship and companionship to erotic sexual relationships (Rupp 2001).

The later development of women's lesbian and heterosexual subjectivities is also demonstrated by the role sexology played in constructing women's sexualities. Throughout the nineteenth century, sexologists claimed that only men were able to be actively sexual and that women's sexualities were a response to, and dependent on, men's initiation. In a parallel to this logic, homosexual women were "female inverts," as "inversion" of the female character into that of a male is what it took in sexology's discourse for a woman to pursue another woman, as supposedly only a man would (Chauncey 1982; Smith-Rosenberg 1989). The shift in the twentieth-century discourses of sexology as well as psychoanalysis, psychiatry, and medicine to conceptualizing women's sexualities as active, self-initiating, and agentic is central to the development of both heterosexual femininities and lesbian women's identities.

While the historical studies presented so far document the rise of heterosexuality among the social sciences, medicine, and psychiatry, culminating in the Freudian distinction and its discursive diffusion into other scientific and popular cultural discourses, other significant historiographical work has documented the everyday relationships between homosexual men and working-class "normal" men, who will become "heterosexual" over the course of the first half of the twentieth century. These shifts in masculinities are partly the result of developments in medical-scientific discourses that pathologized homosexuality and consolidated heterosexuality as a middle-class phenomenon that would later pass on to working-class men's cultures as well. Although expert medical discourses and professionals were culturally esteemed, the behaviors and subcultures of men and women with same-sex desires remained to varying degrees independent from their influences.

In *Gay New York: Gender, Urban Culture, and the Making of the Gay Male World, 1890–1940*, the historian George Chauncey (1994) provides a careful periodization on the rise of heterosexuality as an identity category among working-class and middle-class men. From the 1890s to the 1930s, working-class cultures of New York socially permitted "normal" men to publicly socialize and have sex with other men who were categorized as "fairies" without this stigmatizing these "normal" men as homosexual or morally deviant. According to Chauncey,

> So long as they [normal men] maintained a masculine demeanor and played (or claimed to play) only the 'masculine,' or insertive, role in the sexual encounter—so long, that is, as they eschewed the style of the fairy and did not allow their bodies to be sexually penetrated—neither they,

the fairies, nor the working-class public considered *them* to be queer. (1994, 66; italics in original)

The key distinction is that fairies were the ones marked as socially stigmatized but publicly tolerated womanlike men. From their plucked eyebrows and colored hair to their powdered faces and overall effeminate bodily comportment, fairy men projected public self-presentations that embraced these markers of femininity. Further, "normal" men, who are also called "trade" by their fairy and homosexual sexual partners, of this period are not to be thought of as "heterosexual," at least not yet, as these "normal" men could engage in sexual activity with other men without the cultural opprobrium of the heterosexual/homosexual system. The sexual boundaries between "normal" men (sailors, common laborers, hoboes, and various other transient workers) and fairies were not based on a conceptualization of sexuality as a distinct indicator of personhood; rather, the sexual boundaries between "normal" men and fairies were organized through this period's gender system and the sexual roles assumed in these relations. "Normal" men, according to Chauncey, "were, rather, men who were attracted to womanlike men or interested in sexual activity defined not by the gender of their partner but by the kind of bodily pleasures that partner could provide" (1994, 96).

Regarding middle-class men's culture, the development of a homosexual or queer identity among gender-conventional middle-class men in the 1910s and 1920s led to the establishment of heterosexuality among their nonhomosexual male middle-class counterparts. On one hand, middle-class gender-conventional queer men distanced themselves from fairies' effeminate self-presentations and stigmatized status, but queer men privately acknowledged to themselves and other queer men that they sexually desired men. "Queer" at this time means a conventional masculine gender presentation among homosexually identified men, and it is largely a reaction against the stigmatized status of effeminate homosexual men.

On the other hand, nonhomosexual middle-class men reacted and formed their heterosexual masculinity against both fairies and queer men alike. By claiming that their masculinity was indicated by their heterosexuality—that is, the absence of homosexual desire—"heterosexual" middle-class men emerged in this period of changing gender and sexual formations. According to Chauncey,

> Whereas fairies' desire for men was thought to follow inevitably from their gender persona, queers maintained that their desire for men revealed only their "sexuality" (their "homosexuality"), a distinct domain of personality independent of gender. Their homosexuality, they argued, revealed nothing abnormal in their gender persona. The effort to forge a new kind of homosexual identity was predominantly a middle-class phenomenon, and the emergence of "homosexuals" in middle-class culture was inextricably linked to the emergence of "heterosexuals" in that culture as well. (1994, 100)

Queer men constituted a sizable number of homosexually identified men from 1910 until the 1940s, but since queer men led publicly heterosexual lives, fairies were the ones who took the brunt of antihomosexual prejudice and discrimination. The straight world's lack of knowledge of the middle-class world of gender-traditional queer men meant that they faced less police harassment and hostility than their fairy counterparts (Chauncey 1994, 103).

At this same time, the black community in Harlem was home to working-class and middle-class subcultures of black gays and lesbians. Celebrated blues singers, such as "Ma" Rainey, Bessie Smith, and Gladys Bentley (who married her white lesbian lover in a talked-about ceremony), all sang about "sissies" and "bulldaggers" to their knowing audiences. While black New Yorkers were ambivalent about public displays of homosexuality, they embraced it in performers and at the annual drag balls held in Harlem. "Nothing reveals the complexity—and ambivalence—of the attitudes of the black press and Harlem as a whole toward gay men and lesbians more than the Hamilton Lodge ball, the largest annual gathering of lesbians and gay men in Harlem—and the city," notes Chauncey (1994, 257). The drag balls were the most publicly talked-about events of homosexual life at this time and received favorable, if not sensational, coverage in the black press.

From 1900 to 1930, black middle-class men of the period navigated the shift from a Victorian industrial entrepreneur notion of masculinity to one based in the rising consumer capitalist economy. The historian

Martin Summers (2004), in *Manliness and Its Discontents: The Black Middle Class and the Transformation of Masculinity, 1900–1930*, discusses the heterosexual/homosexual divisions and their effects on the masculinities of aspiring middle-class black men. Summers compares the "normal" black male members of the Prince Hall Freemasonry, a black fraternal order that created a social network among black men based on their shared sense of class standing and masculinity, to the middle-class black homosexual male artists of the Harlem Renaissance. Both the Prince Hall Freemasons and Harlem Renaissance artists were experiencing a changing definition of masculinity, moving from one based in industry to one "more defined by the consumer goods one owned, the leisure practices one engaged in, and one's physical and sexual virility" (8).

Summers implicitly describes the Prince Hall Freemasons as "normal" or nonhomosexual men who defined their masculinity by being married and providing for their wives and children: "When black Masons invoked their positions as protectors of, and providers for, women and children, and spearheads of commercial development within the black community, they were engaging in the formation of a gender identity that was rooted in notions of production" (42). Gender identity is central to the inchoate formation of a heterosexual identity among the Freemasons.

In contrast, Summers views the African American and Afro-Caribbean men of the Harlem Renaissance as contesting the black middle-class "normal" masculinity of the Prince Hall Freemasons. This contestation is based on the Harlem Renaissance men's homosexuality. Some of the most celebrated black male artists of the Harlem Renaissance, such as Langston Hughes, Wallace Thurman, Richard Bruce Nugent, and Countee Cullen, belonged to the vibrant black homosexual subculture in Harlem (Garber 1989; Summers 2004). However, while this visible black gay subcultural presence contested black middle-class norms of respectability and heterosexual conformity, they also provoked outbursts from Harlem pastors like Adam Clayton Powell.

> Homosexuality, they [the black middle-class] argued, was only one of the
> ills of rapid urbanization but it was the most dangerous obstacle to the
> reconstitution and stabilization of the black family. One of the tireless

crusaders against gay and lesbian subculture was Adam Clayton Powell, pastor of Abyssinian Baptist Church in Harlem. Powell attempted to
root out homosexuality not only from urban leisure spaces but also from
more respectable institutions such as the church. (Summers 2004, 194)

Here, then, pastors like Powell created an antihomosexual discourse
among the black middle classes and aimed to enforce a respectable
black masculinity as strictly heterosexual. As a result, black masculinity,
heterosexuality, and middle-class status aligned in the stigmatization of
black homosexualities.

Alongside these shifts in Victorian masculinity that allowed men to
develop sexual selves and erotic desires in different ways, whether as
"normal" or conventionally gendered, on one hand, or queer and masculine versus fairy and feminine, on the other, women were just beginning to create sexual subjectivities and a sense of consciousness around
their new erotic desires. By rejecting the Victorian model of femininity and its emphasis on reproduction and sexual restraint, American
women fomented a sexual revolution from 1890 to 1930. Historians
observe the appearance of three groups of women who exhibited the
newfound freedoms in "manners and morals" of the period: working-
class wage earners, young middle-class "flappers," and the second generation of independent feminist "new women" (Allen 1931; Meyerowitz
1988, 1990; Ryan 1983, 2006; Peiss 1983, 1986). These groups of women
were central to the historical rise and formation of heterosexuality as
connected to, but separate from, gender identities. All three groups of
women were orientated to intimate relationships with men, but among
the second generation of "new women" were famous lesbian writers of
the time, and some working-class women participated in homosexual
subcultures as well.

As the sexualization of women produced nascent conceptions of heterosexual and homosexual feminine selves, the older nineteenth-century "female world of love and ritual" between female friends, companions, and clandestine lovers—that is, "romantic friendships" between
women—became suspected of "female inversion" and stigmatized as
a form of female homosexuality (Faderman 1981; Smith-Rosenberg
1975; Rupp 2001). No longer could "romantic friendships" be seen as
sexually innocent, simply platonic, or unassociated with lesbianism;

the romantic friends themselves as well as the expert discourses of sexologists, psychoanalysts, and medical psychiatrists started to view same-sex friendships and intimacies as possible or actual forms of lesbian identities and relations. However, the homosexual suspicion and stigmatization that surrounded "romantic friendships" were uneven in their application among women who displayed "normal" gender presentations as well as those from different social classes and races, as "romantic friendships" continued to include a variety of relationships—from friendships to sexual relationships—between women into the twentieth century (Rupp 2001).

As a result of the influences of the first sexual revolution on American women, according to the historian Joanne Meyerowitz (1990),

> women began to adopt more sexual, or at least less modest, styles; shorter skirts, cosmetics, bobbed hair, and cigarettes, once the styles of prostitutes, all seemed evidence of a larger change in mores when adopted by "respectable" working- and middle-class women. Men and women mingled freely in new commercialized recreation industries and in workplaces. And surveys of the middle class revealed increases in premarital intercourse. (274)

This sexual revolution and the rise of young working-class women wage earners, who adopted these new sexually permissive attitudes and styles of dress and sought fun in cheap amusements, were connected to the second industrial revolution, which occurred from 1880 to 1920 in urban centers. Disfavoring the previously predominant kind of work available to women as domestics, urban wage-earning women sought positions in the new workplaces of the office, department and retail store, and factory (Peiss 1986; Meyerowitz 1988).

As the economy shifted to an increasingly consumer-based organization, women's and men's leisure pursuits did as well. The new social entertainments and leisure activities included popular theater, dance halls, and nickelodeon cinemas. These leisure activities were accompanied by the mass production of automobiles, which procured a new kind of privacy for women and men. Urban entertainments, along with automobiles, created new spaces for women's and men's heterosocial interactions and their heterosexual self-developments, as these new

spaces provided separation from the family and workplace and promoted heterosocial interactions in these urban geographies (Peiss 1983,
1986; Zaretsky 2004).

From middle-class flappers who went slumming in working-class
districts to middle- and upper-class "new women" who lived in these
neighborhoods and observed their working-class counterparts' behaviors, more affluent women's heterosexual practices and subculture were
influenced and shaped by those of working-class wage-earning women.
This group of working-class women wage earners included black and
white women lodgers who lived in the furnished room districts of
urban centers apart from their families (Meyerowitz 1988, 1990; Peiss
1986), native white and immigrant wage earners who lived at home
with kin (Peiss 1986), and their more sexually permissive "charity girl"
peers (Peiss 1983, 1986).

Living outside traditional communities and family supervision,
working-class women lodgers, who constituted one out of five urban
wage-earning women, negotiated sexual conventions and boundaries
in the context of economic necessity, as they worked in low-paying jobs
that barely met their basic expenses (Meyerowitz 1988, 1990). Meyerowitz (1990) describes the patterns of their sexual practices:

> Heterosexual relationships in the furnished room districts included "dat-
> ing," "pick ups," "occasional prostitution," and "temporary alliances."
> Like professional prostitution and marriage, these were economic as well
> as sexual and social relationships. . . . By entering sexual relationships,
> however, they could supplement their wages with free evenings on the
> town, free meals in restaurants, and sometimes gifts and money. (280)

The woman lodger became a symbol for urban reformers. On the one
hand, she represented a type of endangered womanhood in need of
protection, but on the other hand, some Hollywood movies romanticized her as a chaste but sexually exciting independent woman who
sometimes caught the eye of rich male suitors (Meyerowitz 1990).

While women lodgers, also known as "women adrift," later became
popular characters in novels, movies, and magazines, showing the
struggles but also the excitement of living as independent working-
class heterosexual women, they were at the same time a model of

nonmarital and nonprocreative heterosexuality, one that went against the dominant model of wifely and motherly duties in the domestic home of the heterosexual family (Meyerowitz 1988). If women lodgers struggled harder to make ends meet than their female peers who lived at home, then it was paradoxical that women wage earners who lived at home also depended on men "treating" them to the city's amusements. This is due to the fact that many of these women's parents claimed their daughters' incomes as part of the family's earnings (Peiss 1986).

Although applying the term "charity girls" to all working-class wage-earning women would be a mistake, the term was underworld slang used to describe working-class women who traded sexual favors for a night out on the town with a male companion. The importance of the term is that it highlights the fluidity of heterosexual respectability among working-class women who sought a good time by visiting a city's restaurants, dance halls, theaters, and amusement parks. In other words, "charity girls" represented a form of working-class female morality that fell between the degraded "fallen women" and the utmost sexually chaste ladies.

Alongside their working-class peers, female flappers emerged out of middle- and upper-class white families, and these young white women took advantage of these new urban spaces and media as well, rebelling against their parents' repressive propriety (McGovern 1968; Meyerowitz 1990; Ryan 1983). With their adventurous heterosexuality, female flappers also signaled a notable departure from the ideal of a restrained sexual self. According to one historian's classic description, a flapper

> smoked, drank, worked, and played side by side with men. She became preoccupied with sex—shocking and simultaneously unshockable. She danced close, became freer with her favors, kept her own latchkey, wore scantier attire which emphasized her boyish, athletic form, just as she used makeup and bobbed and dyed her hair. (McGovern 1968, 317)

To say the least, the flapper daughter was not her Victorian mother.

With the rise of flappers, there was a resexualization of American middle-class women, allowed for the first time to be erotically heterosexual. For example, nineteenth-century sexologists and medical doctors discussed female deviancy as "inversion," a broad category of deviant gender behavior that included homosexual desire as only one aspect. Now they focused on female deviancy as "homosexuality," which was now coupled with heterosexuality (Chauncey 1982). Before the sexual revolution of the early twentieth century, Victorian women were generally viewed as passionless, asexual, or passive sexual beings. Only men (and female prostitutes), not respectable, sexually chaste women, displayed aggressive sexual desires. During Victorian times, sexologists and medical doctors, then, thought that only an "inverted" woman would pursue another woman, as it took a masculine character to be sexually active and aggressive in Victorian culture.

However, once inversion gave way to homosexuality in the early twentieth century, both lesbians' and heterosexual women's sexual characters were capable of being active and more like men's ostensibly aggressive sexual character. Chauncey analyzes this shift through changes in sexology and the broader culture:

> For if it no longer was considered a deviation from the norm for a woman to initiate sexual relations, then it no longer needed to be considered an inversion of her sexual or social role to do so. But once all women were considered able to experience and act on sexual desire, medical concern shifted logically from the *fact* of women's sexual activity to their *choice* of sexual and social partners. . . . Indeed, the resexualization of women—in one sense a progressive development—was used to tie them to men, as the culture increasingly postulated the importance of women's sexual desire as a basis for their involvement in heterosexual institutions such as marriage, which their employment supposedly rendered less of an economic necessity than before. The new complexity— and restrictiveness—of sex/gender roles was epitomized by the flapper, who was at once both sexually precocious and profoundly heterosexual. (1982, 143–44; italics in original)

With the increasing recognition of lesbianism in American society, heterosexual women's prior same-sex relations, particularly romantic friendships, and same-sex social institutions, such as women's colleges and settlement houses, were no longer viewed as solely indicative of asexual relations and spaces of female bonding; rather, these relations and organizations were now regarded with suspicion as potentially lesbian (Chauncey 1982; Rupp 1989a; Smith-Rosenberg 1989).

Alongside the white female flapper, who had left behind her Victorian female predecessors, was the white male flapper, who similarly rejected many aspects of the Victorian model of manhood as embodied by the white Christian gentleman. The white male flapper introduced a lustful heterosexuality into male masculinity. Whereas the white Christian gentleman valued character, married a woman of virtue, but visited prostitutes for sexual release, the male flapper maintained his predecessors' focus on character, but looked for sexual and intellectual companionship with women, emphasizing fun and a promiscuous sexual ethic (White 1993). In contrast, the tramp bohemian completely disavowed the Christian gentleman ideal. The tramp bohemian embraced an ethos of underworld primitivism, where a wild sexuality and violent masculinity promoted fraternizing with other men while avoiding commitments, sexual and otherwise, to women (White 1993, 180–81).

In addition to the sexual liberalism of the white female and male flappers, the second generation of feminist "new women" contributed to the sexual revolution among women by rejecting the asexuality of the first generation of feminist "new women" (Ryan 2006; Smith-Rosenberg 1989). This second generation included both heterosexual and consciously lesbian-identified women. Born in the 1870s and 1880s, they came of age in the first decades of the early twentieth century. Among the most famous are Margaret Sanger, Isadora Duncan, Gertrude Stein, and Radclyffe Hall. Hall, although British, wrote arguably the most famous and influential lesbian novel of the period, *The Well of Loneliness*, which was published in 1924 but became a touchstone for generations of lesbians throughout the first half of the twentieth century in America (Newton 1993; Smith-Rosenberg 1989; Rupp 2009).

Whereas the first generation of "new women's" asexual character and image as "repressed old maids" protected them from the stigma of homosexuality, the "new women" of the 1920s opened themselves up to the rhetoric of male sexologists, doctors, and politicians who sought to discredit them as social troublemakers seeking male privileges and as perverted "mannish lesbians" to be reviled and shunned (Faderman 1991; Newton 1993; Smith-Rosenberg 1989). These characterizations and their cultural purchase led the historian Carroll Smith-Rosenberg

(1989) to argue that the 1920s "new women" were eventually marginalized and came to be viewed as social failures and outcasts:

> Investing male images with feminist meanings, they [the 1920s "new women"] sought to use male myths to repudiate male power—to turn the male world upside down. They failed. By the 1930s, women and men alike had disowned the New Woman's brave vision. The New Woman herself, shorn of her connection to older feminists, of her political power, rhetoric, and influence, became a subject of misunderstanding and ridicule. (265)

The label "lesbian" became a powerful way to discredit any woman professional, reformer, educator, or feminist ideologue by the 1920s, making an anti-lesbian discourse a way to enforce heterosexuality and traditional gender roles among women in general (Faderman 1991; Smith-Rosenberg 1989).

However, the anthropologist Esther Newton (1993) argues that while the rising visibility of the mannish lesbian and the charge of lesbianism led partially to the undermining of the early twentieth-century women's movement, it also helped to create spaces, discourses, and identities for consciously lesbian women, helping to form lesbian subcultures in American culture at this time:

> To become avowedly sexual, the New Woman had to enter the male world, either as a heterosexual on male terms (like Emma Goldman and eventually the flapper) or as a lesbian in male body drag (the mannish lesbian/congenital invert). Feminine women like Alice B. Toklas and [Radclyffe] Hall's lover Una Troubridge could become *recognizable* lesbians by association with their masculine partners. (291; italics in original)

Nonetheless, among these working-class women workers and their female flapper and feminist new women peers, the early twentieth century witnessed the power of compulsory heterosexuality in its high rates of marriage and the occurrence of marriage earlier and earlier in the lives of American women. "The proportion of never-married women fell precipitously after 1900, from as high as 20 percent for women who came of age in the late nineteenth century to well less than 10 percent for women born after 1900. . . . the mean age of marriage fell steadily after 1890 until in the 1950s it reached an all-time low of 20.2 years" (Ryan 1983, 242).

Although a culture of sexual liberalism was expanding sexual expression among white working-class and middle-class heterosexual Americans by the 1920s, allowing them some sexual exploration before marriage, this dynamic remained uneven in its development across the lives of black Americans (D'Emilio and Freedman 2012; Cahn 2007). Rather, mainstream American society and the culture of sexual liberalism constructed blacks' sexualities as hypersexual. In the context of the legacy of slavery, blacks were ideologically constructed as less civilized than whites and demeaned with descriptions of their sexualities as animal-like.

Historians of black women's experiences of migration to the north argue that rape, the threat of rape, domestic violence, and a desire to take control and care of their children, along with economic considerations, fueled black women's migration before and during the Great Migration (Carby 1986; Hine 1989). Needing to protect themselves from sexual violence and refuting notions of a promiscuous nature, black women developed a politics of respectability (Higginbotham 1993; Mitchell 1999; Wolcott 2001). Aimed at garnering respect from white society and within their own black communities, black female respectability imposed social constraints on working-class blacks' behaviors, bringing them into line with middle-class values of heterosexual propriety as well as industriousness, thrift, good manners, and proper deportment (Wolcott 2001).

Sexual pathology continued to be the recurrent historical frame through which black women's heterosexualities would be positioned in relation to white America (D'Emilio and Freedman 2012, 277–99). For example, due to their lack of economic opportunities in northern cities like Chicago and New York, black women became associated with prostitution. By the 1930s, in New York, black females accounted for over half of the arrests for prostitution (D'Emilio and Freedman 2012, 296–97). Given the association of black women with prostitution and the popularity of "slumming" by whites in black neighborhoods and clubs, black women's heterosexualities were stigmatized as wild, exotically different, and primitive (Collins 2004; D'Emilio and Freedman 2012; Heap 2009).

In counterpoint to this pathologizing of black heterosexual women, Hazel Carby (1986) documents black women blues performers who rejected hypersexual codings of black womanhood. Through their songs, blues performers narrated black women's experiences of northern migration from the South. Drawing on black communal expressions of call and response, singers like Bessie Smith, "Ma" Rainey, and Ethel Waters sang about women being left behind as their men migrated. Their songs were filled with stories of separation, migration, and the difficulties of dealing with men's infidelities in heterosexual relationships. Some blues singers like "Ma" Rainey also sung about their lesbian relationships in boastful songs like "Prove It on Me Blues," naming the streets frequented by lesbians in Chicago as evidence of the subculture's vitality (Carby 1986; Meyerowitz 1990). Black women blues singers, though, could be subversive figures, playing against the politics of respectability that most black women felt compelled to exhibit in order to counter stereotypes of themselves as promiscuous (Carby 1992; Garber 1989; Mitchell 1999, 2004).

During this time, black reformers and activists focused on racial uplift and destiny by promoting the heterosexual reproduction of healthy or "better babies" by black heterosexual families. In response to the threats of lynching and ritualized rape, black reformers promoted heterosexual marriages and families with healthy offspring as key to racial advancement. The historian Michele Mitchell (2004) explains this development among black reformers and activists:

> [P]referred behavior was associated with middle-class and aspiring-class values in that it firmly placed sexuality within the realm of marriage and family; and, as more and more black women decided to limit their pregnancies, they were encouraged to bear a healthy number of "well-born" babies by a particular and vocal cohort of racial uplift activists. (106)

To bring this discussion to a close, if the Jazz Age strikes us as a surprising period of sexual tolerance, where "normal" men and women mixed with homosexuals in bars and restaurants, at annual drag ball events, and in a variety of other louche public locations, then the backlash against this "deviancy" and the sexual and racial "slumming" that went with it probably proves unsurprising. As the Great Depression set in, antigay attitudes, state policies, and local policing began to clamp down on the previous public places where homosexuals had socialized and congregated. A conservative gender and racial order reacted against the gender nonconformity of fairy men and butch women and built the closet of homosexual oppression in the next period in order to protect heterosexuals from homosexuals' deviancy and to establish the supremacy of heterosexual identities, relationships, and institutions (Canaday 2009; Chauncey 1994, 2004; Heap 2009).

Heterosexual Hegemony and the Rise of the Closet, 1930s–1960s

The rise of the closet as a state formation across the country occurred through a variety of laws and policies that were put in place from the late 1920s through the 1950s. After the end of Prohibition in 1932, many states made it illegal for bars and restaurants to serve lesbians and gay men (Chauncey 2004, 7). In 1934, the Production Code of the Hollywood film industry banned depictions of homosexuality; the ban remained in place until 1966. Similarly, in 1927, New York State passed a "padlock" law that prohibited gay male and lesbian characters from being portrayed in Broadway plays. Since Broadway was the staging ground for new plays in America, this exclusionary policy meant that a generation of theater production would be shaped by this censorious antigay law (Chauncey 2004, 6).

What the closet's laws and policies meant for everyday Americans is that a system of sexual identities—homosexual and heterosexual— was being constructed in place of and in relation to the previous era's gender system of organization. With the rise of heterosexuality as a new discourse of men's and women's self-identities, the exclusion of all same-sex contact became the key element of the definition of heterosexual identities. However, the gender system did not disappear but continued to serve as an informal set of classification codes in popular culture and common stereotypes of heterosexual and homosexual identity practices.

For men, over the course of the 1940s, 1950s, and 1960s, the terms "fairy," "queer," and "trade" started to be replaced by the predominance of "gay," which, like "queer" before it, emphasized a masculine gender self-presentational style among homosexual men. The disappearance of "trade" or working-class "normal" men—that is, men who were not homosexually identified but who would accept homosexual men's sexual advances—along with the new establishment of gay as the preferred homosexual identity category over fairy and queer, represented the development of sexual object choice and its accompanying hetero/homo binary as distinct from the previous gender system, where homosexuality was conceptualized as gender inversion and emblematized by the figure of the fairy (Chauncey 1994, 20–21). Now, "normal" working-class men, who had previously had sex with homosexuals without being viewed as homosexual themselves, were viewed as "latent" homosexuals. This system of sexual identities confined homosexuality to a "deviant" minority and heterosexuality to the "normal" majority. As it was for their middle-class counterparts, being "normal" or "heterosexual" for working-class men now meant the total absence of both homosexual interest and behavior (Chauncey 1994).

Furthermore, heterosexuality became a key part of gender boundaries for the middle classes in the twentieth century. Heterosexual identities helped to reinforce dichotomous gender roles for men and women. Likewise, the norms and conventions of gender identities were central to the construction of heterosexual identities, as gender displays took on a new significance in indicating normative heterosexual identities. Gender codes and identities became and continue to be codes of heterosexual/homosexual behaviors, interests, and styles.

Whereas the society of the nineteenth century exhibited a clear delineation in the worlds of white men and women, where white men dominated the public worlds of work and politics and white women were largely confined to the home as wives and mothers, the first half of the twentieth century witnessed women struggling for civil and political rights, specifically suffrage, as well as joining the workforce and attending college in sizable numbers. Men were moving from farm and blue-collar occupations to white-collar ones, where the salient qualities were seen as "feminine" traits, such as the ability to project a good presentation of self, to adeptly manage interactions with clients, and to work well with others in teams (Goffman 1959). The gender division was in flux; while men were becoming "feminized" through white-collar occupations, women were increasingly entering into predominantly male bastions, such as college, the workforce, and government (Chauncey 1994; D'Emilio and Freedman 2012, White 1993).

Heterosexuality, then, played an essential role in the legitimation of a traditional gender order. For example, the most famous sociological theorist of the time, Talcott Parsons (1954), argued that men were "instrumental" in their role as family providers, and women were "expressive" in their roles as mothers and wives. Parsons warned that if these functional roles were deviated from, there would be role "strain" or "competition." Thus, heterosexuality made dichotomous gender differences between men and women seem natural and part of a functional social order. Heterosexual families in this discourse were needed to produce the country's future citizens; ideologically, this reduced gender divisions to a heterosexual procreative imperative (Chauncey 1994; D'Emilio and Freedman 2012; White 1993). Men and women were, then, necessarily and justifiably different in order to reproduce the family, the nation, and even humanity in general.

The association of heterosexuality with traditional gender conventions and identities also helped to form a culture of homophobia. A whole symbolic system of homosexual codes circulated through hegemonic notions of gays and lesbians as gender deviants. Homophobic practices separated heterosexuals from homosexuals, denying the latter public spaces, social recognition, and legal rights (Chauncey 1994; D'Emilio and Freedman 2012; White 1993).

As a heterosexual social order developed, a procreative heterosexuality continued to tie men and women together in marriages and families. Heterosexual men, however, started to contest the expectations of being a breadwinner for a wife and family. The new discourses of bachelorhood and sexual promiscuity legitimated a nonprocreative model of heterosexual masculinity for men. Similarly, heterosexual women grew increasingly dissatisfied with being confined to the roles of wife and mother. Women became more sexualized, started to be increasingly capable of economic independence, and aimed to become active partners in "companionate marriages."

As these shifts were occurring among men and women and these new models of nonprocreative heterosexuality became increasingly predominant, sexual images of women in popular magazines started to proliferate as well. In fact, the growth of sexual images of women in popular magazines throughout the twentieth century "was one component of a broader transformation toward a modern sexuality that assigned a heightened value to nonprocreative heterosexuality," argues Meyerowitz (1996, 9). The term "cheesecake" started to circulate in 1915 to indicate acceptable mass-produced representations of variably naked women, while "borderline material" indicated images that pushed the line between "respectable cheesecake and illicit pornography" (Meyerowitz 1996, 10).

In an important US Post Office legal hearing on whether *Esquire* magazine could legally deliver its cheesecake pictures through the federal mail system, American society witnessed the increasing cultural support for nonprocreative heterosexual identities. In 1946, the US Supreme Court ruled that the postmaster general, Frank C. Walker, could not censor magazines like *Esquire* for their scantily clad images of women. In winning its case, *Esquire* called on a female social worker and a female child welfare activist for supportive testimony. These two professional women supported the sexualized pictures of women as ordinary, flattering, and indicative of a healthy heterosexual femininity.

They described the images as commonly accepted, modern, healthy and lovely imagery, admired by girls and women as well as boys and men. They avoided the obvious gender asymmetry that we notice immediately today: that only women were portrayed with their clothes off and that the pictures were created by men for heterosexual male pleasure. (Meyerowitz 1996, 18)

Cheesecake and borderline material proliferated across mass media publications after this court decision, setting in circulation a highly sexualized white heterosexual femininity for women to embody and for men to consume without shame.

The debate over cheesecake images was recapitulated in the letters African Americans sent to *Ebony* and *Negro Digest*. From 1945 to 1957, African American letter writers debated issues of the racial stereotyping of black sexuality as animalistic, protested the devaluing of black women's beauty, and raised concerns over their respectability. In the debate among African Americans over the representation of black heterosexual women's sexualities, Meyerowitz observes that

African-American women also argued the pros and cons of sexual images within the context of American racism. Since the early years of the slave trade, white men had used racist stereotypes of African "animal" sexuality to justify the sexual exploitation of black women. And some of the most hard-core pornography presented nonwhite women as exotic objects of titillation for white men. From the end of the nineteenth century, middle-class African-American women activists had worked strenuously to counter these racist stereotypes and to publicize a contrasting image of black women as morally pure. (1996, 19)

Although most African American women objected to these cheesecake images, other African American women and most of the men defended the images as a sign that black women's beauty was finally receiving the recognition it deserved and had long been denied. In the context of the exclusively white cheesecake media images that predominated in popular American culture of the time, some even viewed black cheesecake images as part of racial advancement (Meyerowitz 1996, 18–20).

Similarly, from the start of *Playboy* magazine in the 1950s, women wrote letters supporting the image of the topless "Playmate of the Month" as a model of sexual allure and expressing their enjoyment of the magazine and its ethic of sexual fun (Meyerowitz 1996). Moreover, the development of *Playboy* in the establishment of heterosexuality for American men was a watershed event in the construction of straight masculinity.

Before the arrival of *Playboy* and its dissemination of the image of the lascivious heterosexual male bachelor, men in the 1950s found themselves uniformly expected to marry and to support a wife and children, by ideally earning a "breadwinner" wage (Ehrenreich 1983). White men, though, were chafing against the "trappings" of marriage and their role as the family "breadwinner." "If adult masculinity was indistinguishable from the breadwinner role," the feminist scholar Barbara Ehrenreich notes, "then it followed that the man who failed to achieve this role was either not fully adult or not fully masculine" (20).

The conformist culture of 1950s America drew on the specter of homosexuality to keep heterosexual men in line (D'Emilio and Freedman 2012; Seidman 2002). This conformity was partly enforced through the stigma attached to men who did not follow the breadwinner route as homosexuals. "Fear of homosexuality kept heterosexual men in line as husbands and breadwinners; and, at the same time, the association with failure and immaturity made it almost impossible for homosexual men to assert a positive image of themselves" (Ehrenreich 1983, 26).

However, with the rising popularity of *Playboy* magazine, a cultural alternative was offered in place of the family man role and its breadwinner work ethic. Although heterosexual men should still work hard at their careers and make money, playboys need not get married and give control over their wages to wives. Instead, *Playboy* encouraged heterosexual men to lead the life of a lascivious bachelor. Ehrenreich provides this insightful quote from Hugh Hefner on the alluring image of bachelorhood that the magazine proffered and publicly legitimated for its readership:

> We enjoy mixing up cocktails and an hors d'oeuvre or two, putting a little mood music on the phonograph and inviting in a female acquaintance for a quiet discussion on Picasso, Nietzsche, jazz, sex. (1983, 26)

Heterosexual men, in the eyes of *Playboy*, should be consumers who dated and had sex with women without the confining commitment of marriage. One might call heterosexual men who emulated *Playboy*'s bachelor model immature, but one could no longer label these men possibly homosexual. In other words, *Playboy* magazine served as a cultural model of heterosexual masculinity orientated to nonmarital sexual relations. *Playboy* encouraged heterosexual men to stay bachelors and have casual sex. More importantly, it provided proof of a lustful heterosexual masculinity through subscription to its magazine and the new cultural model of heterosexual masculinity it represented.

Historical revisionist accounts of *Playboy*, though, find a more complicated message in the magazine's portrayal of heterosexual women. The historian Carrie Pitzulo (2011) argues that in its efforts to carve out a model of heterosexual masculinity beyond the roles of husband and father, the magazine supported hedonistic pleasure and a nonprocreative version of heterosexuality for both men and women. While the magazine objectified women's bodies, it also encouraged heterosexual women to take up the sexual privileges of men in its image of the sexually entitled "girl next door" who enjoyed sex.

Alongside the new icon of the lascivious heterosexual bachelor, science emerged as a surprisingly provocative purveyor of sexual information and its dissemination in American society with the unexpected best-seller success of Alfred Kinsey's dryly written, but substantively exciting, studies of American men's and women's sexual practices. Regarding men's sexual practices of the time, Kinsey's report, published in 1948, showed "that masturbation and heterosexual petting were nearly universal, that almost ninety percent had engaged in premarital intercourse and half in extramarital sex, and that over a third of adult males had had homosexual experience" (D'Emilio and Freedman 2012, 286). In contrast to the dominant image of mainstream America as sexually conservative and reserving sex for marriage, Kinsey's study documented a surprising variety of sexual practices among heterosexual men.

While Kinsey's report on the frequency of men's nonmarital sex practices eased many white men's sense of sexual "deviance," black men's migration to northern cities did nothing to mitigate the pernicious stereotypes of their heterosexual masculinities as dangerous, violent, and hypersexual (McGruder 2010). Escaping the Jim Crow segregation and threat of lynching in the South, black men wound up facing disproportionate arrests and harsher punishments for rape in the criminal justice system of northern states. "Between 1930 and 1964, ninety percent of the men executed in the United States for rape were black," observe D'Emilio and Freedman (2012, 297).

Black men were also often blamed for the dissolution of the black family due to their lack of sexual morals and their irresponsible ways. Given the perceptions of black rates of unemployment, black fathers' absence from the home, and black families' dependence on welfare for survival, black people's sexualities, particularly black heterosexual men's, were viewed as exemplars of disorder, pathology, and immorality (D'Emilio and Freedman 2012, 295–300).

Meanwhile, with the publication of Alfred Kinsey's report in 1953 on American women's shocking practices of masturbation and significant rates of premarital and extramarital sex, the 1960s picked up on and mainstreamed this trend of casual sex among nonmarried heterosexual women. The author Helen Gurley Brown and her book *Sex and the Single Girl*, published in 1962, exemplified this new sexually permissive attitude among heterosexual women of the 1960s. Brown promoted an ethic of sexual fun, answering Hugh Hefner's call for heterosexual male lasciviousness and nonmarital sex with a message that sex is power and that a woman should exercise this power by being just as uncommitted to marriage as any man, at least until her youthful looks faded (D'Emilio and Freedman 2012, 303–4). Brown went on to be the editor of *Cosmopolitan* magazine, which unsurprisingly became a kind of female version of *Playboy* for straight women. In addition, the pill arrived on the cultural sex scene, and it dramatically lessened fears of pregnancy and anxieties of becoming an unplanned parent, proving unsurprisingly popular among women (and men) in a new era of sexual permissiveness.

Historical shifts in heterosexual femininities need to be understood through the rising visibility of lesbian identities in the 1950s. Lesbian identities have historically served as a source of stigma in enforcing narrow definitions of heterosexual femininity (duCille 1989; Duggan 2000; Faderman 1991; Rupp 2009). And with the rise of a lesbian subculture, particularly the butch/femme working-class bar scene and the first lesbian organization, Daughters of Bilitis, in 1955, American society witnessed a growing consciousness of homosexual and heterosexual feminine identities. By the 1950s, American culture overwhelmingly enforced normative heterosexuality through the use of polluting images of lesbians as psychologically sick, socially deviant, and representative of the outer bounds of human abnormality (D'Emilio 1989; Faderman 1991). The Cold War in particular enforced an image of homosexual women and men as possible communist traitors due to their potential to be blackmailed by Soviet spies for their stigmatized sexual identities. Consequently, heterosexual Americans, particularly the heterosexual nuclear family, became the emblematic representation of patriotic, loyal citizenship, while gays and lesbians were potential enemies of the state (Lewis 2010).

In their study of lesbian bar culture in Buffalo, New York, Elizabeth Kennedy and Madeline Davis (1993) document a working-class subculture of butch and femme lesbians who felt oppressed by the enforced secrecy and discrimination against them and thus desired to break out of the "closet" of oppression they experienced in the 1940s and 1950s. Butch lesbians experienced a deep sense of themselves as "queer," marginal, and the targets of homophobic harassment and oppression, while femmes "did not experience themselves as basically different from heterosexual women except to the extent that they were part of gay life" (Kennedy and Davis, quoted in Stein 1997, 17–18). Thus, gender-traditional presentations of self were a way for women to pass as heterosexual if lesbian, and they remained a central force in maintaining compulsory heterosexuality among women, particularly by stigmatizing masculine lesbian gender displays.

Illustrating the defensive status of feminism's association with lesbianism in the 1960s is the liberal heterosexual feminist Betty Friedan and her breakthrough best seller, *The Feminine Mystique*, published in 1963. Friedan sought to bring attention to a postwar ideology of gender subordination that kept heterosexual women repressed as housewives and denied them permission to pursue careers and lives outside the home. Historians, though, question the accuracy of Friedan's characterization of postwar gender ideology as uniformly opposing women's participation in paid work and politics (see Meyerowitz 1994b; Ryan 2006). Historical revisionist accounts argue that the gender ideology of postwar women's magazines, as well as Friedan's defense of early feminists and their "emphasis on femininity and domesticity (and the two were often conflated), seems to have cloaked a submerged fear of lesbian, mannish, or man-hating women. . . . She [Friedan] attempted to legitimate the early feminists by repeated insistence that most of them were feminine, married, and not man-hating" as well as by excluding many lesbians from her book's narrative and later the National Organization for Women, which she founded for women's rights, but to the exclusion of the "lavender menace" (Meyerowitz 1994b, 1460).

The 1950s were the end of an era of conformity in American history. The grievances of sexual, gender, and racial minorities that had been ignored and overlooked would be heard and publicly aired in boycotts, marches, and riots, as well as in courtrooms, workplaces, and governmental bodies. The next decades would bring forth a civil rights movement that would inspire women and lesbians and gay men to challenge gender and sexual oppressions in unparalleled ways, building their own communities, organizations, and social movements in the process of transforming gender and sexual norms, expressions of identity, and their communities' marginalized statuses. Heterosexual and homosexual boundaries would be contested, and the cultures of straights and gays would no longer remain so separate, distinct, and unknown to each other.

Challenges to Heterosexual Hegemony and the Decline of the Closet, 1960s–1990s

From 1920 to 1960, a culture of sexual liberalism dominated the erotic lives of heterosexual Americans. It promoted limited sexual experimentation on a pathway to a lifetime marriage for many heterosexual American men and women. With the decline of a culture of sexual liberalism, the 1960s witnessed the rise of a culture of sexual pluralism, where practices of premarital sex, cohabitation, divorce, and nonprocreative casual sex, especially with the availability of the birth control pill, made heterosexual and homosexual intimate practices start to look more and more alike (D'Emilio and Freedman 2012; Faderman 1991). With the growing strength of a national LGBT movement during this period, heterosexual hegemony faced a set of wide-ranging struggles in expressions of sexual and gender identities, relations, and, more crucially, political movements against homophobia and normative heterosexuality.

Alongside sexual pluralism, gender norms and dynamics changed with the rise of second-wave feminism and a new generation of women workers in the labor force. Although poor and working-class white women and black women had a long history as wage earners in America, now middle-class white wives and their daughters were the new entries into the workplace during the 1960s and 1970s, and at unprecedented levels (Hochschild and Machung [1989] 2012). While heterosexual women's femininity was not socially enhanced by working, as work remained associated with masculinity, heterosexual women did gain power in their marriages through their economic contribution to the family (Hochschild and Machung [1989] 2012, 131). As a result of heterosexual working women's new financial power in the family, heterosexual men's social statuses suffered a blow. No longer could heterosexual men see themselves as the lone provider for the family. Consequently, the roles of husband and father lost some of their normative standing in constructing an ideal heterosexual masculine status among straight men. Most heterosexual men also could no longer afford to enact their role as a family patriarch due to men's declining wages and salaries in an uneven and alternately stagnant economy. Since the 1970s, heterosexual couples and families have increasingly needed dual incomes to be financially stable, let alone to purchase homes and send their children to college (Collins 2009; Ehrenreich 1995; Gerson 2010).

To replace the traditional masculine roles of breadwinner husband and father, other forms of heterosexual masculinity became prominent. One of these, of course, is the heterosexual bachelor. Heterosexual bachelorhood, as cultivated by *Playboy* magazine's ideology of promiscuity and sexual fun, was reinvigorated and presented as an alluring model of straight masculinity to both married and single heterosexual men (D'Emilio and Freedman 2012, 303). Alongside the heterosexual playboys, the hippies of the late 1960s and 1970s inaugurated a different and androgynous model of straight masculinity. Hippie men with their long hair, beaded jewelry, and shapeless clothing blurred gendered norms of style and presentation between men and women (Ehrenreich 1983). Popular fashions for men's clothing also commoditized the "androgynous drift" of the hippie style for mainstream American male consumers. "In the early seventies, retailers redid their stores as discos. . . . In men's clothing, the old austere division between business and sports clothes broke down with the coming of bell-bottomed pants, tie-dyed shirts, denim jackets and broad, outrageously colored ties" (Ehrenreich 1983, 114).

Meanwhile, changes in homophile politics, the first political homosexual groups in the United States, which fought for reform and accommodation in the 1950s and 1960s, would give way to liberationist lesbian and gay politics in the 1970s that demanded attention and expressed anger against their oppression in a new way. Prior to the Stonewall riots of June 1969, lesbian and gay political organizing had been confined to a small number of protesters during the political events of the 1950s and 1960s. While these homophile groups succeeded in challenging discriminatory statutes, gaining the support of the American Civil Liberties Union, and picketing the White House to protest the federal ban on gay and lesbian employees, their homosexual identity politics were narrowly focused and circumscribed in their effects on American society in the 1950s (D'Emilio and Freedman 2012). During this period of homophile politics from 1950 to 1969, gay men and lesbians generally "came out" only to other gay people and passed as straight at work, with nongay friends, and with their own families as well. After Stonewall, gay liberationists refashioned "coming out of the closet" to mean coming out to heterosexuals. This was new, and it made everyday acts of coming out the strategy and goal of the movement (D'Emilio 1989). Reframing lesbian and gay identities as public demands for recognition by society at large had social, cultural, and political consequences for gays and straights and started the dismantling of the closet of state repression. By making coming out to straights the strategy and goal of LGBT social movements, Stonewall politics effected a revolutionary social and cultural shift, and it is this social-historical development that conditions today's social integration of LGBT persons and the newfound mass media visibility of LGBT images.

The success of the new politics of coming out is demonstrated by the huge growth in gay organizations throughout the country. As the historian John D'Emilio (1989) observes, "On the eve of Stonewall, after almost twenty years of homophile politics, fewer than fifty organizations existed. By 1973, there were more than eight hundred lesbian and gay male groups scattered across the country" (466). With the solidifying collective sense of lesbian and gay identities and the number of growing organizations, there came a series of movement victories in the 1970s. For instance, the American Psychiatric Association removed homosexuality from its list of mental disorders in 1973, while half the states removed sodomy statutes from their penal codes during this decade as well (D'Emilio and Freedman 2012, 324).

As gays and lesbians claimed public recognition and demanded rights and respect, heterosexual men and women faced a series of choices in deciding how to accommodate this new out and visible gay "minority." For instance, lesbian feminists, emerging alongside second-wave feminist organizations, opened up the boundaries between heterosexual women and lesbians in an unparalleled way. The sociologist Arlene Stein (1997), in *Sex and Sensibility: Stories of a Lesbian Generation*, documents a generation of "new gay" women, many of whom had been heterosexual housewives, girlfriends, and mothers, who came out through consciousness-raising groups and a woman-centered culture, based in bookstores, community centers, political groups, and annual music festivals. This generation of "new gay" women was focused less on sexual desire for women than on making women the social and political center of their lives (Faderman 1991; Stein 1997).

Lesbian feminists created a specific form of feminism that argued against viewing lesbianism as simply a sexual desire or identity, but rather pushed for thinking of it as a totalizing cultural project to remake women's lives. They highlighted lesbianism as a form of woman identification. This sensibility is best captured by the classic statement, "The Woman-Identified Woman," written by the cultural collective Radicalesbians (1970). In it the authors argued that lesbianism was more about political and social identification with women's values, experiences, and interests than an erotic desire. As a result of the overlap and cultural collapse between feminism and lesbianism, Stein (1997) explains, "the new discourse of lesbian feminism enabled many women who had never considered the possibility of claiming a lesbian lifestyle to leave their husbands and boyfriends—some for political motives, others in expression of deeply rooted desires, many for both reasons" (41).

From the emergence of political and legal organizations (such as the National Gay and Lesbian Task Force, the Human Rights Campaign, and Lambda Legal Defense) to the development of domestic partner benefits to the passage of gay adoption laws and the spread of antidiscrimination ordinances across the country, the decline of the closet as a form of state repression is seen in the rights, changes in state policy, and recognition garnered by lesbians and gay men throughout the 1970s and 1980s.

It is in the context of the decline of the closet and the rise of a post-closeted culture that I explore shifts and changes in the social construction of heterosexual identity performances. That is, heterosexual men and women negotiate the establishment of their identity statuses in an era of lesbian and gay tolerance, visibility, and rights, and their performances of heterosexual masculinity and femininity are increasingly varied as a result. From their relations with lesbian and gay coworkers and acquaintances to friends and family members, heterosexuals face a set of choices in deciding what kinds of boundaries to employ in their interactions with LGBT individuals. They may choose to be supportive (antihomophobic), indifferent (that is, maintain the normative heterosexual status quo), or unsupportive (homophobic), or they may combine these possibilities in their attitudes, interactions, and relationships with LGBT people today.

3

Straight Men

Renegotiating Hegemonic Masculinity and Its Homophobic Bargain

If being homophobic is still one of the clearest ways for straight men to signal their straight identity status, then one of my central questions was, How does this identity practice change in contexts where lesbians and gay men are out and other straight individuals disapprove of hostile homophobic attitudes? Although homophobia persists, I argue that straight men, like Eric Ward, a white man in his twenties, use boundaries of social distance from gay individuals, symbols, and spaces to more tactfully and subtly project being straight. Eric's straight identity practices include not wearing light-colored and tight-fitting shirts because of the "gay look" he thinks they convey, and he avoids going into gay bars, has no gay friends, and says he more "tastefully" engages in the homophobic banter of his friends and stepfather.

In contrast, Jason Robson, a black man in his twenties, mixes urban styles of dress (e.g., hoodies and sportswear) with metrosexual ones (e.g., tight shirts and fitted jeans). Unlike Eric, Jason has close gay friends and goes to gay bars on occasion. In fact, the first time I met Jason's girlfriend was when they were hanging out in one of Orangetown's downtown gay bars with their gay couple friends. In this chapter, I show that straight men are neither simply antigay nor uniformly pro-gay, but rather that there is a multiplicity of homophobic and antihomophobic stances that they draw on in constructing their sexual-gender identities, their identity practices that enact boundaries of social distance, and their relationship to gay individuals, symbols, and spaces.

By heterosexual masculinities, I mean configurations of sexual-gender practice and discourse that refer to the identity categories heterosexuals and men and are organized in relation to the structures of sexual and gender orders (Connell and Messerschmidt 2005). Heterosexualities generally, but not necessarily, align with sexual behaviors and desires orientated to the other—as opposed to the same—gender. Masculinities are gender practices that generally refer to men and male bodies, but may include women and nonmale bodies as well (Pascoe 2007; Schippers 2007).

Straight Masculinities, Hegemonic Masculinity, and Antihomophobias

Scholars of masculinities underscore the importance of studying heterosexual masculinities in relation to homosexual ones (Carrigan, Connell, and Lee 2002; Connell and Messerschmidt 2005; Kimmel and Messner 2010; Segal 1990). Raewyn Connell (1987, Connell and Messerschmidt 2005) has developed the concept of hegemonic masculinity to illustrate the normative status of heterosexuality, arguing that "the most important feature of contemporary hegemonic masculinity is that it is heterosexual, being closely connected to the institution of marriage; and a key form of subordinated masculinity is homosexual" (Connell 1987, 186).

Hegemonic masculinity captures the historically predominant and still salient pattern of normative heterosexual masculinity based in homophobic practices. Hegemonic masculinity among high school boys, for example, is demonstrated by their use of the "fag" epithet. High school boys use the "fag" discourse to insult and police other boys' gender expressions of masculinity. The "fag" epithet signals a boy's lack of masculinity and associates his masculine expression with homosexuality, femininity, and a form of male shame (Pascoe 2007).

Although the concept of hegemonic masculinity captures the historically predominant pattern of masculinity and is thus a key principle in the social construction of straight masculinities, I both expand on and challenge the assertion that homophobia is a central organizing

principle of contemporary straight masculinities. To be sure, homophobia is central to the construction of many boys' and men's sense of
masculine status, identity, and power, but most of these studies of
straight masculinity focus on adolescent boys in school settings (e.g.,
Epstein and Johnson 1998; Kimmel 2003; McCormack 2012; Pascoe
2007; Plummer 2001) or young men in college (Anderson 2009). This
focus imposes clear limits on this important body of masculinities
scholarship.

For example, one might think that high school boys and college-age
men are emotionally immature and sexually insecure, and while this is
obviously more pronounced among high school boys, it still accurately
characterizes young college men as well (Arnett 1994; Grazian 2007;
Mishkind et al. 1986). For these reasons and others that I will elaborate on regarding the development of antihomophobic practices, my
book moves us further toward understanding how adult straight men,
ranging in age from twenty-two to fifty-six, construct their straight
masculinities.

Like the previous scholars, though, I document homophobic attitudes and actions as central to the construction of some straight men's
identities. However, I complicate conceptions of homophobia by showing they can be not just about prejudicial attitudes toward gays but also
a response to being identified as possibly nonstraight because of less
conventionally masculine styles of clothes, such as tight-fitting shirts
or pink-colored ones, as pink is a color with a highly feminine association. I underscore that context and self-definition remain primary
in my approach to interpreting straight masculinity's meaning-making
practices; consequently, a pink shirt when worn by an "alpha male" may
have a double-edged meaning, indicating his ability to embrace a highly
feminine color due to his masculine reputation. In effect, a pink shirt
may enhance, not diminish, an "alpha male's" straight masculinity.

Other straight men defined their homophobia toward gay men as a
reaction to being sexually objectified or "cruised" by another man, and
it is this both imagined and real objectification that precipitates their
feelings of homophobic prejudice. Throughout this chapter, I highlight how homophobic practices are being reframed due to a context of
increasing homosexual tolerance that pressures straight men to down-
play prejudice toward lesbians and gays in public settings, and to reserve

its expression for their interpersonal social circles, where it's still taken for granted and is not socially sanctioned as unacceptable behavior.

Homophobic prejudice notwithstanding, in this chapter I show that in today's post-closeted culture, patterned exceptions have emerged in relation to, and as a contestation of, hegemonic masculinity, and consequently straight masculinities do not necessarily rely on homophobia for their establishment (McCormack 2011; McCormack and Anderson 2010). I argue that we must now explore the development of antihomophobias or pro-gay acts on the part of straight men in post-closeted contexts. I define antihomophobias as practices that aim to counter prejudice and discrimination against gays and lesbians as well as practices that may expose, and sometimes renounce, straight status and privilege. In this chapter, I show that black and white straight men's antihomophobic stances trade on the prestige of being tolerant of gays and lesbians, with black straight men's antihomophobias in particular drawing on their experiences with racism.

Straight Identity Practices and the Continuum

This chapter examines the construction of straight masculinities through in-depth interviews with fourteen black and fifteen white straight men. I document a range of interactional practices through which these men enact straight masculinity, from those who rely on homophobic practices to maintain an unambiguous straight status to those who embrace antihomophobic practices that contest boundaries of social distance between gays and straights and thus subvert normative heterosexuality. My discussion of these practices derives from interview data, and I take the practices the men report to me as conventional ways of speaking and acting that they treat as matters of commonsense knowledge and everyday competence. By social distance, I mean the practices these men use to negotiate boundaries in associating or disassociating themselves from stigmatized practices or individuals. I develop an analytical continuum to map a range of heterosexual masculinities based on interview data with black and white heterosexual men. The continuum moves from homophobic heterosexual masculinities (which the model of hegemonic masculinity theorizes) to antihomophobic ones (which contest the hegemonic model).

First, as I map expressions of heterosexual masculinities, I describe the hegemonic masculine pattern: straight men who engage in homophobic practices that define homosexuality as socially inferior to heterosexuality. Homophobic practices involve the construction of boundaries that establish social distance from gay individuals, signifiers, and social spaces. By putting distance between themselves and gay men, straight men aim to signal an unambiguous straight masculinity.

Furthermore, I analyze the way race subtly and complexly shapes heterosexual men's reported homophobic and antihomophobic practices. I illustrate how black straight men on the homophobic end of the continuum draw on their racial status and religious beliefs to legitimize homophobic stances, while their white straight male counterparts invoke social views of gays as deviant and abnormal to justify their homophobias.

In the second section, I map a range of straight men's antihomophobic practices, moving from men who establish weak normative straight boundaries to those who blur them. While both black and white heterosexual men who construct weak boundaries view gays as equals, heterosexual men in the weak boundaries category aim to retain their straight status and privilege. Black straight men who espouse antihomophobic stances posit a shared sense of understanding of oppression due to their racial status. This allows black straight men to communicate a sense of solidarity across the sexual line of homo/heterosexuality, in order to support gays' and lesbians' struggle for equality. However, overall, black and white straight men in the weak boundaries category aim to maintain their heterosexual status and privilege. In contrast, a small number of white straight men (four out of the total twenty-nine interviewees) renounced their straight status and privilege by blurring boundaries between heterosexuality and homosexuality in some contexts. Finally, I elaborate here and in the conclusion on the sociological significance of my analyses and the value of the continuum for linking (micro) straight masculine identity practices to the (macro) production of the social institutional orders of sexualities and gender.

This continuum documents boundaries of social distance to illustrate that straight men construct their identity partly through the degree of distance they establish from gay signifiers, individuals, and spaces.

Consequently, the continuum provides both the logic of the order of each case and the centrality of practices of homophobia and antihomophobia in the management of straight masculine identity practices. Beyond its use as a means of organizing the data, the continuum shows how straight men's (micro) identity practices link to the (macro) social institutional orders of sexualities and gender.

The practical sociological value of the continuum is that it provides a way of talking about the recurring identity practices and strategies that straight men enact in a variety of situations and contexts to project themselves as straight. To that end, straight men who primarily rely on homophobic practices aim to reproduce the sexual and gender hierarchies that constitute hegemonic masculinity. Their everyday identity practices of straight masculinity, essentially, aim to naturalize these hierarchical orders and return us to the closeted dynamics of the past.

The men interviewed self-identified as black or white straight men with the exception of one of the black men, Darryl White, who I have excluded from the analysis, as he did not identify as straight but as a "sexual being." He also reported having relationships with both women and men. Although Darryl is of interest in thinking about issues of sexual fluidity and black men's sexualities, he remains an outlier in my sample and obfuscates my focus here on straight masculinities. Table A.1 in the appendix provides each respondent's age, marital status, educational attainment, occupational status, religious affiliation, and position on the continuum.

I present an analytical continuum of straight masculinities, using the concepts of homophobias and antihomophobias to map the sample. This continuum emerged from the analyses of the interviews, but I present the range and breadth of the sample. The analysis is divided into three empirical sections: (1) homophobias and strongly aversive boundaries; (2) antihomophobias, weak boundaries, and maintaining straight privilege; and (3) antihomophobias, blurred boundaries, and surrendering straight privilege.

Homophobias and Strongly Aversive Boundaries

I begin my analysis by exploring the reported straight identity practices of those men who could be categorized as expressing straight masculinities by enacting boundaries of homophobic social distance. Straight identity practices are the words and deeds that the men use in attempting to perform a straight status. The concept of straight identity practices, constituted through practices of masculinity and homophobia/antihomophobia, is sociologically significant as it is expressed across a wide range of contexts and social relationships, such as an individual man's work, family, and friendships. This identity status is part of everyday, mundane social interactions. In this section, I argue that one main way straight masculinities are constructed is through straight men's expressions of homophobia, which create boundaries of social distance between themselves and gays.

In the context of a post-closeted cultural dynamic, I qualify the notion that enacting a normative performance of gender unquestionably constructs an unambiguous straight identity (West and Zimmerman 1987). Performing straight identities is often partly constructed in social interactions through normative gender performances, but normative gender performances are not reducible to performances of straight identity. In other words, although a conventional gender performance remains a key way to project a straight status, it no longer promises in any certain terms an unquestionable straight identity for the individual in question.

Furthermore, straight identity performances claim power and privilege through their own catalogue of identity practices that, while socially grounded in gender, are not reducible to it. For example, straight identity practices include the traditional practice of wearing a wedding ring, claiming a marital status as a husband or wife, and simply expressing sexual or romantic interest in the other gender; these acts are all taken as indicators of a straight status. However, in today's context of gender and sexual identity diversity, lesbians and gay men often embody and enact gender-conventional displays in their own identity performances, while many straight men and women embrace less conventional gender practices in expressions of themselves. In short, normative gender performances are far from foolproof performances of straight identities in these cases and contexts.

Nonetheless, I underscore the point that because of male privilege at large, failing at straight masculinity is more significant for individual straight men than an "unsuccessful" performance of straight femininity is for individual straight women. For instance, Pascoe's (2007) study of the "fag" discourse is a demonstration of the explicit policing of straight masculinity by high school boys of themselves and other boys, and she finds that it has no parallel among high school girls. Rather, "slut" and "ho" are the choice epithets high school girls use to discipline one another's establishment of a respectable straight femininity. This dissimilarity in gender policing demonstrates that the salient stigma for girls is based in the discourse of sexual promiscuity, where the insult "slut" references the loss of feminine virtue and (hetero)sexual purity, not the loss of a straight status or suspicion of lesbianism (Pascoe 2007, 52–59). I hasten to add that I do not mean to suggest that anti-lesbian epithets are absent from straight women's homophobic stances, but rather they are less prominent than insults like "slut."

Nine of the twenty-nine straight men fall into the "strongly aversive" category of the continuum. Six of these men are black and the other three are white. Each expresses homophobic views that define homosexuality as socially and morally inferior to heterosexuality. This is the key characteristic that I used to establish their inclusion in this category. In their most hegemonic form, these homophobic practices reproduce heteronormativity, as the men seemingly want to recast homosexuality as a closeted identity that does not deserve respect, recognition, or legal rights.

"I'm a hardcore, 110 percent heterosexual [and] that means having sex with members of my own gender is an impossibility," says Rodney Smith. The intensity of the qualifying words "hardcore, 110 percent" stands out in Rodney's self-definition of his sexual identity.

Raised in a conservative Southern Baptist tradition, Rodney, an African American male in his thirties, is married with children and works as a teacher. Rodney views homosexuality as morally wrong and projects a straight identity through his homophobic practices:

> I think that anybody who knows me, if they are gay, they would know that it's a good idea not to tell me that they are . . . because my moral foundation is such that there are some social vices, moral vices that I don't want to be around. . . . Let me give you an analogy: homosexuality is to the family what cancer is to any living tissue of the body.

Rodney's homophobic talk invokes religious connotations, describing homosexuality as a "moral vice" condemned by his "moral foundation." Gay individuals are morally polluted, and therefore he uses social distance from them to establish an "unpolluted" straight masculinity for himself.

Although Rodney knows that many Americans now view homophobia as mean-spirited and wrong, he resents the term "homophobia" for criticizing individuals who condemn homosexuality. He feels at odds with currents in American culture, particularly the values of his white liberal school district, which increasingly construct gays as normal people who deserve tolerance and respect.

> Homophobia is a verbal sword for homosexuals. It's their nuclear weapon. If you somehow want to make homosexuality wrong, immoral or bad, then it's automatically because you fear it. In my mind that's what homophobia is, it's a weapon used by homosexuals to paint heterosexuals in one big paint stroke.

Rodney views homosexuality as socially degenerative and morally wrong, but his homophobia is racialized as well. For him, individuals who are openly gay are white, not black. The black community condemns homosexuality, he says, and open displays of it. Consequently, he feels a sense of racial betrayal when he meets an openly gay black man.

> One of the traits among African Americans is that we wear our clothes loose. This guy had the exact opposite. He had the tight jeans on. Red flag number one. All right, different folks, whatever. Just because you're black doesn't mean you have to like rap music and all that stuff. Dude starts talking about how he was in prison and I was "word" [an expression of respectful acknowledgment]. And then what he liked [sex with men]. And then from that point on it was a wrap. The conversation was over. Because morally speaking, black people are pretty socially conservative . . . and to see an openly gay black man was blowin' my mind.

In recalling the interaction, Rodney points out how this gay black man deviated from black cultural codes by wearing tight jeans, and this deviation signified his homosexuality. In effect, Rodney is appealing to racial masculine norms of clothing style (i.e., baggy jeans and oversized shirts) in order to establish what counts as a black masculinity. His conception collapses black conventional masculinity with a heterosexual status and leaves little room for an openly gay identity among black men. Thus, a black man admitting to being gay shocked Rodney. Although he had started talking to the man out of a sense of racial belonging, his discovery of an openly gay black man contested his perception of a social world where blacks, if gay, are closeted or reticent about admitting it in public.

In post-closeted contexts, where homophobia is less tolerated, explicitly homophobic expressions are avoided. In Rodney's case, he works in a school district with gay colleagues. Although he exhibits a strong homophobic attitude in private life, his dominant attitude toward gays at work is one of tolerance. Consider the following situation with his school's assistant principal. Rodney found out that his assistant principal is a lesbian after a student in his class told him that she, the assistant principal, had flirted with his student's mother:

> One of the kids' parents allegedly was hit on by her [the assistant principal] and the kid came back and told me. But I mean it doesn't necessarily impact as far as our [his and the assistant principal's] personal relationship is concerned. She's [the assistant principal] never brought it up to me. I've never brought it up to her. And it doesn't matter in my mind because her sexuality, just like my sexuality is my business, her sexuality is her business. It has nothing to do with the job. I mean if we're porno stars that might be an issue. But we're educators. So, what does that have to do with what we do behind closed doors?

Here Rodney avoids making any degrading comments about his assistant principal's homosexuality. The homophobia that he expresses at other points in the interview is missing when talking about a colleague, and a superior, at his workplace. He seems compelled to show respect toward a nonheterosexual colleague and is conscious of how overtly homophobic statements are potentially damaging to his reputation and promotion. As a result, his strategy here is to make sexuality a private matter outside the purview of his public workplace relationships.

For example, other teaching colleagues have come out to him as well, and he similarly avoids making any explicitly homophobic statement, saying, in contrast, "As far as my [work] relationships, I mean I can work with anybody. You don't have to necessarily look like me or act like me or believe as I believe. I'm about the bottom line. Let's just get whatever we need to get done, get done." In contrast to his public presentation of self at work, in private life Rodney is quick to express his general disgust and intolerance toward homosexuality. This is one example of how homophobic intolerance is practiced in post-closeted cultural contexts: that is, public work relations may follow a strategy of tolerance, while private life is less managed, and overtly homophobic attitudes are more liable to be expressed.

In sum, in public spaces like his workplace, Rodney feels pressured to enact a modicum of tolerance toward gays while privately deriding them. The increasing tolerance of gays and the rise of a post-closeted culture now cast Rodney's homophobic talk as hateful, mean-spirited, and illiberal. Straight men like him often feel compelled to project a veneer of tolerance toward gays in public spaces in order to maintain a socially acceptable status among colleagues. Although some straight men I interviewed expressed strong homophobic attitudes, it was more common for them to construct a straight masculinity through boundaries of social distance.

In a post-closeted culture, straight men negotiate a pervasive sign system that codes gendered practices as indicative of a heterosexual or homosexual identity. Masculine/feminine practices are the grid for a heterosexual/homosexual sign system that is overlaid on them (Hennen 2008; Pascoe 2007). Embodying a conventional masculinity and being homophobic are strategies that aim to perform a conventional masculinity and, by extension, a straight status. Illustrating this is Eric Ward, a white male in his mid-twenties, who constructs his heterosexuality by avoiding dressing in styles that he views as connoting a nonmasculine and, by extension, gay identity. Eric recalls the following incident where he felt anxious that his gender practices didn't project an unambiguously straight masculinity. Eric's girlfriend thought he could use some stylish clothes, so they purchased a couple of tight-fitting and light-colored shirts. However, after wearing these stylish shirts, Eric decided they gave off a "gay" look and proceeded to get rid of them.

My girlfriend took me out to try to give me a little fashion tip. We bought a few shirts that were lighter-colored and tighter-fitting. I wore them a couple of times and [thought] "I look good. They show off my muscles." And after viewin' some of the shirts that I see some men out there wearing . . . a lot of guys wear these tight shirts. But on me, I threw them away. I didn't like them. I thought, and that's what I said to her, "I think this looks gay." Just not the masculine look that I want.

Heterosexual anxiety about appearing gay is an issue for straight men like Eric who worry that others view certain stylish clothes as indicative of a gay identity. Although avoiding these clothes isn't overtly homophobic, it does reinforce a normative straight boundary that marks certain styles as gay and more conventional masculine styles as straight. Moreover, stylishness may be stigmatized by its association with gay men, and Eric aims to maintain his straight privilege by embodying a conventional masculinity.

Due to Eric's physical attractiveness, his male friends make jokes about his good looks, calling him a "pretty boy," for example. He tells me, "I think there was a point, once in a while where I would be, my masculinity would feel threatened, when buddies of mine would say, 'Hey, pretty boy or hey, Ken.' I'm tall, blond-haired. I don't dress, I don't overly pay attention to how I dress, but I don't look like a bum either." Here Eric's whiteness is referenced by the comparison of him to a Ken doll, Barbie's male companion. While this comparison to a Ken doll is meant to imply that Eric is good-looking, it also could be construed that his attractiveness borders on the feminine. Further, whiteness is also key, as both the phrase "pretty boy" and the reference to a Ken doll allude to feminine forms of white male beauty.

Whiteness gains its privilege partly through its denial of racial privilege and its status as the taken-for-granted but idealized racial identity (Bérubé 2001; Frankenberg 1993; Rasmussen et al. 2001). This privilege means that white men are typically viewed, by others and themselves, as "individuals," not members of a racial-ethnic minority group like blacks, who are situated within a panoply of hypersexualized stereotypes.

Illustrating his perception of popular cultural ideas regarding straight men's sexual fluidity, Eric, in contrast, excludes homosexual desire from his own straight identity. He says that being straight means that "I only like girls. I only like women. I don't have thoughts. You hear people who are heterosexual have thoughts, occasional thoughts about another man. I don't have that. I really only like women."

In contexts where homophobia is less accepted, gender practices become a key strategy for signaling a straight identity. For straight men, masculinity practices are fraught with anxiety due to never being able to live up to an imagined hegemonic ideal. Illustrating the defensive connection between masculinity and heterosexuality, Eric views jokes about him being gay as damaging his masculine reputation. For instance, when asked, "Is it important that others view you as masculine?" he connected this question to a joke about him being gay.

> [My sister and mother] were joking around, saying, "I think that Eric is gay." And I got all upset about it, saying, "How the heck can I be gay? I've been datin' these girls," and then I said, "Who said that?" And she [his sister] said, "Oh, Mom said it." I think that if I'm not viewed as masculine it's only because of how in touch with my feelings I am known to be. I've always been made to feel not that it's not masculine, but it's like emotional intelligence.

Although Eric dismisses the charge of being gay as a joke, he does not surrender his emotional sensitivity in order to avoid a misreading as gay. In effect, Eric is refashioning an idea of a masculine straight self that includes this emotionality. Indeed, his talent for giving advice is something he's proud of. To renegotiate masculinity, Eric designates this emotionality a form of "intelligence," even if it's "emotional intelligence." It is important to note that the labeling of his emotionally attuned behavior as "emotional intelligence" is also a nonhomophobic practice, as it neither produces antigay prejudice nor counters it.

Another instance where he feels self-conscious in managing his straight identity status is when his male friends joke that he might be gay because he teaches middle school children, although he says they are just "bustin' balls." Still, nonhegemonic masculine practices like being a middle school teacher or emotional intelligence are often laden with anxiety for straight men. In masculinity grading, nonhegemonic practices imperil straight masculine standing.

Like Rodney, Eric generally excludes gays from his circle of friends and has never gone to a gay bar. However, unlike Rodney, Eric's homophobia is not based on a religious morality but rather social views of homosexuality as deviant. Whereas Eric says he doesn't engage in the same level of public homophobia as his friends and stepfather, he still participates in their homophobic banter; to not participate codes one as possibly not straight and/or as having a deficit of masculinity. Eric explains his participation and view of homophobic prejudice:

> I'll be sitting with my stepfather or with my buddies who are prejudiced up the ying yang. They've got something to say about everybody. I can kind of chime in but to a little more tasteful level. . . . Homophobia means taking the things that I don't like about certain gay individuals [e.g., effeminacy], taking them at a personal level. When I said that it doesn't bother me personal [sic], someone who is homophobic will look at a way that a guy they deem gay and say that threatens my masculinity and that's being homophobic. They feel that if someone like that is talking to them or is around them that they need to make a comment.

Here Eric tells me that his friends and stepfather are strongly prejudiced, invoking a sexual metaphor with the phrase "prejudiced up the ying yang," an interesting choice of words due to associations of gay men with anal sex. Moreover, he views public comments directed at gay individuals (or individuals perceived as gay) as homophobic, but hedges on his own less public practices. Instructively, his discussion of homophobia illustrates an implicit division among some straight male circles: one either actively participates in homophobic culture and maintains a heterosexual status, or risks losing one's heterosexual standing for being nonhomophobic.

In post-closeted cultural contexts where tolerance and acceptance of lesbians and gay men are promoted, straight men like Eric offer a comparative strategy for justifying their homophobia. He does this by comparing himself to less tolerant and more homophobic men, like his stepfather or other straight male friends. Eric is right; there are violent and more avowedly homophobic straight men than him, but the point I want to underscore is that his comparative strategy makes sense in reaction to a post-closeted culture that pressures straight men to refashion their homophobia due to a culture of gay tolerance. In other words, by telling me that his homophobia is less prejudicial than other men's homophobia, Eric illustrates a key strategy for expressing homophobic sentiments in an age of tolerance.

However, concerns about gay marriage bring to the fore how gay identities violate traditional gender arrangements, particularly regarding families and parenting. For Eric, gay identities are gender-deviant and abnormal, and thus so are gay relationships. And what he takes strong opposition to is the idea of gays parenting children. This became clear when I asked him what he thought of gay marriage.

> Gay marriage. I think it's like this: two men, two women. I'm fine, not a problem with it. Do I think it's natural or normal? No, not really. I don't have a problem with it. The only time I have a problem with it is when children are involved. When it's involving the raising of a child. I think that there is a unique offer that a male and a woman bring to the development of a child. I think that is very important to the child.

From his practices of not wearing "gay"-looking clothes to his participation in homophobic banter to his strong opposition to lesbian and gay parenthood, Eric attempts to secure a straight masculinity through homophobic practices that use social distance from gay individuals to project a straight masculinity, and his homophobic views invoke beliefs that homosexuality is deviant and abnormal.

Unlike Eric, who attempts to project his straight masculinity by closely monitoring his styles of dress, Terry Bogan, a divorced black father in his thirties who works as a security guard, says no one has mistaken him for being gay, and he doesn't worry about his "spiffy" dressing style giving off a gay look. Demonstrating how his conventional masculinity constructs an unimpeachable straight status, Terry says, "People know that I'm definitely a man's man. I'm definitely heterosexual."

He elaborates on how straight men generally intuit that other men are straight or not:

> Sexuality among heterosexual men is definitely a topic of discussion. Because men just look at women. Most men in this society can't even control themselves: a woman walks by, heterosexual men make

comments that [say] they're heterosexual. When you see a man not showing any interest in women, you start to wonder about this guy. But nowadays it has become so openly disrespectful of divine law. People just openly let you know, "Hi, my name is Jack, I'm gay." Nobody hides it. I don't know anyone in the closet anymore.

Here Terry observes that since he and in his opinion most straight men objectify women they find attractive by looking at and showing interest in them, if a man does not act in this manner, other straight men will be cued. He also observes that gays are no longer closeted and that they are often out and visible in public settings; he cites coworkers from previous jobs at phone company call centers to his own out stepbrother, Rick Brown. Although Terry knows that his stepbrother is gay and is acquainted with lesbian, gay, and bisexual individuals, he does not call any of them friends. He's derisive of his stepbrother's partner being referred to as his "husband," stating, "[a] cousin of mine told me he [my stepbrother] had a husband and it made me laugh a little bit."

This homophobic derision is explained by Terry's strong religious upbringing. His father was a Baptist minister and believed in a traditional patriarchal family. This traditional patriarchal attitude also led to conflicts with his ex-wife:

> She [my ex-wife] definitely wanted to be a man. No question about that. Not to say that she was a butch or lesbian. She just wanted to dictate to me how things should be. . . . And my mother wasn't like that, and I just can't tolerate it. If you said to my mother, "Mommy, can I do this?" She would always say, "Ask your father." It was already established that your father is the king of this castle.

Even though Terry does not think that he is homophobic, he views homosexuality as a sin due to his strong Baptist upbringing. He tells me, "I'm not homophobic if you're leading towards that. I don't think if I sit next to a gay person, I'm going to get AIDS." Terry's statement illustrates another strategy for expressing homophobia in today's context of gay tolerance. Paradoxically, Terry's homophobic practice is a denial of being homophobic. However, his statement of homophobic denial is belied by the very statement he invokes in his defense, stating that he doesn't think he can contract HIV/AIDS by sitting next to a gay individual. His statement also invokes a comparative logic: whereas others would be unwilling to sit next to the said gay individual, he would be willing to, and his statement implies that he should get some comparative "credit" for his open-mindedness.

When I ask Terry what homophobia means to him, he says,

> Homophobia means that the person has a personal hatred or disposition against gays. It's self-explanatory. A phobia, like they're frightened of them. Like they're worried that something bad is going to happen if they're around them. I just don't take it to that extreme. It's not my cup of tea, but I don't take it to the extreme that if you sit next to me on the train I don't think that I'm going to die of AIDS. I just don't take it to that extreme.

Further, when I asked Terry what he thinks causes homophobia, he replied,

> The same thing that causes racism. Or any other type of ism. It's a fear of the unknown and it's ignorance. You know to some degree, I don't compare or believe sexism, racism and homophobia are the same. People like to lump those all together but they're very, very different. For someone white to say they hate me because I'm black, I mean that's a terrible sickness too, but it's a little bit different than saying I hate you because you're gay. To me, people are not born gay. It's a personal choice. And it's a choice that comes about to me because of their inability to control their desires. Now being a man, I realize a hand is a hand. So if a man gropes me down here or a woman gropes me down there and they do it long enough and in the right way, I'm going to ejaculate. I realize that. I realize that I can get off with a man or a woman. I choose to get off with a woman. I didn't choose to be black, although I'm proud of it. I didn't choose it. But somebody says I hate you, but I didn't really have any choice in the matter, then that's not really fair to me. People, liberals, lump those all together.

Terry's statement that he prefers having sex with women but can be aroused by men is consistent with his view that sexuality is a choice, as he perceives both heterosexuality and homosexuality to be personal choices an individual makes.

Like many straight men, Terry rationalizes his homophobia by arguing that homosexuality is a moral and social choice that individuals can be blamed for when framed through the template of Christian scripture. When it comes to thinking about race, however, he ignores how American culture socially stigmatizes black people and other people of color; instead, he defines race as solely a biological state, represented by skin color and genetics. Homophobic beliefs, according to Terry's rationalization, are acceptable because homosexuals "choose" to be gay, but since, as Terry explains, he cannot "choose" to be black, racism is both a different kind of oppressive phenomenon and, in his eyes, worse than homophobia. However, he does draw a connection between homophobia and racism as forms of ignorance, illustrating his understanding of what prejudice across the sexual line of hetero/homosexuality involves for minority groups.

Still, his religious condemnation of homosexuality is most clearly demonstrated when I asked him about gay marriage. This is his response:

> Gay marriage, I think, is an abomination. I don't think that should be legislated. My thing is this. I'll be very blunt with you about this. If two men want to have sex, they have to answer to God on the Day of Judgment. That's their business. But I think we shouldn't legalize it in America, in a country that was built on Judeo-Christian values it would be contradictory to legalize two men or two women getting married for the sake of them having some type of rights or benefits of two heterosexual people.

The traditional morality prescribed by Christian scripture is often invoked in opinions that condemn homosexuality. For black straight individuals like Terry, who grew up and was socialized in the Baptist faith, a Christian standpoint is used to legitimate their stance against same-sex marriage and justify their antigay sentiments.

Martin Alexander is a straight black man who did not grow up going to church but joined a black Protestant congregation as an adult. Martin's straight masculinity entails boundaries that are less exclusionary than the aforementioned men. A married black man in his forties with children, Martin works as an energy technician and knows of several rumored gay men and one "out" lesbian at his workplace. Interestingly, he has felt comfortable becoming friends with his openly lesbian coworker, Patty Crocker. He says that his male coworkers are more tolerant of lesbians than gay men and that many of them find Patty attractive:

> I work with a girl who's a lesbian. She's out. It may not be fine with some people, but she doesn't care. Because she's attractive and some guys would like to be with her and she's not interested because she's not into guys. They might get a little upset about that. They are not as bothered as seeing two women together, as they are seeing two guys together. Because they're sexually attracted to a female physique. They don't want to watch two guys.

Indicative of not only the growing visibility of out lesbians and gay men in the workplace, Martin says that lesbians, as opposed to gay men, are more tolerated by straight men in his workplace. However, lesbian tolerance is coupled here with a homophobic attitude that views lesbians as sexual objects for straight men. This tolerance is dubious, if not just a typical kind of gendered homophobia.

I asked him whether having a lesbian coworker or lesbian sister had changed how he viewed homosexuality. Martin replied, "Probably, only because it puts a face on it. Even if I don't agree, it still certainly gives you more tolerance." Here it is clear to see that as gay coworkers claim the right to be out, along with family members and other acquaintances and friends, straight men like Martin feel that these openly gay individuals compel them to be more tolerant.

When I asked Martin what being heterosexual meant to him, he replied,

> That means I'm not attracted to men. I'm not sexually attracted to them. I can remember a time when, that's why I asked you about transgendered. There are some she males or transgender males [sic]. You would never know unless they told you they were. There was this situation where I met somebody and then nothing happened. I met this person. It wasn't

at a gay bar. It was to my knowledge, it was just a regular straight place. The person was very nice, very nice. But you would've never known that [she was a transsexual woman]. I would never be attracted to a man. Doesn't do anything for me, but I find out later that they [*sic*] were.

Martin found himself attracted to and flirting with a transsexual woman he met at a straight bar in Orangetown. Later he found out this person was not a biological woman and was taken aback by the discovery. His attraction to a transwoman made him reflect upon and question his own heterosexuality. If he was attracted to a transsexual woman, then was he attracted to men and not heterosexual but gay? While he says that he is not attracted to men, he did find himself attracted to this transwoman on this occasion, describing her as "very nice." Hence the perplexity this interaction creates for his own conception of straight identity.

Transsexual women are often portrayed in popular media accounts as "tricking" cisgender men (that is, men who experience a match between the gender they were assigned at birth, their bodies, and identities) into having sexual relations with them under the pretense that they are cisgender women. In reports of these incidents, cisgender men respond by murdering the said transwomen in an act of retribution that seems aimed at regaining and purifying their polluted straight masculine identity status (Schilt and Westbrook 2009).

Reflecting on homophobia, racial identity, and straight-identified men who pursue transwomen for sex, Martin emphasizes that because of the continuing lack of acceptance of LGBT persons, some straight-identified black men would rather pursue sex with transsexual women than openly identify as gay themselves. Citing news reports about the celebrity Eddie Murphy's alleged preference for pursing sexual relations with transwomen, he comments,

You heard about Eddie Murphy picking up a transvestite or a transsexual. OK. There's a lot more of that around than people realize. So there's another thing. That's become a whole new phenomenon now in the sense of the openness to it. There's a lot of heterosexual men that are very open to that, where they wouldn't be open to saying they're gay. That's why I think you have people like Eddie Murphy and others who wouldn't consider sleeping with a guy; tranny that's fine. You follow me? You see what I'm saying? There's another phenomenon that people don't realize. It's very true, trust me, it's very true, it wouldn't be the phenomenon that it is. You pick up the paper the *Village Voice*, you look, you'll see that they have a whole section there with she males, trans. It's there for a reason. But most of those people would never consider themselves gay. They're not going to classify themselves as gay.

Martin is right to point out that many weekly newspapers in cities like New York have listings of transwomen who advertise their sexual services to clients. His own experience attests to black straight men who may find transsexual women attractive, even when they themselves would not openly admit to this experience to others.

Although Martin did not grow up going to church, he married a black woman from a strong religious tradition and joined her conservative black Presbyterian church. Due to his religious beliefs, he does not condone homosexuality:

> I think marriage is an institution that was instituted by God for procreation of his creation. A male, female can only come together and have a child. There's no way that a man and a man can have a child together. Would I vote for it? This is what it really comes down to. Would I vote for a same [sex] marriage package? I would probably say no, and I'm not a bigot by any means.

Martin views gay marriage as prohibited by his Christian beliefs, but he still claims to be "not a bigot," indicating his desire to be seen as nonhomophobic despite his own statement opposing same-sex marriage. Still, his statement about not being a bigot indicates that Martin wants to differentiate himself from, say, racists, who are often described as bigots. His statement hints at a connection between racial and sexual prejudices, but his Christianity seems to determine his stance on gay marriage.

Unlike the other black men in this category, Jessie Clayton does not base his disapproval of gay relationships on his religious beliefs. Rather, Jessie defines himself as nonreligious, but views homosexuality as socially abnormal and deviant. For example, he expresses this when I ask whether he thinks same-sex marriages should be allowed. He explains, "I don't think they [state governments] should allow it. Because if they [gays and lesbians] have kids or adopt kids . . . it would mess up the kids. Society to me won't be right."

The last interviewee in this section illustrates how straight men who tolerate gays still experience a homophobic anxiety based on a fear of being an object of gay male desire. William Russo is a white male in his late thirties who joined the army after high school. Similar to the prior men, William's heterosexuality is established through boundaries of social distance that, while not strongly homophobic, generally exclude gays from his close circles. For example, he stated that he had only one gay male friend, who came out to him within the last year, although he had known that his friend was gay for over a decade. William preferred to let his gay friend, Jim Taylor, tell him in his own time, and this in part allowed William to not have to integrate Jim's gay identity into their friendship. It also meant not having to think about whether Jim was sexually attracted to him, an anxiety that William consciously experiences in gay settings. William explains how Jim did eventually come out to him:

> We were just sitting out one night and he [Jim] just said, "Oh by the way, you did know I was gay, didn't you?" I'm like, "Whatever." We [their mutual friends] all knew. We knew he hung out in the gay community. It was just like one of those things where you're not gonna intrude in his personal space and ask. It's just not something you would do. It's like whatever he does he does and that was what it was.

William's minimal, noncommittal response, "Whatever," effectively shuts down any discussion he and Jim might have had about Jim's sexuality. Responding as he did, at least as he explained the exchange to me, William reveals his unwillingness to acknowledge that part of Jim's identity and his lack of comfort in their friendship now that Jim makes a claim to wanting recognition as a gay man.

Besides drawing boundaries of social distance, which generally exclude gays from his social circles, William relies on a hypermasculine gender performance to indicate his heterosexuality. For instance, his head is shaved and he has a solid, jock-like build and attitude. When dating women as well as when interacting with other men, he wants to be viewed as an "alpha male." William states this explicitly:

> I want women to view me as masculine. A woman, especially if I'm dating her, I want her to view me as an alpha male. Women will always go after the stronger male, the one that can provide best for her. I'm not always successful at it, but that's always the direction that I'm moving.

When I ask him in what ways he tries to show this, he mentions a number of things, ranging from his military experience to his career to how much money he makes. In short, when it comes to women and competing for them with other men, William sees every interaction as a potential competition to demonstrate dominance. He does this with men as well. "I like to beat other guys if it involves me making money or me winning. Everything I do with other guys, I feel the need to beat them and that's just what it is. I don't always succeed in that, but that's what I need to do."

William's straight masculine identity aims to reproduce hegemonic norms. For example, at the very beginning of the interview, he told me, "Honestly, in regard to relationships with women, bisexual is preferred. I like two girls." He explains to me that what he means by a bisexual woman is one who will have sex with him and another woman at the same time but have relationships only with men. His straight masculinity is constructed through a sexual objectification of women that reduces their sexualities to his instrumental needs, viewing bisexual women as created to meet his sexual wants and preferences.

William consciously identifies as a "straight, white male, Republican, business [minded], economic conservative, [with] libertarian social values. That sums me up." Even though he does not frame these master statuses as forms of privilege, his naming of them shows an awareness of his multiple identity statuses.

He makes a point of telling me that he is less homophobic than other straight men, as his very willingness to be interviewed demonstrates his tolerant attitude. He says, "I'm more comfortable in more situations. I mean how many straight guys like me are gonna come in and sit and have this interview. Yeah, I don't think I'm a typical guy." Again, a comparative logic operates in this statement, where William says he is less homophobic than a "typical guy," as evidenced by his consent to being interviewed by me, a gay male. In a sense one might say William thinks I should feel grateful or "lucky," as many straight men would not agree to be interviewed.[1] Again, this comparison underscores his tolerance of gays.

Illustrating the complicated ways homophobia and attitudes of gay normalization paradoxically circulate together in post-closeted contexts, William supports the right of same-sex couples to marry.

> I think it's nobody's business other than the people that are getting married. I don't understand how it could be, how it possibly could be as big of a political issue as it got to be. It should be a non-issue. . . . The government should recognize the marriages that come out of wherever [same-sex marriage is legalized].

Wanting to understand how changes in lesbian and gay life are connected to changes in heterosexuals' sense of their identity status and relationships, I ask William whether he thinks being straight is different today than in the past. He says that in the past a straight man had to get married and have children, but today things are different. He notices more heterosexuals who are single for a longer amount of time or who marry but later divorce and are single again.

Since William has never been married and is single and straight, this status creates some tension for him. He knows, for instance, that others sometimes view being single at his age, thirty-eight, as a potential sign of homosexuality. In addition, William generally avoids going into gay bars and fears having a man flirt with him.

> I think as a heterosexual guy you have a phobia of being hit on by another guy. That's largely why we don't like to go, like myself, I don't feel comfortable going to The Pub [a gay bar] for a drink. I've been in there before. My friend Alicia dragged me in there one night, but I felt anxious the whole time.

For many straight men like William, homophobia is less about prejudice toward gay men and is more based on social anxiety about a gay man being attracted to and flirting with them. For instance, William tells me that his gay friend Jim told him that "he looks at guys the way I look at women." And this reversal in being the object of objectification, as opposed to the subject doing the objectification, produces an anxiety that William experiences as a social-psychological threat.

Many of the straight men I interviewed defined their homophobia as based on the uncomfortable feelings they experienced when they perceived gay men as objectifying them, particularly when gazing at their bodies. This definition of homophobia came up repeatedly in the interviews, as many of the straight male respondents do not like to go to gay bars and described a strong anxiety when they were around gay men more generally. The possibility of being flirted with and taken as gay themselves presents a threat or challenge to their sense of themselves as conventionally masculine and, by extension, unmistakably straight.

The psychoanalyst Ken Corbett (1993) argues that one of the fantasies and fears that underlie this homophobic expression is an ostensibly straight man's image of himself as "the object of a man's desire." By "so fantasizing, he must, if ever so briefly, put himself in the place of a man who desires another man." This perspective positions straight men as desiring men, a position only gay men, not straight men, are supposed to consciously fantasize and experience as part of their sexual desires. Furthermore, these straight men perhaps imagine and feel themselves to be wanted the way they would want a woman. As William observes, "he looks at guys the way I look at women." This, then, positions them like women—passive, submissive, docile—when looked at by another man. It makes sociological sense, then, that social distance is and continues to be a key homophobic boundary practice that straight men use to manage their anxiety and discomfort as well as intolerance and animosity toward gay individuals, spaces, and symbols.

Antihomophobias, Weak Boundaries, and Maintaining Straight Privilege

This section explores the antihomophobic practices of white and black straight men. If homophobic practices of social distance from gays are ways to secure straight masculine statuses, then how straight men perform their straight masculinities while being antihomophobic is an interesting sociological question. I map the other side of a continuum of straight masculinities, moving from men who maintain only weak heteronormative boundaries to those who blur them.

Sixteen out of twenty-nine respondents fall into the weak heteronormative boundaries range, while the remaining four men constitute those who blur boundaries. Eight black and eight white men constitute the sixteen men in the weak boundaries category, while four white men constitute the category of men who blur heteronormative boundaries. Although both categories of men exhibit antihomophobic practices that position gays as equals, the key characteristic that defines the straight men in the weak position of the continuum is that they do invoke their straight status to maintain straight privilege. For instance, they often mention their girlfriends or wives in conversations to indicate their heterosexual status, or by having their female friends, girlfriends, or wives accompany them when they patronize gay establishments. In the weak boundaries category, nine out of the sixteen men report having gone to a gay bar, a pride parade, or another gay event. Eight out of those nine state that their girlfriends or wives accompanied them or that they disclosed their straight status when men flirted with them in these contexts.

Straight men in the weak boundaries category promote egalitarian views of lesbians and gay men, but with the assumption that gays are generally gender-conventional. Consequently, they accept the underlying categories of sexualities as heterosexual/homosexual and those of gender as men embodying masculinities and women embodying femininities. In doing so, they take the sexual and gender divisions as natural, but argue that lesbians and gay men deserve respect and rights since many conform to these accepted categories and conventions. They might be considered "reformers" of hegemonic masculinity.

Richard Barrett is a black man in his fifties who has worked as the director of a health care institute for several years. He describes himself as "a very faith-based African American male. Very involved in my church." Challenging the connections among race, religiosity, and homophobia, Richard is a strongly religious man who embraces gay-affirmative values.

During his formative years, before Stonewall, Richard says, he grew up with gay men in his neighborhood and church, but their sexuality was not talked about. Homosexuality was associated with femininity in boys and men, he says. Richard explains that the word "sissy" connoted homosexuality, a marked femininity, and a loss of masculinity for him and his peers: "In retrospect, there were folks in the neighborhood and the church who were gay, mostly men. Folk would describe certain folk, not as being gay or homosexual, but being a sissy. You knew what the word 'sissy' meant, a man with feminine kinds of traits." He acknowledges that homosexuality is a difficult identity for blacks to embrace. He still thinks of the closet, silence, and stigma in terms of how the black community treats homosexuality.

> Well, being homosexual in the black community is still very much a closeted kind of expression. And when I was growing up, it wasn't exposed. There were some folk who were obviously that way, but they were just so in the minority. That whole issue is pretty difficult to dialogue with. And it is associated to some degree with weaknesses.

Indicative of post-Stonewall gay visibility and its accompanying sign system of heterosexual/homosexual identity, Richard describes a time when he worked in a hospital in the 1970s and regularly wore clogs to work. He was single and in his mid-twenties at the time and says that, although he had a girlfriend, many of the female nurses wondered whether he was gay and thought the clogs might be a sign of a homosexual identity. He humorously recalls the incident when his secretary told him that some of the nurses suspected he might be gay:

> My secretary came to me one day and she said to me, "So and so likes you." "Well, hey, I didn't come here for that and plus I have a girlfriend." "Well, then, somebody else likes you too but you don't seem to have time for any of them." Well, I said, "True." And they [the nurses] also said because you wear those clogs they want to know if you're gay. I said, "No, I'm not." I just chuckled at her. She said, "I told them that you weren't, but they just said he wears those clogs." And it was the clogs more so than anything else. Wearing clogs in the '70s, it was just the thing. It was fashionable. But folk put one and one together and came up with fifteen. My secretary and I, we, laughed about it.

Richard later married in his thirties and says he does not know of a time since the clog incident when he was suspected of being gay.

Although Richard is a devout Christian, he supports same-sex marriage. He notes, however, that the Bible views homosexuality as a sin, but thinks that hating gays is even more morally wrong:

> I have a very religious background. The Bible defines it as a sin, but so is hate a sin. Could I belong to a congregation where the pastor was gay? I struggle with that. You would not catch me at a rally opposing gay marriage. I mean they can raise families as well as anyone. I mean sexual practice. What's next? Height? We've done the race thing.

Richard points out that while the Bible condemns homosexuality, it also condemns hate. Distancing himself from those who oppose same-sex marriage, he disavows using religious morality to justify denying gays' rights. Even though he would struggle with having a gay pastor, he doesn't view gays' struggles for civil rights as different from blacks' struggles. Gay visibility and cultural integration have created a movement that black heterosexuals engage in. Although previous studies have shown that blacks' religiosity conditions and supports their homophobic beliefs (Herek and Capitanio 1995; Schulte and Battle 2004), this isn't the case for Richard and three other religious black straight men in this category of the continuum. Rather, Richard's religious beliefs in part shape his support of same-sex marriage and lesbian and gay families, as he sees hatred of lesbians and gay men as against Christian values. Still, at the same time, his ambivalence regarding integrating gays in church as ministers demonstrates the limit of his antihomophobia.

The next respondent, Jeff Rapaport, is a thirty-seven-year-old white Jewish male who draws weaker boundaries of social distance from gay and lesbian people. He and his wife live in a mixed gay/straight neighborhood, and they are acquainted with many gay individuals. In fact, he also goes to gay bars with his wife and is flattered when gay men flirt with him. Jeff says he mentions his wife as a last tactic to indicate he's straight. He recounts a time when this happened:

> I was talking to someone the other day and he was hitting on me when I was sitting on the steps [of my house]. And I was trying to figure out a way to tell him I wasn't interested. I didn't want to be rude to the guy. But

finally I just said something like, "My wife wouldn't like me going out to Magnet [a gay bar] with you."

Although they make no moral distinction between straights and gays, social and sexual behaviors are coded as straight or homosexual for Jeff and his wife. For instance, Jeff explains that his wife thought he might be gay since she did not physically arouse him for a period of time. He explains, "I'll tell you a funny story. I was taking medication one time and I was having a hard time performing. And my wife thought that maybe I was gay just because I wasn't attracted. I think people even close to you can feel that way. And it was just a temporary thing, but it was problematic."

Gay visibility entails a cultural coding of sexual acts and performance, bodily comportment, styles of dress, linguistic style, and various lifestyle choices as gay or straight. That even Jeff's wife suspects that he is homosexual indicates the pervasiveness of homosexual codes and the diffusion of a homosexual/heterosexual sign system into everyday life.

Jeff doesn't think that gender behavior indicates someone's sexual identity, unless the person is extremely gender-nonconformist. Still, out of habit he avoids certain behaviors:

I would say that I don't go like this [*makes a limp wrist*]. Because I think that's traditionally, if you do that, then people will say [you're gay]. It doesn't mean anything either, but stereotypically that's in my head. I don't cross my legs, you know, the real close cross.

Here, his coding of behaviors like crossing one's legs indicates that he views enacting practices coded as feminine as devaluing a man's masculine display and eliciting others' suspicion that he is homosexual.

Further, Jeff claims he doesn't consciously avoid wearing particular clothes in order to not be viewed as gay, but he codes men who are more fashionable than himself as gay. He knows that some heterosexual men are fashionable, but the heterosexual men in his social circles are not. "I'm not really very fashionable in the first place and I accept that about myself. So, I don't really have any fear of what I'm wearing being seen as gay." Everyday gender practices from clothes to particular behaviors are coded as heterosexual or homosexual for Jeff.

Interestingly, in reflecting on his own personal and social privileges, Jeff readily acknowledges his white male privilege, but is less able to articulate its relationship to any form of straight advantage. In relation to job opportunities, he says,

> When you are a white male, there's certain ways that you have opportunities that other people don't. So I think it's kind of like you have to acknowledge that. . . . For instance, what I mean is like when you look for a job the white male who's interviewing you is more inclined to hire you because there's that commonality. I think there's a whole old boys' network; it still is in existence. And it's not necessarily formal. It's more that people know people and they recommend people. So I think even from just an overall society perceptive, it's different if you're white. . . . A lot of gay people, you would never know that they're gay, so therefore they're getting the same kind of treatment. I think there are certainly [gay] people who are discriminated against, but I guess that my thinking for the most part [is] if you're gay [and a white male] and you go in and try to get a job, I think it's that maybe just being white and being a male will get you in the door in places you couldn't if you were black and male. And whether you're gay or straight, unless it's completely obvious, it wouldn't matter, you'd still get in that door. So you may not get the same treatment when you're there and you may not get to be able to be open about being who you are but you can get in there.

Jeff articulates several important points. First, he acknowledges that race and gender privileges play roles in one's job opportunities. However, he compares racial and gender statuses to sexual identity status and implies that sexual identity has a different set of social cues that are less salient than race or gender. That is, race as marked through skin color is a different and typically a more salient identity marker than sexuality. Moreover, he states that white gay men may also choose to not disclose their sexual identity status in ways that African American men cannot similarly manage in the disclosure of their race. While straight privilege has real and important ramifications in workplaces, Jeff underscores how racial inequality is often more salient for Americans than sexual inequality.

Like many of the straight men with weak boundaries, Jeff also registered anxiety over gay male gender-nonconventional behavior when I asked about TV shows he watched with gay characters. Gay male representations that are not gender-conventional exhibit a nontraditional masculinity; that is, they challenge a binary gender order of men as masculine and women as feminine. Acceptable gay images for many straight men are ones that exhibit traditional masculine displays. For example, regarding the characters on the now syndicated TV sitcom *Will & Grace*, Jeff commented that Jack is "so overly gay. I thought that it was kind of stereotypical and is a bit much, but then you have Will to offset it, who was your normal kind of guy for the most part."

In sum, Jeff's masculinity grading practices not only enforce gender normativity, but heteronormative boundaries that code gay men as embodying feminine practices and straight men as consistently masculine. The limit of Jeff's antihomophobia is demonstrated by the subtle strategies he uses to project his heterosexuality as traditionally masculine. By purposefully mentioning his wife or having her accompany him to gay spaces or by avoiding certain gendered behaviors, Jeff aims to project his straight status or recuperate it and its privilege.

Mark Wilson, the next respondent, is an African American male in his thirties who grew up in a working-class neighborhood. Like Jeff, Mark doesn't maintain strong boundaries between straights and gays. For example, when he was married he would go to gay clubs with his wife, but now he sometimes goes with female friends. Yet, despite Mark's lack of strong boundaries between gays and straights, he still thickly codes straight or gay identity practices through masculinity and refracts these masculinity practices through racial and social class lenses. While there is some diversity of clothing styles in his social circles, Mark still expects other black and Latino straight men to wear loose-fitting T-shirts and baggy pants or jeans that sag down over their waist. He demonstrates that a post-closeted cultural coding of straight/ gay identity practices frames black straight men's perceptions of other men of color and their embodiment of racial norms in styles of dress:

> Culturally, for African/Latin men we usually wearing those baggy jeans, the boots. Just a certain look that we've become accustomed to giving off. If I see another African American or Latin American brother, he might

be doin', what's one of the artist, the Lenny Kravitz thing. He may be fully aware of himself and just don't wanta assimilate to what everybody in the hood is wearing. So, automatically that draws attention. Something's up. It may be the jeans won't be as baggy. He might not have a thermal or hoodie on. He might have a nice shirt on. He might even tucked in the shirt. A lot of times I know for a fact brothas look at the level of education as well. Because everyone speaks a certain lingo. There's a certain type of dialect that's spoken. But you have someone else come in that's been afforded education and dress a little bit differently because consumer-wise they're conscious, it throw people off and they try to figure him out.

In effect, Mark is appealing to racial norms of clothing style (i.e., baggy jeans and oversized shirts for blacks and Latinos) in order to establish a straight masculine identity. However, Mark acknowledges that styles of dress vary among black and Latino men. For instance, class status as indicated through consumption habits often alters the style practices that black and Latino straight men model as well.

Racial straight masculine style codes can be extremely nuanced, even exacting in their attention to detail. Richard Majors (2001) and C. J. Pascoe (2007) both note the emphasis African American boys and men place on the politics of appearance in performing their straight masculine statuses. For Majors, the "cool pose" encompasses a black man's demeanor, speech, clothing, hairstyle, walk, and whole bodily self. For example, the sagging jeans or pant styles young African American men often display embody this cool pose, performing a hyperstraight masculinity by paradoxically displaying their underwear, often boxer shorts, from the back, with their pants hanging off their buttocks. This is not the most conventional style practice one might imagine in the abstract, but given the context of black men's associations with hypersexuality, their surplus of straight masculine symbolic capital compensates for these displays of their underwear-clad rear ends. Whereas, in gay contexts and on gay men, butt-revealing pant styles would most likely be read as sexually provocative, even suggesting a desire for anal sex. Here, in contrast, the audacity it takes to embrace this style practice marks black men as so exaggeratedly straight and masculine that they seem in part to dare others to stare at their asses or mistake them for being gay at the risk of the threat of violence, real or implied. Moreover, nonblack boys and men now copy this aesthetic of sagging pants or jeans, referencing this black style practice and aiming to acquire some of its symbolic capital for themselves.

Mark's friend Brian Lane, for instance, exhibited typical black masculine style practices but with gender-nonconventional elements, and, in this case, it was these minute style elements that raised Mark's doubts about Brian's heterosexuality:

> A buddy of mine. Cool dude, but there was just something about him. I was doing security in the clubs. Just one night, it bothered me the first time, and I didn't say anything. And the second time, I said, "Fuck it, we're cool." I don't wanna offend him. There were just certain times. I don't know if it was a compelling feeling. I just wanna ask him. In the hood, we got brothas, he a playboy, but he [Brian] was like a pretty boy. And it was like he would wear the baggy jeans and the boots and everything, but every time you see him everything was pressed, ironed. I mean there wasn't a wrinkle. He wouldn't wolf out [grow his facial hair]. No mustache. The thing that called attention to me once was I seen his eyebrows and they were really creased. I'm like, "Let me holler at you. I don't want to offend you or nothin' at all like that, but are you gay?" He went off on me. He kept asking me, "Why would you say that to me?" And I apologized.

Despite Brian's adherence to black masculine style codes, it's his non-normative masculine style practices (e.g., ironed clothes, plucked and stylized eyebrows) as a "pretty boy" that stand out to Mark. Even though Mark views gays and straights as social and moral equals, his masculinity grading practices enforce not only gender normativity, but also normative straight boundaries that code gay men as somewhat feminine and straight men as consistently masculine. The depth and detail with which masculinity practices are graded illustrate an elaborate gender sign system. The fusion of gender and sexual identity practices has the effect of making masculinity, along with normative straight boundaries, the key site of sexual identity politics in everyday life.

In addition to employing normative masculinity practices and codes, the public disclosure of a straight identity is the easiest strategy for signaling and reestablishing one's heterosexuality. For example, if Mark encounters women he knows at a gay club, he readily declares he's straight if they ask him.

> I've frequent[ed] a lot of different clubs. And I'll go inside of a club, because, shit, liquor is liquor. I've been to a few clubs that's been labeled a gay club. And [straight] females will see me and they'll come over and say, "Yo, you gay or you straight?" And I'm like, "No, I'm straight." "Then what the fuck you doin?" I say, "Yo, you've seen these specials?" And I'm in there drinking up a storm.

Despite his recognition of gay prejudice, Mark doesn't view straight identity as a privilege or grasp the subtle reclamation of straight privilege embedded in "coming out" as straight in a gay context.

Nonetheless, Mark's pro-gay values are remarkable given his father's overt animus toward homosexuality. Mark recalls how his gay cousin, Bruce, was beat up by his own father for being gay and Bruce had asked to stay with Mark's family, but Mark's dad refused to offer shelter to Bruce. As Mark recalls, "My uncle had beat him [Bruce] up . . . because he found him and I guess his male friend in the bedroom. And we had received a phone call because my older cousin [Bruce] had want[ed] to come stay with us in Queens. My father was like totally against it and he and my mom got into this big beef."

Perhaps even more unlikely is that Mark first became friendly with black gay men while he was incarcerated as a juvenile offender. When I asked him, "What does homophobia mean to you?" he related this story:

> For instance, when I was incarcerated I used to have real long hair. And for a while I had a couple of female friends coming up and doing my hair but when you're incarcerated, they send you all over the goddamn place. . . . But what you always find . . . a lot of times the gentlemen, who took on the thing of being homosexual, they can braid the hair. That was

their hustle. [I said,] "fuck it, I'm gettin' my hair done." I used to speak to them. A lot of them, they were just really down-to-earth dudes that just like dudes. . . . It took a whole year of me rockin' the afro, not being able to do nothin' with it. So I had homophobia for a year.

With limited options in prison, after a year Mark turned to the black gay men who made money in prison by styling hair. By realizing that these men are, as he puts it, "down-to-earth dudes that just like dudes," Mark moved past his adolescent perception of gays as abnormal and deviant.

To this day, though, Mark employs weak boundaries to establish his straight identity. For instance, his detailed coding of his friend Brian's nonhegemonic practices illustrate how filled with meaning masculinity practices are for him. This notwithstanding, Mark's anti-homophobic practices allow him to feel comfortable socializing in gay spaces. In contrast to straight men who purposefully avoid gay spaces, symbols, and individuals, Mark establishes softer and less exclusionary boundaries of social distance. The limit of Mark's antihomophobia is demonstrated by the subtle strategies he uses to project his straight masculine status. Similar to Jeff who is accompanied by his wife, Mark, by having a woman accompany him or by readily disclosing his straight status in gay spaces, aims to project his straight standing and thus its privilege.

The last interviewee I discuss in the weak boundaries category is Jason Robson. Born in 1979, Jason is a single young black man who was raised by his mother and experiences being a (heterosexual) black man as his most salient identity:

> Me being a man and just me being black just automatic throws out the vision of black man. So that would be my identity, the strongest identity I have. It's not something I try to figure out how to portray to everyone that, "Hey, I'm a black man." It's just something that they see me as. So I just let people see me as what they want to see me as until they find out who I am.

His black identity positions him within an array of racialized heterosexual stereotypes, whether it is women acquaintances jokingly inferring he has a large penis or male friends insinuating that his associations with women are sexual, not platonic. Jason's racial identity hyper-het-erosexualizes his masculinity. For instance, this comes across when he says, "I mean if you see me around a lot of times you see that I always hang around with girls. They [straight men] never questioned my [straight] sexuality. A lot of people just assume that I have a lot of girls, both guys and girls." He continues, discussing how he prefers being friends with women. "I'd rather hang around with all girls. That's where I see bisexuality in guys because they like to hang around with other guys. When you hang around with just guys all the time, all they're talk-ing about are girls."

I asked him, "But most straight guys wouldn't hang around with just girls, right? That would be a stereotype for gay men?" Jason explained, "That could be a stereotype for gay men, but in my case a lot of people seem to just think I have a lot of girls and I'm hooking up with all these girls. They never assume that I'm gay because I hang out alone with girls."

Jason's straight masculinity practices are generally conventional, so his black identity acts as a kind of trump card against homosexual suspicion, exaggerating his straight masculinity, as seen through his friends' assumptions that he is "hooking up with all these girls." He perpetuates this by letting other men think he has sex with his women friends. Jason thus partly constructs his straight masculinity through the sexual objectification of women.

Jason's pro-gay values are illustrated by his active choice to befriend gay individuals. In college, for example, he chose to live in a dorm suite with a gay student and became close friends with him and his boy-friend. When I ask Jason why he is not homophobic, he relates his expe-riences of being a racial minority and sees his management of racism as analogous to how gays must manage homophobia:

Because I'm black and if you look at it from the standpoint of at one time black people were discriminated against by everyone, why would you discriminate against somebody else? Just put yourself in their shoes because you actually can. Because black people are still discriminated against.

For him, being antihomophobic is analogous to being antiracist; he empathizes with the discrimination that gays experience as similar to discrimination against himself and blacks in general. Jason draws on his black racial status to understand the stigma of homosexuality that gays must negotiate in everyday life. Further, he identifies as an atheist, and so there is no religious basis for condemning homosexuality. Unlike Richard's discomfort with the idea of a gay pastor, Jason's support of gays is unequivocal.

Finally, Jason is often told by female friends that he has a metrosexual style. He says, "Well, I don't wear tight jeans because they're not too comfortable. Tight shirts I do wear, but the first thing that people think is, 'Oh, he has a good body.'" Although young black heterosexual masculine styles are often associated with urban styles of oversized clothing, Jason's style of dress takes on a metrosexual aesthetic. This theme of codes of metrosexuality is one that I will return to when discussing the next respondent, comparing the two heterosexual men's racial refractions of metrosexuality.

Antihomophobias, Blurred Boundaries, and Surrendering Straight Privilege

In developing the concept of antihomophobic practices as plural, I show that there are multiple forms of antihomophobia in circulation among the respondents. While the straight men in the weak boundaries category distance themselves from homophobic expressions and variably counter antigay prejudice and discrimination, they still aim to maintain their straight identity status and privilege. Straight identity statuses and their accompanying privileges are part of a system of heteronormativity, which produces and reproduces heterosexual domination and homosexual subordination. In order to claim straight privilege and receive the benefits of straight group dominance, straights must claim a straight identity status. Following masculinity scholars' conception of gender inequality and privilege, I claim that, whatever other consequences they might have, and regardless of what individual straights intend, straight identity practices, which include the claim to a straight status, have the effect of reproducing an unequal sexual order and straight privilege (Schrock and Schwalbe 2009, 280).

The last respondents are the white straight men who constitute the far end of the continuum. In addition to countering homophobic prejudice and discrimination, they purposefully blur boundaries between heterosexual and homosexual identity statuses. By allowing themselves to be viewed as gay in some situations, they surrender their straight status and its accompanying privilege in these interactions. It is this key point that constitutes the further development of their antihomophobic practices beyond combating homophobic prejudice and discrimination, as their blurring of identity status boundaries challenges the reproduction of straight privilege in a heteronormative sexual order.

I qualify their boundary-blurring practices by noting two important conditions. First, they generally blur boundaries in informal public contexts, such as in gay bars or restaurants with gay and straight clienteles, but these practices also do occur in formal public contexts, such as in a college classroom. Second, these straight men retain a sense of knowledge and a certain advantage over others since they are the only ones who know what their sexuality is when they blur sexual identity boundaries.

Matt Becker is a single thirty-year-old white male who grew up in a working-class family. Unlike Jason, whose racial heterosexual masculinity situates him in terms of hypersexual straight stereotypes, Matt's straight masculinity is refracted through a white racial lens that codes his heterosexuality with the status and prestige of normality. However, like Jason, Matt has a lot of women friends with whom he enjoys spending time alone.

> I've always been a guy who's had a lot of friends who were female, and exclusively friends. I mean I go out with four, five, six girls, which is a little abnormal in the sense of what guys think is typical. I've gotten into plenty of conversations where it would be girl talk. I don't mean any of those stereotypical things: but girls get together and they sit around and they talk about their feelings. And guys, as a very general experience of mine, don't do that.

STRAIGHT MEN   >>   125

Although Matt is conventionally masculine, his straight women and gay male friends joke that he is gay or "metrosexual." (Chapter 5 provides a fuller discussion of metrosexual masculinities and their non-normative implications.) When I ask him what he thinks that means, he says, "the way that I interpret the term is a straight male who has a lot of the perceived characteristics of a homosexual male—tidiness, neatness, style with their dress."

Matt describes going to gay bars and feeling comfortable. He does not need to disclose his straight identity to turn down men who flirt with him. His antihomophobia means not reclaiming straight privilege by "coming out" as straight:

> If somebody comes up to me, hitting on me, then I'll say, "Not inter-ested." And I don't mean I'll brush them off. I don't need them to get away from me. No different than me being at a nongay bar or club, or a girl approaching me who I'm not attracted to and me saying, "Sorry, not interested," or making small talk for a few minutes and then moving on.

Being antihomophobic, Matt has a number of gay male friends with whom he goes to gay bars for drinks. Interestingly, Matt and Jason both exhibit similar qualities. They are gender-conventional men, have close gay friends, and straight women tell them that they're "metro-sexual." However, it is Matt who is singled out as being possibly gay. It seems that whereas Jason's heterosexual masculinity is marked as hypersexual because of his black identity, Matt's heterosexual mas-culinity is unmarked by his white identity. Moreover, since homo-sexuality is often racially associated with whiteness, this association reinforces how others view Matt's metrosexual behaviors as possibly homosexual, whereas Jason's similar behaviors don't elicit the same response. That is, Matt's stylish appearance is coded as possible evi-dence of a gay identity while Jason's fashionable dress is not. This is similar to what Pascoe (2007) found. She observes that "because Afri-can American men are so hypersexualized in the United States, white men are, by default, feminized," and practices attentive to appearance expose white men to suspicions of homosexuality in ways that they don't among black men (71). Finally, while Matt has gay male friends jokingly tell him he's gay and has been flirted with at gay bars, Jason assumes that gay men in gay bars don't think he's gay, as he has never been approached by a gay man.

Two more individuals illustrate antihomophobic practices that prominently blur gay/straight boundaries. Alan Waters is a married forty-year-old white community college instructor who championed a domestic partner policy at the conservative community college where he teaches. Like Matt, he is comfortable with the possibility of his identity being read as gay. In his classes, Alan often includes gay subject material, aiming to create a classroom space that affirms antihomophobic values. He also purposefully allows students to perceive him as possibly gay by using the word "partner" instead of wife.

> Sometimes students make assumptions about their teachers and sometimes I let them linger in uncertainty to think about their own ideas. I would refer to my "partner" and they would assume "partner" means gay and I wouldn't always clarify that for them. Students would say, "Oh, don't use the word partner, people will think you're gay." And I'd say, "Okay, what's the issue with that?"

Nick Lynch, my last interviewee, goes even further in blurring boundaries of social distance between straights and gays in everyday life. By allowing himself to be viewed as gay at times, Nick, a single white male in his early twenties, contests heteronormativity by surrendering his straight status and privilege. For Nick, being straight "means that I'm only emotionally and physically attracted to the opposite sex. Guys have never given me an erection." The boundary he uses to establish his heterosexuality is to profess a strictly heterosexual desire. By defining heterosexual identity as based on sexual desire, he rejects the equation of conventional masculinity and heterosexual status.

Illustrating his antihomophobia and refusal to claim straight status and privilege, Nick also doesn't disclose his heterosexuality when men flirt with him. He says, "I get that confusion all the time working in the bar scene. I have guys and girls come on to me. So I know for a fact that I don't protrude a straight, exact heterosexual or homosexual, identity. I realized that the lines are so blurred these days that you really can't tell who's gay and straight."

Further, because Nick doesn't view masculinity as tightly connected to heterosexuality, he isn't defensive in being viewed as gay. The detachment of masculinity from heterosexuality partly explains his ease in blurring boundaries. Nick's acceptance of others viewing him as gay is demonstrated by how he deals with the aggressive flirting of gay men at gay bars.

> Homosexuals don't make me feel uncomfortable. The only time I ever feel uncomfortable in a bar is when somebody is a little bit too forward and that happens with straight people and gay people. Although in this area, I do find it a little bit more among the gay community. Gay men are a little bit more forceful if they find you attractive and they're drunk at a bar. I don't have women grabbing my ass and touching my chest at a straight bar. But if I go to someplace like Magnet [a gay club] with a couple of friends, it's bound to happen. It doesn't bother me. I almost expect it, but definitely a little bit more forward.

Nick's antihomophobic practices of blurring heteronormative boundaries were atypical. Most straight male respondents use varying degrees of social distance to project a clear straight masculinity. The rarity with which respondents disentangle masculinity and sexual identity demonstrates Nick's knowledge of gay men's diverse masculinities and his understanding of the subtle homophobia enacted by this conflation. Nick grew up in a context of lesbian and gay visibility, and his enactment of straight masculinity reflects young Americans' sense of comfort with post-closeted gay life (Seidman 2002).

The Continuum, Antihomophobias, and Shifts in Hegemonic Masculinity

Based on these interviews, I am suggesting that straight masculinities are shifting and do not necessarily rely upon homophobic practices. Consequently, it is important to rethink accepted models like Connell's (1987, 1995) theory of hegemonic masculinity and Kimmel's (2005, 2008) model of masculinity as based on an unchanging homophobic dynamic. Decades of lesbian and gay political activism (Armstrong 2002; Seidman 2002) have increased gay visibility and produced

Table 3.1. Continuum of Straight Boundaries of Social Distance (Men)

Strongly Aversive Boundaries	Weak Boundaries	Blurred Boundaries
Rodney Eric Terry Martin Tom Jessie Jerome Heath William	Paul Richard Toby George Milton John Derek Jeff Mark Michael Marvin Joe Carl Chris Robert Jason	Matt Ken Alan Nick

attitudinal changes toward tolerance and acceptance. This is conditioned by the formation of a straight culture that now appeals to anti-homophobia in order to claim an enlightened status. The continuum I have described defines a range of everyday interactional practices that straight men use to reject, resist, or accommodate an antihomophobic stance in their performances of straight masculinity. Table 3.1 provides a visual representation of the entire continuum and where each individual man falls on it.

Based on the homophobic boundaries of social distance that straight men construct between themselves and gay individuals, spaces, and signifiers, the continuum provides a grading of straight masculine practices and shows how race intersects with these identity practices. This grading documents both the homophobic and sexual identity practices that heterosexual men use to establish their straight masculinities and to maintain its privileges. The left side of the continuum, which I labeled the strongly aversive boundaries category, is constituted by various enactments of straight masculinity that involve straight men disassociating themselves from gay individuals and style practices perceived as gay and feminine, to managing anxieties about being an object of gay male desire.

Documenting relationships along the axes of race, gender, and heterosexuality, the continuum shows that black and white straight men in the strongly aversive category enact similar kinds of homophobic stances in the boundaries of social distance they establish between themselves and gay individuals and signifiers. In the context of increased tolerance toward lesbians and gay men, these straight men feel pressured to exhibit a modicum of respect and tolerance for openly gay people. Besides Rodney, the other five black straight men in this category did not want to be seen as prejudiced against gay people, as they drew on their experiences with racial prejudice to empathize to some degree with the prejudice lesbians and gay men experience. However, as the literature would predict (Herek and Capitanio 1995; Schulte and Battle 2004), five of the six black men in this category invoked their religiosity as their rationale for their homophobic stances. In contrast, the remaining black heterosexual man and the three white heterosexual men invoked social views of homosexuality as an abnormal and deviant identity to justify their homophobic practices.

In contrast, in the middle of the continuum, which I labeled weak boundaries of social distance, four out of eight black straight men identified as religious, and these black men *did not* invoke their religious morality to condemn gays. For example, Richard, a highly religious black man, stated that hatred is a sin from his Christian standpoint. Rhetorically, Richard drew on his religiosity to support gay rights and equality. Furthermore, all of the eight black men in the weak boundaries category, whether they identified as religious, nonreligious, or atheist, use their experiences with racism to understand the homophobia gays must negotiate in everyday life. This understanding of the link between racial and sexual oppressions conditioned these black straight men's gay-friendly stances and their support of lesbian and gay friends, kin, and coworkers.

In the middle of the continuum, we are witnessing variations in heteronormativity, where heterosexual men variably accommodate homosexual normalization (that is, viewing gays as normal and worthy of respect), but gender-conventional displays remain a factor in this accommodation. These heterosexual men, then, maintain hegemonic masculine norms by basing their respect of gay men in particular, and all men in general, on whether they enact traditional masculine displays and disavow feminine ones (Schippers 2007). Some also enact hegemonic practices by constructing women as sexual objects. Furthermore, they subtly maintain their heterosexual status and privilege, performing it through a traditional masculine practice or by calling attention to their heterosexual relationship. For example, when heterosexual men in the weak category patronize gay establishments, they are typically accompanied by their wives, girlfriends, or female friends, who in part project their heterosexual status.

Nevertheless, the black and white heterosexual men in the weak boundaries category exhibit antihomophobic stances by respecting lesbian and gay identities and relationships, befriending openly gay people, and supporting gays' legal rights. Being antihomophobic, then, is also a gender and sexual identity strategy that trades on the prestige of being tolerant, enlightened, and empathetic in order to claim a gay-friendly straight masculine status in the context of lesbian and gay visibility, the cultural integration of gay people, and Americans' liberalizing attitudes toward homosexuality (Hicks and Lee 2006; Loftus 2001). The audiences for antihomophobic stances include these men's friends, family members, and coworkers.

Exhibiting the most dynamic antihomophobic practices among the respondents are the four white straight men at the far end of the continuum who surrender their straight status and privilege and blur gay/straight identity boundaries by allowing themselves to be viewed as gay at times. They describe situations where they go to gay bars with gay friends, not heterosexual female companions. They also do not feel compelled to disclose their heterosexual identity to avoid having men flirt with them or in defensively correcting perceptions of themselves as possibly gay. Perhaps these men lean in part on their white and middle-class privilege to compensate for the loss of a heterosexual status when others view them as gay. In contrast, black heterosexual men lack racial privilege and instead must negotiate stereotypes of hypersexuality (Collins 2004). The social identity costs of blurring gay/straight identity practices for black straight men, then, are higher, as their heterosexual masculinities are stigmatized by their racial status, whereas white privilege affords the prestige of normality to compensate for the stigma of homosexuality that these four white men take on in some situations and contexts.

Moreover, the continuum links (micro) heterosexual masculine practices to the (macro) production of the social institutional orders of gender and sexualities. On one hand, the continuum demonstrates how homophobic heterosexual masculinities variably reproduce gender and sexual normative social orders. At their most hegemonic, homophobic heterosexual masculinities aim to return to a social order where heterosexual identity is unquestionably dominant while homosexual identity is repressed and circumscribed to a double life of public invisibility and private shame; this is akin to the closet dynamics of pre-Stonewall culture. These identity practices, then, affirm the theory of hegemonic masculinity.

At the other end of the continuum, we are witnessing the development of antihomophobic heterosexual masculinities, which at their most counterhegemonic aim to subvert the reproduction of normative heterosexuality and normative masculinity. We might ask, then, Does the concept of hegemonic masculinity adequately theorize these heterosexual men's changing interactions with gays? That is, if one of hegemonic masculinity's central principles is the notion of a hierarchal relationship between straight masculine practices and subordinated gay masculinities, then how are we to theorize the development of the antihomophobic practices of straight men who contest masculine and heterosexual normativity? Although only four of the heterosexual men surrendered heterosexual privilege and blurred boundaries between heterosexual and homosexual identity statuses by letting themselves be taken as gay at times, they are, and point to, a vanguard of heterosexual men who are challenging the institutional orders of gender and sexualities. The current model of hegemonic masculinity would theorize these men as rejecting its norms of homophobia and the subordination of women and femininities.

Although these four antihomophobic straight men embody conventional masculinities, they do not reinforce a normative masculinity. The association of masculinity with male bodies does not automatically enforce gender normativity. Rather, these antihomophobic straight men adopt a variety of nonnormative masculinities, as seen by their inclusion of gay men and surrendering of straight status and privilege. Further, they do not use the gender strategy of performing a conventional masculinity to indicate their heterosexuality, as they are nondefensive when gay men flirt with them and when they are taken for being gay. Still, I qualify this analysis of their surrendering of straight identity status and privilege and blurring of boundaries by noting that the ability to claim a straight identity is a readily available practice for them in situations where they feel defensive in being perceived as nonheterosexual. This notwithstanding, recuperating a straight masculine status is itself subject to a reiteration of sexual and gender practices, practices that are not entirely under any one man's control and are conditioned by the social context in the widest sense.

In sum, investigating configurations of straight masculinities and their relations to homosexualities is important for furthering our understanding of sexual and gender identity practices in the context of today's unprecedented levels of lesbian and gay visibility and social integration (Seidman 2002).

I return to a discussion of straight masculinities, specifically metrosexual masculinities, in chapter 5, exploring in more depth the narrative accounts of some of the straight men presented here. In the next chapter I analyze the identity practices of the black and white straight women I interviewed, showing how their identity practices are both similar and different from the straight men's practices I explored here.

4

Straight Women

Doing and Undoing Compulsory Heterosexuality

Are straight women less homophobic than straight men? Like other researchers (LaMar and Kite 1998; Loftus 2001), I find that the homophobic stances of the straight women in my sample are less defensive than the straight men's. Nonetheless, I do find homophobic prejudices among straight women. In particular, their antigay prejudice comes to the surface regarding the issue of same-sex marriage and granting social and legal recognition to lesbian and gay couples. For example, Beth Moore, a twenty-six-year-old white married woman, disagrees with the idea that gays should be entitled to the civil right to marry. As a Christian, Beth views marriage as a religious institution and does not think lesbian and gay relationships are morally equal to straight ones. While she supports civil unions for same-sex couples, she maintains a Christian worldview that does not respect a secular society in which the granting of lesbians' and gay men's legal rights is a question for the country's courts, legislatures, and ballot boxes.

Straight women, also unlike straight men, did not report a preoccupation with how their styles of dress would be interpreted by others. In fact, many of the most pro-gay women told me stories of trying to persuade homophobic straight male friends to lighten up and be less worried about a gay man flirting with them. Erica Harris, a twenty-two-year-old black woman, recounts taking straight male friends to gay bars in Orangetown to show them that their perceptions of gays are one-dimensional. Erica wants her friends to realize that by being comfortable interacting with nonstraight people they might enlighten themselves and in the process enjoy the company of people who are different from themselves.

The question I explore in this chapter is specifically how heterosexuality shapes women's femininities.[1] This question is often implicitly addressed, or altogether absent, in scholarship on women's formations of gendered selves (for exceptions see Jackson 1999, 2006; Hamilton 2007; Richardson 1996). While past scholarship in gender studies has focused on analyzing the gender practices, discourses, and identities of women's gendered subjectivities, it has paid less attention to the relationship between women's gender practices and their heterosexualities. The research also does not generally distinguish between women's heterosexual "behaviors" and their "identity practices" as heterosexual. This chapter provides an account of the multiple and recurrent social situations in which these straight women's identity practices take place.[2]

Through the frame of a post-closeted cultural dynamic, this chapter's analysis intervenes in the systems of compulsory heterosexuality and male domination. On the one hand, I provide an account of the homophobic practices and claims to privilege of some straight women. On the other, I explore how other straight women enact antihomophobic practices but maintain straight privilege, while others reject straight privilege and develop what I call a queered straight identification.

I present case studies of black and white straight femininities.[3] Aspects of the lives of straight women are sketched with the purpose of illustrating a series of positions on a continuum. As in chapter 3, I introduce a continuum to map straight women's practices, specifically the homophobic and antihomophobic stances that they construct in establishing boundaries of social distance from gay and lesbian individuals, symbols, and social spaces.

The following analysis divides straight femininities into three sections. The first section explores the homophobic end of the continuum and how straight women in this category enact homophobic stances generally based on their Christian religious beliefs that condemn homosexuality. The second section analyzes those straight women who fall into the weak boundaries category; it illustrates a series of antihomophobic stances by straight women who contest homophobic prejudice and discrimination but do not blur normative boundaries of heterosexuality. The blurred boundaries category is discussed in the last section. Here, I focus on a more "activist" set of straight women whose identity practices blur identity boundaries between heterosexuality and homosexuality. These straight women begin a discussion of women who self-define their identities as straight but enact queered identifications in their willingness to engage in sexual relations with other women and promote sexual equality.

As in chapter 3, I show how race shapes and frames straight women's homophobic and antihomophobic stances. On the homophobic end, black straight women generally draw on their racial status and Christian faiths to justify their homophobic beliefs, while their white counterparts use notions of lesbian and gay sexualities as deviant in their rejection of lesbian women's and gay men's claims to recognition and rights. However, I also document exceptions to this pattern, illustrating how one of the white straight women invokes her Christianity in disapproving of same-sex marriage and one of the black women cites her Caribbean culture and family's views of homosexuality as socially abnormal in legitimizing her prejudicial attitudes. On the antihomophobic end of the continuum, and similar to my findings regarding black straight men's antihomophobic stances drawing on their experiences with racism in affirming gay life, I show that black straight women reference a shared understanding of oppression based on their racial status in articulating their reasons for supporting lesbian and gay equality.

Theorizing Straight Femininities: The Continuing Relevance of Compulsory Heterosexuality

The sociologist Raewyn Connell (1987) argues that women enact normative femininity, or what she calls "emphasized femininity," by generally being supplicants to men, particularly in the workplace, as well as by establishing their roles as wives and mothers as central to their sense of selves. Emphasized femininity, she states, is "the display of sociability rather than technical competence, fragility in mating scenes, compliance with men's desire for titillation and ego-stroking in office relationships, acceptance of marriage and childcare as a response to labor-market discrimination against women" (187).

In reformulating emphasized femininity, or what she calls "hegemonic femininity," the sociologist Mimi Schippers (2007) argues that it is important to foreground the hierarchical relationship between masculinity and femininity in its construction. She states that hegemonic femininity "consists of the characteristics defined as womanly that establish and legitimate a hierarchical and complementary relationship to hegemonic masculinity, and that, by doing so guarantee the dominant position of men and the subordination of women" (94).

Although not explicitly using Connell's concept or Schippers's reformulation of normative femininity, I call attention to their understanding of gender inequality in relations between men and women. While their concepts center the dynamics of masculine domination and feminine subordination, they do not highlight the centrality of heterosexual normativity in constructions of women's gender identities in the ways that the concept of compulsory heterosexuality does. By employing the late Adrienne Rich's ([1980] 1993) concept of compulsory heterosexuality in order to theorize how heterosexuality organizes normative femininity, I argue that compulsory heterosexuality does a better job of capturing the dynamics of straight feminine identity practices for my purposes.

Rich's conception of compulsory heterosexuality as a political institution highlights how heterosexuality is a structural norm and system of power that creates hierarchies that differentially value, reward, and enfranchise heterosexuals over nonheterosexuals. More than this, her concept captures how male domination works to make heterosexuality compulsory for women in different ways than for men, due to women's different structural positions in social institutions, particularly in normative roles as wives in marriages and mothers in families. Rich ties her concept to social institutions as well as representations in culture, thus providing a rigorous sociological account of how gender and sexual orders work together in support of compulsory heterosexuality.

While I use the terms "normative heterosexuality" and "heteronormativity" interchangeably, my use of "compulsory heterosexuality" in regard to the construction of straight women's identity practices is meant to theorize the co-construction of gender and sexualities as dissimilarly structured for straight women than they are for straight men.[4] The concept of compulsory heterosexuality captures for me the related, but not reducible to each other, relations and orders of male domination and normative heterosexuality straight women face in doing their sexual-gender identities.[5]

In other words, Rich maintains that the norms, relations, and institutions that organize the lives of women as wives and mothers, as well their historical economic dependence on fathers and husbands, enforce the norm of heterosexuality on women in qualitatively distinct ways than they do on men. In the straight construction of women as subordinates who face unwanted sexual advances from men at work, on the street, or even in their own homes as wives, compulsory heterosexuality makes salient the connections between systems of male and heterosexual domination and the oppressive processes through which women are forced into, subordinated through, and circumscribed by heterosexuality. "Women have married," Rich explains, "because it was necessary, in order to survive economically, in order to have children who would not suffer economic deprivation or social ostracism, in order to remain respectable, in order to do what was expected of women . . . because heterosexual romance has been represented as the great female adventure, duty, and fulfillment" ([1980] 1993, 242).

In sum, Rich's theory argues for a tight connection between male domination and the enforcement of heterosexuality on women, and the concept of compulsory heterosexuality embeds two claims. First, the concept claims that women's desires, roles, and identities are defined as dependent on relations with men; thus heterosexuality enforces gender differences and binary conceptions of sex and gender. Second, it claims that a binary gender order makes heterosexuality seem as if men and women are "natural," necessary, and compulsory complements to one another as a result of the reduction of species survival, reproduction, and romantic relationships to heterosexual relations (Butler 1990, 1992; Rich [1980] 1993; Seidman 2009).

However, over the last third of the twentieth century, lesbians and gay men have become integrated into a variety of social institutions; thus, while normative heterosexuality's dynamics still subordinate gay men and lesbians, American society is witnessing the weakening of compulsory heterosexuality in social institutions, such as corporate workplaces, multiple mass media outlets, and in county, state, and federal courtrooms where legal changes now support and condition the inclusion of out lesbians and gays as well as their representations within these spheres (Eskridge 1999; Gamson 2002; Ghaziani 2011; Raeburn 2004; Seidman 2002; Stein 2010; Walters 2002; Weeks 2007).

Moreover, compulsory heterosexuality not only subordinates lesbians and gay men but also normalizes and circumscribes the recognition of the multiple forms of heterosexualities that exist. Taking a Foucauldian approach, we may see compulsory heterosexuality as producing differences, conflicts, and hierarchies among heterosexualities at the level of identity, culture, and politics. For instance, a heterosexual normative model of identity, which links itself to monogamy and procreation within marital relations and views sexuality as a private matter, claims a hierarchical position over nonmonogamous, nonmarried, nonprocreative, and nonprivate sexual practices in the lives of these *other* straight men and women as well as gays, as the rest fail to meet the normative standard of this specific formulation of heterosexuality (Richardson 1996; Rubin 1984; Seidman 2009, 2002). In this sense, scholars should think of "normative heterosexualities" in the plural, recognizing the multiplicity of hierarchies among heterosexualities in its normative construction.

Focusing on how heterosexuality shapes women's femininities, I show that the continuing analytical purchase of the concept of compulsory heterosexuality is that it points our attention to the differential structural enforcement of heterosexuality on women. It shows the ways in which bisexual, lesbian, and queer women's sexualities in today's context are often variably caught and resituated in processes of commodification and heterosexist dynamics. Often these heterosexist dynamics are situated from the standpoint of straight men, as seen in mass media representations such as straight male pornography or in public displays of same-sex kissing by ostensibly straight women who use these acts to titillate straight men, explore nonstraight behaviors in straight spaces, or identify as bisexual or "heteroflexible" (Clark 1993; Hamilton 2007; Rupp and Taylor 2010).

For example, the sociologist Laura Hamilton (2007), in her study of Greek fraternity parties at a Midwestern university, finds that heterosexual women will kiss other women to garner heterosexual male attention. She quotes one college woman as saying, "'Guys said, 'Do it, do it!' just screwing around. . . . [They] were like, 'These girls are going to kiss!'

So you think you're cooler and guys think you're cooler'" (164). Here, same-sex intimacy between women with straight men watching confirms the women's heterosexual statuses, as opposed to creating doubt or suspicion of them as lesbian or bisexual (Rupp and Taylor 2010). To underscore the point, it almost goes without saying that the converse situation of two straight men kissing with women watching at, say, a college sorority party would not generally confirm the straight status of these individual men.

Whereas research shows that straight men tend to be more verbally and physically demonstrative in their homophobic displays than heterosexual women (Herek 1988; Gallup 1995), Hamilton's study calls our attention to the homophobic practices that straight women use to avoid, marginalize, and exclude lesbians in order to remain unstigmatized by their presence in college. Hamilton and other sociologists demonstrate that straight femininities draw on specifically gendered practices, such as bodily capital (the value of one's body's shape), beauty, and charm in garnering straight men's recognition and bolstering the value of their straight femininity in erotic markets (Bernstein 2007; Bettie 2005; McCall 1992).[6]

Compulsory Heterosexuality and Strongly Aversive Boundaries

Continuing to use the continuum of straight identity practices to map a range of interactional practices through which straights enact boundaries of social distance, in this section I analyze the identity practices of the eight out of the twenty-nine straight women who fall into the strongly aversive category. Five of these women are black and the other three are white. My conceptualization of identity practices, again, draws on the in-depth interviews I conducted with fourteen black and fifteen white straight women.[7] I take the practices that the women reported to me as accounts of their conventional ways of speaking and acting. These accounts are matters that they treat as commonsense knowledge and everyday competence. For further information, table A.2 in the appendix provides a description of the demographic characteristics of the straight women respondents, listing their religion, age, occupation, and position on the continuum as strongly aversive, weak, or blurred.

Unlike the homophobic straight men who fell into this category, straight women in the strongly aversive category use identity practices that are more understated, subtle, and nuanced in establishing their straight identities in interactions with lesbians and gay men. For instance, all of the eight women who fell into this grouping stated that they have lesbian or gay acquaintances, friends, coworkers, or even family members who are part of their circle of friends or extended familial relations. Many of them also reported having gone to gay bars on occasion, stating that they did not feel particularly anxious about being viewed as possibly lesbian or bisexual while there. Nonetheless, all of these eight straight women express homophobic views that define homosexuality as socially and morally inferior to heterosexuality, and it is this key characteristic that establishes their coding into this grouping on the continuum.

Again, the continuum provides a way of analyzing the identity practices of straight women and the different ways they perform their straight feminine identities in recurrent situations. Straight women in this group contribute to the sociohistorical reproduction of the existing sexual and gender orders that essentially take the orders for granted as natural, normal, and morally right. The micro–identity practices of these women's straight femininities are part of the reproduction and maintenance of the social institutions that enforce heterosexual and male domination in contemporary American society.

Although I use the same analytical frame of homophobic to anti-homophobic practices in categorizing where each woman lies on the continuum, I emphasize the unique dynamics that qualitatively reshape these practices and their work in the social construction of straight femininities. Straight women's practices of homophobia have less to do with constructing strongly aversive boundaries of social distance; instead, the issue of same-sex marriage and its condemnation due to religious worldviews proved salient in their homophobic practices.[8] In part, the social capital women gain through marriage, the establishment of families, and statuses such as wife and mother are informing these straight women's homophobic prejudices, as the desire to maintain these privileges emerges in their homophobic responses to this issue (Bourdieu 2001; Chodorow 1978; Hays 1996; Moore 2011).

Like the homophobic practices of the straight men in chapter 3, at their most extreme, these straight women's homophobic practices reproduce the norm of compulsory heterosexuality that would turn homosexuality back into a closeted identity that does not merit respect, recognition, or rights. Generally, these respondents invoked Christian religious beliefs to justify their homophobic practices. Religious views act as a clear moral compass, dividing the world into sacred and profane divisions (Alexander 1988; Durkheim [1915] 1995), and for these straight women religious beliefs have an aura of being beyond reproach. However, as sociologists we must view religious practices as choices; thus, individuals and their faiths must be held accountable for the positions they hold on social issues.

For four of the five black women and one of the three white women in this group, Christian religious judgments, compulsory heterosexuality, and homophobia intersect in prejudices that construct only heterosexual identities and relationships as morally right, good, and blessed, while homosexual ones are constructed as morally wrong, bad, and damned. The issue that most clearly brought this to the fore was same-sex marriage. At the time of my interviews in 2004 and 2005, the Massachusetts State Supreme Court had just rendered its decision legally sanctioning same-sex marriages on 18 November 2003 and started issuing licenses on 17 May 2004, making it the first state to legalize gay marriage.

In post-closeted culture, straights face competing cultural logics: on one hand, they negotiate a logic of the cultural normalization of homosexuality, which promotes tolerance, acceptance, and a liberalization of attitudes toward gays. On the other hand, straight individuals may draw on homophobic cultural logics, which are often based in social-psychological schemas of abnormality and unhealthiness or religious ones of Christian immorality and sinfulness. Homophobic and anti-homophobic practices and discourses exist side by side in the complex contexts of today's post-closeted culture; they are competing logics and discourses that configure and reconfigure the changing environment of contemporary sexual identity politics in American society. In my interviews, this complex context is illustrated by the way practices of cultural normalization or antihomophobia and homophobia are combined in the same heterosexual person.

Consider Martha Lewis, a fifty-four-year-old black woman who wears her hair in small dreadlocks to her shoulders. She recently went back to college and finished a BA and a master's degree in Christian counseling in 2000. Martha has been married and divorced twice and has a thirty-seven-year-old son from her first marriage and a twenty-five-year-old daughter from her second. She is conventionally feminine in appearance and wore professional dress attire when I interviewed her at work.

At the beginning of the interview, Martha tells me that she has enjoyed socializing in gay bars with straight women friends in the past. She relates this story:

> The women I went out with, we were all heterosexual. . . . We were just out and a friend of mine who, this particular friend has a lot of friends who are homosexual and knows where they go hang out to party. So she said it was a really neat place and I said, "Well, come on. Let's go." So we did. A couple of ladies asked us to dance and we would do that. But, my one friend she got hit on. Well, she is the one friend who has the homosexual friends, so maybe they had seen her out and maybe assumed. That could be it, but my other friend and myself were never hit on. We were asked to dance and we had a great time, like girlfriends dancing.

Her ease in socializing in gay establishments led me to initially think she would be supportive of gay and lesbian people. Similarly, when she tells me about a gay male friend whom she met in her social work program, saying, "A classmate of mine . . . who is homosexual, we still stay in touch. I love him very much and we really got to talk a lot," I am led to believe that she is strong in her support and acceptance of lesbian and gay individuals and their relationships.

However, toward the end of the interview, when I inquire further about other lesbian or gay individuals who have come out to her and her thoughts on their identity, relationships, and the issue of same-sex marriage, she explains that she views homosexuality as a choice that is wrong in the eyes of God and her Christian faith. Given Martha's age, fifty-four, and the fact that she grew up before Stonewall, her account below of her friend's lesbian relationship and her position against making same-sex marriages legal demonstrate that Martha's tolerance of lesbian and gay life has clear limits, as she defines gay relationships and marriages as abnormal, morally wrong, and a sin according to a Christian morality. However, her defensiveness and reliance on a Christian morality to justify her homophobic practices show that a post-closeted cultural dynamic compels Martha to explain or justify her practices and attitudes toward gays. She does not want to come across as hateful toward them, even if she thinks homosexuality is morally wrong. In her account below, she explains that her friend who was her nail technician, who was also a black Christian woman, started dating a woman but eventually realized that it was an immoral act for her as a Christian.

> A dear friend of mine, she and her daughter own a shop and she was my nail tech and they're both Christians and as time went on, I found out that her daughter was having an intimate relationship with another female, but she knew better. She had been raised in the church, but it was a choice that she made. So there again it comes down to your choice. And she felt very comfortable in this relationship but as time went on, she got to where she wasn't comfortable anymore because she knew that it wasn't right.

Martha's narrative sounds like a contemporary version of an older Christian story of temptation: the daughter "knew better," she says, than to be involved with a person of the same sex. Perhaps same-sex relations are analogous to other sins like marital infidelity in a post-closeted culture for Christians like Martha. Both are sins in Christian terms, but not punishable with total damnation.

However, since being homosexual is a choice condemned by Christian scripture, Martha reinforces the normative standing of compulsory heterosexuality as based on her Christian worldview by refusing to support lesbian and gay civil rights in general and the right of gay couples to marry in particular. When I ask her, "With people coming out to you, and in knowing gay people, has that made you more supportive of gay rights?" she says,

> No. One of the things I'm looking at right now is that they [gays] are trying to jump on the bandwagon of civil rights. And civil rights is because of your skin color, not your sexual orientation. They can look at you and

not know you're a homosexual but they can look at me and they know I'm an African American. So civil rights. I don't find myself being supportive of those [gay] issues. It's your choice. I'm born this way. That's something that the repercussions are yours. I'm not going to jump on the bandwagon for you.

For her, being lesbian or being a woman in a relationship with another woman is to enter a non-Christian existence defined by sin. Furthermore, Martha views civil rights as a term reserved for racial minorities like blacks, as these minorities in her mind did not "choose" to be born with darker skin. The logic of choice and free will, though, is not an acceptable legitimating strategy for Martha's strong Christian religious beliefs that condemn homosexuality. As the interview progressed, I pushed Martha to defend her notion that sexuality was a choice by asking her whether she viewed her own heterosexuality as a choice or was it just homosexuality she thought of as a choice. As a result of my questions, she became defensive but also perhaps more candid in her responses. Here is our exchange:

> JAMES: Okay, so in your mind then the problem with homosexuality is that it is against Christianity?
>
> MARTHA: I didn't say it is a problem. Why did you say that, "the problem with homosexuality?"
>
> JAMES: Well, if you see it as a choice that is wrong, then . . .
>
> MARTHA: Who am I to say if it is right or wrong? It is just my choice. I think we all have choices. Then we have to suffer the consequences of those choices or reap the benefits of those choices. I am not God so I am not going to say anything. It's just that I choose to be heterosexual. Your choice is your choice and that is something that you have to work out with God. Because when you are before God, the playing ground is all level so [*clears throat*] excuse me, it is not a problem. Right or wrong, it is just what the Bible says. I didn't see him say he made Jack and Jack or whatever. He even says it was an abomination, so we will just go from his word, and his word is kind of specific there, but again it is a person's choice.

Religious teachings are a core principle of her belief system, and many devoutly religious Americans like her base their judgments on a polarizing logic according to which behaviors, identities, and relations are either morally pure or impure. So whether or not Martha actually views her own heterosexuality or others' homosexuality as choices, as she says, remains dubious for me. Nonetheless, under the pressure of my questioning and with a growing sense of defensiveness, her quote demonstrates that she views homosexuality as "an abomination" because it goes against Christian scripture. Her religiosity, in short, is the fulcrum on which her homophobia turns.

Christianity and the traditions of the church continue to hold value for many black people, particularly on the issues of homosexuality and same-sex marriage, of which blacks express stronger disapproval than whites do (Braumbaugh, Nock, and White 2008; Moore 2010a). Consequently, at the end of the interview, when I ask Martha what she thinks about the same-sex marriages being performed at city halls by justices of the peace, Martha's disapproval of them proves unsurprising. "So if it is a same-sex marriage, whether it is performed in a church or not, same-sex marriage is a same-sex marriage. I mean, to me, I consider it wrong." It's important to point out that heterosexuals like Martha do not separate church and state in disapproving of the political struggle lesbians and gay men who desire to marry undertake in fighting for that right. That is, for some, their Christian morality does not respect a secular society that aims to confine religious beliefs to the private sphere while leaving legal rights to be decided in the public sphere of the courts and legislatures.

If Martha based her condemnation of homosexuality on religious grounds, many of the black straight women I interviewed felt that these sentiments were representative of many members of black communities, which they characterized as intolerant of openly gay and lesbian individuals. For instance, Ghanima Powell, a twenty-year-old black college student from a Methodist background, says, "It's less accepted to be homosexual in the African American community than it is outside of it. That's what I see."

According to recent polling data, the proportion of blacks who report being openly LGBT is higher than the proportion of white Americans who openly identify as such (Gallup 2012). Still, in terms of sheer numbers, openly LGBT whites are more numerous. As the United States becomes increasingly made up of people of color over the next decades, we should also expect to see this demographic shift represented in perceptions of LGBT people and communities too.

Similarly, Sandra Morgan, a forty-three-year-old black woman with a strong Christian faith, explains that she learned of how unacceptable and dangerous it is to be queer in a black community when her transgender male-to-female (MtF) cousin was killed while she was growing up. "Within the Caucasian community," Sandra says, "homosexuality is a lot more accepted than it is within the black . . . or non-Caucasian community. I mean they'll kill you. So often times they [queers of color] will leave their communities and go into the Caucasian community because it's a lot more accepted there."[9]

Kelly Jones, a thirty-three-year-old black woman who grew up in Atlanta, Georgia, explains the relationship among religion, black communities, and homophobia the most concretely. Growing up in a strong religious community, Kelly attended a predominantly black Methodist church. She says that the organist at her church was rumored to be gay, but that this rumor was never confirmed by her, other church members, or the suspected man himself.

> The person who was the organist [was suspected of being gay], and in a black church the musicians [are] kind of a higher position and [the congregation] wouldn't treat him that badly. They were just kind of indifferent. . . . It would never be stated that he was definitely gay. Never. . . . [He] never actually showed up with a friend or a companion. It's [homosexuality] less acceptable in the black community.

Kelly's description of her church's homophobic practices illustrates the informal boundary of social distance established between the congregation and the suspected gay organist. The boundary hinges on the congregation never confirming the organist's homosexuality and on him never openly declaring he is gay. To come out as gay in this context means risking excommunication, as this religious community demands the invisibility of the closet for gay individuals if they desire to be respected and recognized at all.

Furthermore, Kelly says that due to her strong religious beliefs, her family's teachings, and the community she grew up in, she is hard-pressed to consider gay and lesbian relationships as equal to

heterosexual ones. "I don't perceive of a gay relationship as a true relationship," she says. And although she had a close lesbian friend in college, Kelly would not live in the same house with a lesbian roommate.
She says she would not be comfortable with a lesbian roommate in her
shared living space.

When I asked Kelly what she thought of same-sex marriage, she dis-
tinguished between marriages performed by a justice of the peace and
those performed by a religious figure.

> If it's strictly from the legal point of view and you do it at the justice of
> the peace, I can understand that. That has nothing to do with religion
> and probably you want to get married for the same benefits that hetero-
> sexual couples have so you can get health insurance and things like that.
> I can understand that. I can see that. I think it would be preposterous to
> get married in a religious place.

Here Kelly hedges on whether she condones gay marriages or not. She
seems to indicate that she supports same-sex marriages performed outside religious contexts. Unlike Martha, Kelly draws a distinction that
seems to support same-sex marriages performed in nonreligious settings. In the context of a post-closeted culture, where gays demand
respect and rights, Kelly's incorporation of some degree of tolerance
and recognition of gays and lesbians moves her to adopt a more egalitarian stance toward gay marriage than Martha's position.

Another important dimension of homophobia in the contexts of
post-closeted culture is the way heterosexual women judge the sexual
identity performances of men. In contrast to studies of heterosexual
women's homophobia toward out lesbians, which indicate that they
use social distance strategies in disassociating themselves from homosexual women (Hamilton 2007), heterosexual women's homophobia
toward gay men or men they suspect of being gay often invokes gender stereotypes of these men's "improper" performance of masculine
conventions. For example, Kelly tells me that she is unable to detect
whether a woman is lesbian or not, as she thinks gender performances
are generally too heterogeneous among women to tell, and she herself eschews conventions like wearing dresses or using a lot of makeup.
However, for men, Kelly employs masculine conventionality or a lack

of it in assessing a man's sexual identity. One of her friends asked her for her opinion regarding a man she was attracted to; Kelly relates the situation:

> A friend of mine, she wanted to go to this bar and she said, "What do you think of the bartender? Tell me what you think about him." I said, "Well, he's gay." She's like, "Are you sure?" I said, "Yeah, I'm sure. . . . " He was very outspoken, flamboyant clothes, more so the way he spoke. He talked with his hands.

Kelly's assessment points to this man's verbal and bodily expressiveness ("outspoken" and "talked with his hands"), along with his choice of attire ("flamboyant clothes"), indicating a system of symbols that tightly links gender practices to sexual identity. Moreover, social distance is less salient, if not entirely absent, in her account, as cross-gender homophobia requires a close scrutinizing of the suspected homosexual man in decoding his masculine performance.

Like the previous straight women, Beth Moore, a twenty-six-year-old white woman who describes herself as a strongly religious Christian, also takes issue with gays and lesbians being able to get married. Like Martha and Kelly, Beth defines a marriage as a relationship that is religiously sanctioned. And since Christian scripture condemns homosexuality, Beth does not support gay marriages, although she would support civil unions for gay men and lesbians:

> I don't agree with gay marriage. I think that marriage is a religious thing. I think that civil unions are different than marriage, but I also think that marriage is something that is consecrated by a priest in a church. To me, it seems like more or less a religious thing, whereas a civil union, like being married by a judge or something like that; it's not the religious aspect of being, I mean you're still in a union; it's still a union. I just think marriage has religious connotations to it.

While religious beliefs and attitudes toward same-sex marriage capture an important aspect of homophobic practices, the interactions between straights and lesbians and gays provide another significant indicator as well. For example, Beth described being friends with her lesbian teammates with whom she played hockey in college. However, when her lesbian teammates started dating, she was the last to know. She says, "I was kind of the last to know of our group of friends. So I had kind of figured [it out]. [Due to] the time that they were spending together and just talking to our other friends, I kind of figured it out before they told us what was going on." Although it is hard to be sure of why Beth's lesbian teammates told her last, it seems plausible to assume that they might have avoided telling Beth if they thought she would be disapproving of their relationship. Lesbians and gay men may use boundaries of social distance between themselves and homophobic straights as well, trying to avoid potential acts of disrespect and misrecognition of their relationships and lives.

Regarding homophobia and black identities, homophobia among blacks is often reasoned to be part of the larger American culture and to be one of the few privileges black heterosexuals have to hold on to in daily life (Lemelle and Battle 2004). For instance, the black feminist scholar Barbara Smith argues, "Heterosexual privilege is usually the only privilege that black women have. None of us have racial or sexual privilege, almost none of us have class privilege, maintaining straightness is our last resort" (quoted in Collins [1990] 2000, 125–26).

Religion, though, plays a key role in the homophobic practices of black people (Griffin 2006; Pitt 2010), as blacks define religion as very important in their lives in comparison to whites (82 percent compared to 58 percent in a 1999 Gallup study). Religiosity is also generally stronger among black woman than black men, as black women attend church at higher rates than their male counterparts (Blow 2008). And blacks as a group tend to belong to more conservative Protestant denominations, such as Baptist and Pentecostal affiliations, faiths with evangelical views that are strongly condemning of homosexuality in comparison to more liberal Protestant ones, such as Methodist and Episcopalian (Laumann et al. 1994; Martin 2009). Both religious affiliation and religiosity, then, play an important role in homophobic practices among some black women and men (Durell, Chiong, and Battle 2007).

Although most of the black straight women I interviewed justified the norm of heterosexuality in relationships and marriages through a Christian morality, there was one exception to this among the five. This exception is Nia Gray, a twenty-one-year-old black woman who is a graduate student in Orangetown. Raised by a working-class Jamaican mother, along with her twin sister and nine other siblings in Brooklyn, New York, Nia views heterosexuality as a central aspect of her self-identity. When I ask why heterosexuality is "very" important to her, Nia says,

> Because considering the fact that I want to have children. I want to have the whole ideal family life. I want to get married. I want to have a husband there who will rub my back, my feet, and all of that stuff. I think that it will create more of a balance in my life. I think being with a female would create an imbalance.

Nia defines straight identity as including marriage, children, and an "ideal family life" while viewing homosexual identities and relations as excluding those possibilities.

Although she has gay and lesbian acquaintances, Nia feels that homosexuality is socially and morally inferior to heterosexuality. For example, one of the first individuals to come out to her was a close childhood friend, Lori Keith, whom Nia considered to be like family since they had grown up together. Nia told me that when Lori came out to her, she let Lori know that she would still be her friend. I asked Nia whether she had become more supportive of lesbian and gay people because of that experience. This is our exchange:

NIA: I think it just made me question where I stood as far as that issue was concerned, considering that, OK, this is somebody who's like my sister. Am I so close-minded that I'm just gonna say forget her? Forget all that we've been through? I was like nah, nah, I'm not going to do that. And I just decided that I don't exactly support it, but I tolerate it. I tolerate it.

JAMES: What's the difference for you between support and tolerate?

NIA: Support, meaning I endorse it. Tolerate is like, OK, I don't like it, but I'm willing to put up with you because you're family or because we've been through so much. I wouldn't cut you out of my life just for that. So like I said, I wouldn't endorse it. I wouldn't be a supporter, like, yay, gay and lesbian rights, they should get married and all that stuff. I wouldn't do that. No.

For some straight women like Nia, having contact with close friends who are lesbian does not translate into stronger forms of support, such as supporting their right to marry.

However, the issue of how Nia "successfully" performs a straight identity in everyday life is an anxious topic for her. Nia is a petite young black woman, who by her own admission prefers to dress casually in jeans and sneakers and to forgo wearing skirts, high heels, or cosmetics. Since she says that she cannot tell if a woman is a lesbian unless the woman is extremely stereotypical, Nia says that the only way another individual would know that she is straight would be by her telling them directly or talking about men. With the increasing visibility of LGBT individuals and the withering of the closet, post-closeted contexts create situations where anyone is viewed as possibly being lesbian or gay. Therefore, Nia fears that this pattern of LGBT visibility means that the traditional presumption of a straight sexuality will be further undermined and will put more pressure on her to more conventionally perform her straight femininity.

Several women have flirted with Nia and tried to seduce her, by asking her whether she was interested in them sexually, as in the case of her childhood friend Lori, or by inviting her to have a bottle of wine and talking about having had sex with another woman and enjoying it, as in the case of her summer roommate Yolanda Jones. And while Nia has turned down each woman's sexual proposition, she still fears being tempted to have sex with a woman and worries about becoming bisexual, although she says she has never had sex with a woman. She tells me,

I just hope that me personally I don't get turned out. That's my fear. I don't want to get turned out. But I know it can happen. . . . I don't think that all people who turn gay choose it; I think that full-blown lesbians, yeah. But then there's bisexuals [sic] who based on experience gives me a doubt and just think, "I want to be pleased, whether it's by a man or a woman. I don't care." And I think that's based on experience. And like I said, I've even thought it and that's only because it's so prevalent now. I feel like even my own sexuality is being attacked because I'm getting women who are coming at me this way.

Because Nia does not enact a clear straight feminine identity performance, her main way of projecting her heterosexuality is to draw boundaries between straights and openly lesbian and gay people in her social circles. Consequently, she has a mostly straight group of other black friends. By condoning her friends' homophobic jokes, she reinforces her status as heterosexual. That is, since her identity practices do not clearly perform a clear straight femininity, Nia relies on social distance and homophobic displays to do this work for her. For example, she and her friends joke that one of their black male friends, Toby Davis, is gay or bisexual. She says that they joke around with Toby by telling him that he is a "homo." Although she says they do this just for fun, it is also because Toby is a friend to a group of openly gay black men. While Toby denies being gay, his friendships with gay men are a clear sign for Nia and their friends that Toby might be gay. Moreover, she says that in their circle of friends, straights do not socialize with openly gay men. And to do so is to have one's straight identity questioned and doubted.

Nia, then, does not generally include gays and lesbians in her social circles, says she would not go to a gay bar, and notes that Toby was an object of derision for her and her friends because he did. For example, she stated that in their dorm room in college, "when those guys [the gay friends] would come over, they wouldn't chill with us. They would go in their room and talk or whatever. And then after they'd leave, then we would start teasing him. Well, it wasn't really me, but I was there too. And I would laugh at it. I was kind of a part of it."

And yet Nia's straight femininity is a source of tension for her on a number of levels. For her, normative straight femininity is too confining, limiting, and even oppressive. From her strong personality to her appearance with her hair in dreadlocks, Nia feels in conflict with the normative boundaries of black straight femininity.

For example, when I ask her how she thinks of her own self-identity in general, Nia says, "Different from other females. I consider myself more masculine in my mind and certain things that I chose to do, sports, just my aggressive tendencies. I consider myself a masculine female." When I ask her for an example of how she feels like a masculine female, she elaborates.

> For example, if I felt that there was an attack on my family, I would be the one to go to the guy and be like, "Yo, don't mess with my stuff." Like

as far as defending my family. That's just one example. . . . And if there's any problems with the family, they would, everybody would be looking at me like, "So, what you gonna do?" Like my sister was having a custody battle with her baby's father and he was trying to take advantage of her and I just got so upset to the point where I attacked him. He was trying to keep my nephew from my sister. I'm like, that's not right. So I physically attacked him, I'm just not afraid to get physical. That's what it is and people associate that with having masculine tendencies. . . . I just wish that it wasn't so strict and limited where I could be masculine, but yet not be acting like a man. I just wish that there was more room for that in feminine behavior.

Female masculinity in Nia's case is partly defined by her physically violent practices and willingness to fight for her family (see Jones 2010 on "ghetto chicks" and fighting). Scholars use the term "female masculinity" to mean the enactment of masculine practices by girls and women (Halberstam 1998; Pascoe 2007). If physical aggression and violence are coded as masculine practices, then Nia's use of the term references this meaning but also calls attention to its connection with her racial and social class statuses as well.

Having grown up in a working-class black neighborhood in Brooklyn, Nia understands how black individuals must negotiate danger on the streets on a daily basis. Physical violence is part of the code of the street; it is where legal authority breaks down and working-class black urban women and men struggle to achieve respect for themselves in everyday life by fighting and defending themselves physically (Anderson 1999). In this case, Nia describes intervening in her sister's custody battle by physically fighting with the child's father.

Nia's female masculinity is connected to both her working-class background and her growing up without a father to help provide support and protection for her and their family. Living in a neighborhood in Brooklyn where crime and a dangerous street life were negotiated on a daily basis, Nia explains this to me:

NIA: But I think generally black women, for the most part I'm not saying all, but you know we have a harder time; we see a lot more. The communities that we grow up in; it's the things that we're exposed to

> as far as crime, absentee fathers, absent fathers, and just witnessing crime in your neighborhood.
>
> JAMES: Like your other friends growing up, their fathers weren't with their mothers?
>
> NIA: Based on my experience, no. They're not there. . . . Either it's because they died or incarcerated—and incarcerated is the big one—died, incarcerated, or on drugs. There's always a few where the father is there and he's not always the best one, but me and a lot of friends that I knew, yeah, we grow up without dads.

In addition to the dynamics of social class, an absent father, and growing up in a dangerous urban neighborhood, Nia's female masculinity is also clearly about the intersections of gender, race, and sexual identity practices. Against normative white straight femininity, which values being nice and kind (Gilligan [1982] 1993; Martin 1996), and black middle-class femininity, which values respectability, decency, and the embodiment of straight femininity through non-Afrocentric styles (e.g., relaxed and straightened hair versus dreadlocks or braids), Nia's female masculine practices perform a less legible black straight femininity when seen through the lenses of both black and white middle-class standards of straight femininity (Collins [1990] 2000; Jones 2010).

Female masculinity, which is often associated with lesbian aesthetics and styles (see Halberstam 1998; Pascoe 2007; for a counterexample, see Kazyak 2012 on rural female masculinity as normative), codes Nia's identity practices in such a way that she feels frustration at how others may fail to recognize her as straight. Her female masculine practices communicate a possibly bi or lesbian sexuality to the women who flirt with and pursue her sexually. She, consequently, resents her own non-normative gender practices, the women who find her sexually attractive, and the few groups and spaces that value her black female masculinity.

In understanding her homophobic attitudes, though, Nia primarily associates her negative views toward homosexuality with her Caribbean cultural background and says that her mother and family would not accept her if she was lesbian.

> Because you know in our community they, we, they don't stand for that [homosexuality]. I'm from a Caribbean background and all the sounds

that they make concerning homosexuality, all gay people are supposed to die. And kill them, shoot them, all that stuff. Yeah, that definitely makes it hard for people to come out because it's like a death sentence almost to come out with it. Like they'll [my mother and family would] tell me I need spiritual guidance; I'm lacking in some area. I'm unbalanced, that I'm an unbalanced person. Yeah, it'd be hard. It would be very hard.

Nia is clear that a homosexual identity would bring shame, rejection, and a kind of social death to any individual who would be openly gay or lesbian in her Caribbean culture and black community in Brooklyn, as she knows that her childhood friend Lori was disowned and shunned by her family and friends, including Nia's mother.

Nia's story illustrates an individual who tolerates but does not support her lesbian friends or their struggle for legal rights. Her homophobic practices are based on views that grew out of her Caribbean family's values and the larger black community she grew up in, which rejects homosexuality and perceives it as an unacceptable identity. For her, heterosexuality is important for achieving the ideal family life she wants, but since Nia neither projects a clear straight femininity in everyday life nor wants to be viewed as possibly lesbian, she establishes her heterosexuality by maintaining an almost strictly straight group of friends, condoning their homophobic prejudices, and generally excluding openly lesbian and gay people from her social circles. Although Nia expresses a strong homophobic attitude based on her family's cultural background, it was more common for straight women in this group to invoke their Christian beliefs to justify their homophobic practices.

In general, though, if virulent homophobic attitudes are less present in American society today, a trend indicated by survey research (Hicks and Lee 2006; Loftus 2001), then boundaries of social distance that are informal, often invisible to the casual observer, and naturalized in social interactions make sense. These boundary practices perhaps make homophobia more insidious and less visible in everyday life, but they also create space, tolerance, and a modicum of respect for lesbian and gay individuals and their relationships.

Furthermore, religious worldviews should not be thought of as removed from social prejudices, nor as exempt from being viewed as a form of homophobia if they are based in a Christian as opposed to a secular morality. Christian religious traditions are social traditions that help to constitute the beliefs and actions of religious individuals, but these individuals, along with their faiths, are still accountable for their attitudes and actions. In other words, religious justifications for homophobic stances should not render them as permissible prejudices, removed from analysis and critique. Furthermore, as I will show in the next section, religious identities among straight women do not always uniformly mean that they will adopt a homophobic set of beliefs. Some Christian straight women (and men) interpret Christian scripture and their church's religious practices in ways that condemn homophobia, even welcoming lesbians and gay men as members of their religious communities.

Shifts in Compulsory Heterosexuality: Weak Boundaries, Antihomophobic Practices, and "Fag Hags"

The identity practices of straight women who integrate lesbian and gay friends, fellow church members, coworkers, and kin into their social circles are an important social force in promoting antihomophobic practices and supporting a post-closeted cultural dynamic that offers new relational arrangements from friendship to religious alliance to workplace collegiality in straights' and lesbian and gay individuals' lives. Unlike the previous respondents, these straight women engage in antihomophobic practices that position gays and lesbians as equals deserving of respect, recognition, and rights. The fourteen out of twenty-nine respondents who fall into this category describe weaker levels of religiosity overall, and generally strong religious beliefs were a barrier to tolerance and support of gay men and lesbians. Eight white and six black women compose the weak boundaries position on the continuum. However, six out of the fourteen straight women in this group did express moderate or high levels of religiosity, and so I describe these women as a counterpoint to those from the previous section, showing that Christian religious beliefs are compatible with supporting and accepting lesbian and gay individuals and their relationships. Three black and three white women make up the six strongly religious straight women.

The key characteristic that defined one as belonging to this category, and not the next, is that these women did flag their straight status and maintain straight privilege to various extents. For instance, like the straight men in chapter 3, these women used a gender strategy of embodying conventional femininity in performing a straight status in everyday life as a way of maintaining straight privilege. Unlike the next group of straight women, these straight women do not blur normative heterosexual boundaries by letting themselves be viewed as lesbian or bisexual, nor do the majority (eleven out of the fourteen) report experiencing same-sex fantasies or engaging in same-sex acts. The next group, in contrast, blurs normative hetero/homo boundaries and reports various kinds of experiences of sexual fluidity.

Although straight women in this "middle" group are less concerned with lesbians and gay men embodying gender-conventional practices than the straight men in this similar "middle" position on the continuum in chapter 3, these straight women do take for granted and therefore naturalize the homo/heterosexual binary division that views sexual identities as static, uniform, and fixed. This sense of the homo/heterosexual binary is evidenced in their descriptions of gay identities as uniform or fixed and, again, their retention of straight privilege while generally being egalitarian in their views of lesbian and gay people, their relationships, and legal rights.

Furthermore, in this group, straight women who defined their Christian beliefs as important to their self-identities stated that they had joined reconciling Methodist churches that accepted lesbian and gay members or that they simply did not accept their faith's stance on gay identities and relationships.[10] For example, Stephanie Phillips, a black woman who grew up as a teenager in the 1960s in Pittsburgh, and belonged to a traditional black Baptist church back then, explains, "They [her black community in Pittsburgh] were very repressed. They were all religious and everything. There wasn't any shacking up when I was [growing up], then in the '60s, people got married—old and young."

In contrast, Stephanie now attends a liberal Methodist church that she helped to become a reconciling congregation that actively accepts gays and lesbians as members. Within the United Methodist Church, churches that belong to the Reconciling Congregations Program embrace gay members and the adoption of liberal attitudes toward homosexuality (Moon 2004). She tells me,

At my church, the Methodist as a denomination is split between being reconciling and non-reconciling. . . . and so this church is basically white with a smattering of black, but there were myself and maybe ten other people who wanted that church to recognize gays and lesbians straight up by naming them in the mission statement and in doing that, we educate [others about these issues].

Reconciling Methodist congregations signal the growing institutional support for including gays and lesbians within mainstream Protestant denominations (Moon 2004), and straight women like Stephanie are active participants in creating an inclusive religious congregation and a post-closeted dynamic in their religious communities.

While being religious is central to Stephanie's sense of self, as a black woman she links oppressions like racism and homophobia as similar in their effects on racial and sexual minorities:

I am a child of God, period. I think that's my basic core. . . . But understand that two of the people that I loved most dearly, who I shared my spirit with happened to be gay black men who've died [from AIDS]. I think that one died maybe four years ago and the other like seven and he was truly in all the world my best friend and so I put all those phobias and isms in the same basket. . . . I have passion about my work because I have friends who have died [from AIDS].

Stephanie has worked for over fifteen years in the AIDS service organization field. The personal passion she brings to her job emerges from her desire to eradicate the disease, as her closest friends were black gay men who lost their lives due to AIDS-related complications. She illustrates that strongly religious pro-gay black women are fostering equality on many fronts.

Other straight women with religious backgrounds like Margaret O'Riordan maintained their memberships in the Catholic Church but disavowed the Church's stance on homosexuality. Margaret, born in 1970, is married with four kids, attends mass weekly, and belongs to a women's Bible study group, and even studied to be a nun in her early twenties. Not surprisingly, she defines herself as a "hardworking Catholic woman," and her faith remains an integral part of her life. However, on the issue of same-sex marriage and the Catholic Church's stance against it, Margaret and the Church part ways.

> I know the Catholics don't want it. I know that I'm supposed to believe that it's just a man and a woman, but you know God created everybody. So that's the way that it is in my book. . . . I think that everybody should be allowed to do what they want to do and be with whom they want to be with.

Margaret maintains a strong identity as a Catholic, but she deviates from the Church's stance on some issues, while others like Nicole Carey view the Catholic religion as too mired in outdated traditions to be of use in making everyday or major life decisions. Raised Catholic by religious parents, Nicole, a twenty-six-year-old white woman, has abandoned Catholicism and its views on sex and sexuality. Instead, she takes her own feelings regarding sex and sexuality as the ultimate source for deciding what is personally right or wrong. Regarding her disavowal of the Catholic Church's and her parents' prescriptions on sexuality, Nicole says,

> I [was] raised Catholic and that kind of dwindled from me probably [by] the end of high school, when I started to really be able to make my own choices and do my own stuff, but I know there was always that big emphasis on you have to wait to get married to have sex and you can't lead boys on. And it was just very super-conservative attitudes from school, from my parents, everything. And then as I became my own person, my own woman, I just see sexuality as. . . . I just know what's right for me. I just see it as a very individual thing, which is why I totally reject the way Catholicism or my parents or some of the [ideas of the] people I grew up around; how they see it as all people should follow this one way of doing things. I see it definitely as an individual thing, based on your own comfort.

Similarly, Nicole explains that she also takes an individualistic approach to the issue of homosexuality and being friends with lesbians and gay men. When her college friend Tracey Adams came out as a lesbian during their freshman year in college, this was the first time Nicole encountered an individual close to her who identified as lesbian, and she had to decide how she felt about it. She recalls this experience and her thinking in sorting out her feelings toward Tracey being a lesbian, as opposed to her Catholic faith's teachings regarding homosexuality:

> When I knew that Tracey was a lesbian, I was shocked in the sense that, "Oh my God, I didn't know anyone who's ever had this lifestyle." Sometimes things only become real to you when someone you know is actually going through it. So it was brand new for me. But after that I just kind of realized, "Okay, this is Tracey." This is a friend that I've had and I know her. I know the kind of person she is and a lot of those stereotypes that my, I don't want to say my parents put them on me because we literally never discussed it, but just in the sense that I grew up thinking that homosexuality was wrong in the Catholic Church, all that just kind of seemed not real to me. Like, "Okay, but in real life that's not how it is." Although I'm not gay or bisexual, I don't understand why they shouldn't be able to get married, have the rights that married couples do. I mean I can't say whether or not that would have changed if I had never met Tracey or Jane [another lesbian friend and coworker]. I just know that now that's how I feel.

Rejecting her Catholic faith's stance of love the sinner but hate the sin, Nicole explains that her support for lesbians and gays is based on her experiences with being friends with openly lesbian individuals like Tracey. It is clear that straight and gay interactions that lead to friendships are an important part of a dynamic that contributes to the creation of a post-closeted culture (Anderson 2008; Muraco 2006, 2012; Nardi 1999). That is, lesbian- and gay-affirmative stances support and constitute a context where lesbian and gay people can be out and respected members of their communities.

Like many straight women, Nicole takes her heterosexual identity for granted in her everyday social interactions. Currently, Nicole has a boyfriend and typically discusses him with her other straight female friends, and her friends similarly discuss their boyfriends or romantic interests with her. Although her own straight identity is often taken for granted, she does not view a variety of social contexts, such as her college campus or the local downtown bar scene in Orangetown, as exclusively

straight spaces. Since gays are a visible and out presence in these contexts, heterosexual and homosexual identity practices become a salient
issue for Nicole and her friends. For instance, Nicole and her friends try
to decode the gender practices of men in bars to detect whether a man
they find attractive might be gay or straight. Sexual identity practices
are read through masculinity performances and are significant for dating, deciding whom to approach, and the bars they choose to socialize
at in downtown Orangetown, where there are a cluster of both straight
and exclusively gay bars along Main Street and between Market and
Union Streets. This area is understood as a distinct neighborhood in the
history of Orangetown, and I have labeled it "Center City" to signify its
significance accordingly. (See the map of Orangetown in the introduction for a visual representation of where this neighborhood lies in the
city's geography.)

In another example, again demonstrating the pervasiveness of
homo/heterosexual identity symbols, Nicole relates an incident when
she was thinking of setting her friend up on a date with a male acquain-
tance in college but decided not to after suspecting he might be gay,
even though later she saw him dating another female classmate. As she
recalls the incident,

> There was a time when I had thought that some guy was gay and that
> was because of his mannerisms. And I was trying to hook him up with a
> friend of mine. And then I realized, "Oh, I think he's gay." It was sort of
> the way he was in terms of his voice was very high, hit high notes, and he
> talked with his hands a lot. I don't really know what it is. I guess just ste-
> reotypical things that you would associate [with homosexuality]. I just
> thought he might be. So I stopped trying to hook him up with my friend.
> And later on I saw him dating a girl from our school. So, I'm assuming
> that I was wrong and he is heterosexual, but I don't know.

Similarly, Tracey, her college lesbian friend, stopped socializing with
Nicole and their other heterosexual female friends after she met her
girlfriend. Nicole feels that this was in part because Tracey sensed—
correctly, according to Nicole—that some of their mutual heterosexual
female friends were not comfortable going to gay bars or with Tracey's
lesbianism in general. When I ask Nicole whether she would be OK

having only gay or lesbian friends, her straight identity does become salient in her choice of having a group of close female straight friends and in socializing in establishments that attract a straight crowd. This is how she responds:

> To be honest, I don't know that I could be friends with only gay or lesbian people because I would feel that there were just certain things I wouldn't have in common, that I couldn't relate to them as well. If that was my situation, then, no, I would definitely be going to gay bars in order to hang out and bond with those people. You would have to go. I also assume they would go to regular bars with me, but I would in turn go there as well.

That is, Nicole and her straight female friends prefer to hang out in predominantly straight establishments since they are straight, and some of them are single and interested in meeting straight men to possibly date. Nicole also says that as a result of gays and lesbians being visible on her college campus, she has become more aware of which men she tries to set her girlfriends up with. Codes and symbols of gay and straight identity practices circulate in these contexts as practices to be aware of among her and her friends.

Whereas Nicole has close lesbian friends, Vanessa Marshall's gay friends are mostly men. Vanessa is a twenty-seven-year-old light-skinned black woman who was raised in the Methodist faith, but does not ascribe much importance to religion now. Vanessa moved to Orangetown after finishing her bachelor's degree in merchandising in New York City and now works as a manager at a retail store in the mall. Her close friendships with gay men have had a kind of domino effect, leading her to become friends with their gay friends and so on. This is how Vanessa explains her friendships with gay men:

> Gay guys can have a closer relationship with females, I think [than straight men]. We perceive gay guys like your girlfriends. You tell them things that you wouldn't tell your [straight] guy friends. A lot of straight guys I don't think know how to be friends with a female. They just don't know how to have that relationship. It's either you're sleeping with them or not. You just can't have that relationship. They just can't hang out and

watch a movie. For a lot of them [straight men]. I'm not saying every single straight guy. I do have straight guy friends, but I think a lot of straight
guys can't. And you can have that relationship with a gay guy. You like
the same things. You like the same corny movies.

Here Vanessa tells me that her friendships with gay men can often be
closer and more intimate than her friendships with straight men, who
she thinks more readily want a sexual, not a platonic, relationship.

Vanessa is conventionally feminine, and although she says it is
unusual that she does not date at her age, twenty-seven, she says
that moving back to New York City and saving money to do that are
her goals right now. Since she does not date, as she plans to move
soon, Vanessa says that the only way people know that she is straight
is through comments she makes about men whom she finds attractive and through her conventional feminine appearance. Further,
while she does not avoid or consciously wear anything in particular to
indicate her heterosexuality, she assumes that most people think she
is straight. Even though she is friends with many gay men and goes
on occasion to gay bars with her friend Leonard Bray, she still does
not worry about being taken as a lesbian while there. "A lot of people
already knew me [at the bar]," she explains, "and they knew that I was
just hanging out with Leonard. And nobody tried to hit on me while
I was there."

Because of her close friendships with gay men, Vanessa has become
well aware of gay men's identity practices, some of their different sexual
preferences (e.g., being a top, a bottom, or versatile when it comes to
anal sex), and now routinely notes when she interacts with or thinks
she sees gay men and lesbians in public places like the retail store where
she works.

Sometimes I can tell. I'm not saying I can always tell. I'm not 100 percent, but I can mostly tell when someone is homosexual. . . . I can tell
by the way they talk, the way they act. I'm not being judgmental and
putting a label on anyone, but I'm a pretty good judge. My closest friend
is gay. I know that there are different types. My friend Leonard does act
more feminine and he does wear, not like girls' clothes, but he wears
tight T-shirts and you can tell. Whereas lesbians, especially when they do

dress more mannish and depending on the way they're acting, you can tell that they're lesbians.[11]

Furthermore, she even somewhat seriously questions the heterosexuality of coworkers whose interests make her suspect they might be gay, although one is married and the other is engaged. Her "insider" knowledge of gay life means that she no longer assumes that an outer heterosexual identity indicates an inner heterosexual desire. This is how she explains it to me:

> There are two guys who probably don't know that they're gay. They probably aren't gay, but just their actions. They do act a little bit more feminine. I've worked with them closely. The one guy is always talking about Madonna and just stuff that straight men don't usually talk about or [are] into. It's not necessarily because they're in fashion, but God knows. Just like the stuff, Madonna, different TV shows that they talk about [make them seem possibly gay].

Vanessa's friendships with gay men, then, have made her part of a rich symbolic world of gay and straight identity codes, where gender practices, taste preferences, and social interests indicate a gay or possibly gay identity (Muraco 2012; Nardi 1999). Moreover, within gay subculture, straight women like Vanessa are labeled and readily given roles as "fag hags"—straight women who are open to and supportive of gay men, readily befriending them (Moon 1995; Muraco 2012). While the term "fag hag" is arguably degrading, there exists no popular cultural equivalent label for gay men's friendships with straight men, nor lesbians' friendships with straight women or men. Straight women and gay men, then, have an established social relationship indicated by slang terms like "fag hag," portrayed on past TV shows like *Will & Grace*, and increasingly prominent in post-closeted cultural contexts, as indicated by Vanessa's friendships with gay men that situate her *within* and a part of gay male subculture.[11]

When I asked Vanessa why she was supportive of gay people even before she had so many close gay male friends, she explained, "My mother's just so cool and with her being married to a black man. She has always been accepting of others and she [taught me to not be] judgmental against anyone because of race, religion, or sexuality. It's all about how you're taught. Seriously." As the sociologist France Winddance Twine (2010) shows, white women who marry black men will adopt antiracist stances in protecting their relationship and interracial children from antiblack prejudice. Vanessa explains that her white mother's marriage to a black man, along with her mother's values of tolerance and acceptance, taught her to oppose prejudicial judgments against others. In addition, in thinking about her own experiences as a woman of color, Vanessa remarks, "I think it's very important as a minority to stand out. I still feel that I have to prove myself, not only as a racial minority who's black and white, but as a female. You do have to work harder. Any minority is going to have to work hard for what they have." Vanessa links her racial and gender minority statuses to other minorities' experiences in having to prove themselves in the workplace and other competitive environments, illustrating how her minority identity allows her to empathize with other minorities.

This notwithstanding, Vanessa and the other straight women in this group, it is important to note, aimed to maintain a clear straight identity status and its accompanying privilege by embodying conventional femininity, by expressing sexual interest in men, and by not blurring heterosexual/homosexual identity practices, which might possibly mark them as lesbian or bisexual. I acknowledge, of course, that their straight identity status is also simply descriptive of their felt experiences, but these straight women did not want to be viewed as lesbian or bisexual, nor did the majority of them include conscious experiences of same-sex desires, fantasies, or sexual encounters as part of their self-practices. The limit of these straight women's antihomophobic stances is, then, shown by their performances of a clear straight femininity and the socially vested privileges it grants.

The Declining Significance of Compulsory Heterosexuality: Blurring Boundaries, Antihomophobias, and Sexual Fluidity

The distinction between the previous straight feminine practices and the ones in this section is that these heterosexual women consciously permit themselves to be viewed as lesbian or bisexual in some situations. They purposefully blur boundaries between homosexuality and heterosexuality, and it is this key point that constitutes their antihomo-phobic practices that challenge compulsory heterosexuality. By letting themselves be viewed as homosexual, these women surrender straight privilege and contest the norm of heterosexuality. For example, by asso-ciating with openly lesbian coworkers at their jobs, flirting with women in public, or integrating their sexual experiences with women into their identities, these straight women challenge a sexual binary that divides and reifies heterosexuality and homosexuality into static identities and reinforces lesbian stigmatization and sexual inequality. It is important to note that women in this group defined religion as of minimal impor-tance to their self-identities; they described themselves as having low levels of religiosity or as nonreligious altogether.

All the women I interviewed identified as black or white heterosexual women, with the exception of one of the black women, Naomi Lynch. I have excluded Naomi from the analysis, as she did not identify as het-erosexual. When asked about her sexual identity, she stated, "I like both men and women, but I don't like to be called bisexual or heterosexual." Although women who avoid labeling their sexuality are important for sexualities scholars to study when thinking about identity politics and the issue of sexual fluidity, I have excluded her from this analysis in order to maintain analytical consistency with my study's definition of heterosexuality as based on a woman self-identifying as heterosexual.

A total of seven out of the twenty-nine women fell into this last group, both claiming experiences of same-sex intimacy and blurring normative heterosexual boundaries in a variety of public contexts in daily life. Four are white and the other three are black. Sexual fluidity among these women seems to be conditioned by their antihomophobic practices. In contrast, the heterosexual women in the previous section did not blur boundaries, nor did they generally report experiences of sexual fluidity or make sexual fluidity part of a queered identification. For example, when I asked Vanessa, "Do you think you ever might have a sexual experience with someone of the same sex?" she said, "I can't say never. At this point in time, no. I'm not attracted to women like that. I want a man." This was the typical kind of response to this ques-tion among women in the previous group. (I, however, provide a more in-depth discussion of sexual fluidity among women in both the weak and blurred boundaries categories in chapter 5.)

For the following women, in contrast, sexual fluidity practices ranged from fantasies and thoughts about being involved with a woman to having had sexual encounters with women at different times over the course of their lives. The question, then, is how do these women project a straight identity? Importantly, each one of them does come out as straight at different times to express interest in someone or to decline someone's interest in them. Moreover, they identify as heterosexual, not bisexual, which maintains a heterosexual subjectivity for themselves and the significant others in their lives. Further, if they feel uncomfortable, anxious, or fearful when blurring boundaries, then employing conscious gender-conventional practices is a readily available strategy for reemphasizing their straight status and recuperating its privilege, as is disclosing an interest in men by discussing a boyfriend, husband, or male partner.

At this end of the continuum, the sexual identity practices of these heterosexual women blur boundaries of homo/heterosexuality and enact sexually fluid behaviors that both challenge the homo/heterosexual binary division and draw attention to the socially constructed character of the sexual and gender institutional orders, which their micro–identity practices aim to render fluid, contested, and in flux.

Driving to a neighboring city from Orangetown to interview Jennifer Dowd, I met a single straight woman who thinks of herself as a liberal and politically minded Irish American. Jennifer enjoys her work but also has her own local radio show, where she brings attention to issues ranging from the environment and immigration to the poor and economically disadvantaged. Previously married, she's now single and in her forties. Raised Catholic, she no longer keeps faith with the Church.

Explaining to me how her interactions with lesbian coworkers have indicated to her that she does not clearly perform a straight femininity, Jennifer tells me that she isn't concerned about being recognized as heterosexual in any number of public contexts, such as at her previous workplace or in a restaurant with lesbian and gay friends. For example, Jennifer's last job was at a chemical company, and as she started to get to know her colleagues, she was approached by two lesbian coworkers, who she intuited might have a romantic, as well as collegial, interest in getting to know her. One of the women, Susan Davis, who was out at work, flirted with Jennifer, inviting her out on a lunch date. Jennifer chose not to "come out" as straight at work to Susan, stating that she did not feel it was appropriate to discuss personal relationships in that context. However, on their lunch date, Jennifer did let Susan know that she wasn't interested in women. Commenting on why she thinks her lesbian coworkers perceived her as lesbian, Jennifer says,

> I don't scream as some straight woman; that's for sure. I always thought just having short hair was perceived as being somewhat gay. The other thing is I think sometimes just being single people think, "Oh, well, maybe," if the person's not married that they're gay. I don't think it's all that clear-cut whether somebody's gay or straight looking. I think some people are more to the type, like a woman who's got very long hair, wears frilly skirts and has long polished fingernails is seen as definitely heterosexual, whereas I have short little stubby fingernails. I'm more of a hippie and I'm not into makeup, which I think is read as gay a lot.

Although Jennifer says that she has not changed her appearance to avoid being viewed as lesbian, her statement illustrates that she recognizes a certain set of gendered practices as codes for lesbianism (i.e., short hair, nonpolished nails, an absence of makeup), and she codes being married, having long hair, wearing makeup, and conventionally feminine clothes as gender identity practices that project a normative straight femininity.

Although Jennifer maintained unclear boundaries between herself and lesbians at this workplace, it was in part because she does not feel that she would have faced discrimination for being viewed as a lesbian there: "It was a very safe, comfortable place, and I didn't feel like I was going to be discriminated against on the job if people thought I was gay. So, it was just a matter of their social perception, which wasn't really all that important to me."

Further, if being perceived as a lesbian meant she had a strong personality as a woman, then Jennifer was fine with that stereotypical association. "If people thought I was gay in part because I was single or in part because I was sort of a strong personality and because I was fighting a kind of very male structure, [then] that didn't seem like such a bad thing." Age enters here into Jennifer's performance and self-image, though, as being in her forties makes salient her single status as possibly indicating a lesbian identity; whereas when she was in her twenties, her age might not have been relevant to the question of whether she projected a clear heterosexual status.

If some heterosexual women avoid lesbian coworkers or the numerous identity practices associated with them (e.g., short hair, a lack of makeup, androgynous clothing styles), then others like Jennifer show why some heterosexual women don't construct strong or weak boundaries but rather embrace a blurred positioning (Dellinger and Williams 1997; Stein 1997). In the context of this workplace and Jennifer's characterization of it, having "a strong personality as a women" or being seen as "fighting a kind of very male structure" was associated with lesbian identifications and claiming forms of respect, authority, and voice for women employees at this chemical company. These attributes are positive qualities that women workers trade on in negotiating recognition and reward in the workplace.

Indicative of Jennifer's liberal values and desire to not reinforce the stigmatization of homosexuality through heterosexual privilege, she recognizes that

> as a heterosexual, I'm certainly not the underdog in any way, shape, or form. And that's where having gay friends gives me some kind of a reference point as to how the entire world doesn't function the way straight people think it does. I haven't really analyzed my straightness even though it makes perfect sense like when it comes to being middle-class. There isn't a lot of imagination about anything in a middle-class neighborhood.

Here Jennifer draws an analogy between heterosexual privilege and class privilege, something that goes unnoticed and unanalyzed, a norm that one judges oneself against. Of course, Jennifer acknowledges that most Americans do identify others by their sexual identity, but that she does not feel the need to flag her sexuality for homophobic reasons. Rather, she is interested in another individual's sexuality only if she wants to date that particular man or does not want to lead a woman on. For her, sexual identity has personal meaning for dating or sharing experiences and is driven by pragmatic, not moral, concerns of wanting to be understood as heterosexual in specific situations, not as a defensive effort to avoid the stigma of lesbianism. In other words, her straight femininity is not a source of status and privilege she rigorously aims to maintain, and so Jennifer consciously allows others to perceive her as possibly lesbian or bisexual in a range of situations and contexts.

Although she has never been sexually involved with a woman, she did find herself attracted to a female coworker at a past job. Part of her antihomophobic practice entails recognizing homophobia as a "fear of gay people, whether it's a fear of being gay yourself or just somebody's existence is challenging yours." She realizes that by recognizing her own sense of homosexual desire or fear of that desire she embraces a non-stigmatizing judgment toward lesbian and gay sexualities. Same-sex desire isn't something one should be ashamed of, Jennifer implies.

If Jennifer sometimes blurs boundaries by associating with lesbian coworkers, Erica Harris goes even further in her everyday life. Erica routinely breaks down boundaries of normative heterosexuality, blurs identity practices of straight femininity, and enacts an active antihomophobic practice in her everyday life.

Erica is a twenty-two-year-old black woman who manages a local restaurant on Main Street in Orangetown. In everyday life, Erica challenges boundaries between gays and straights in two main ways. First, her straight, lesbian, and gay friends and coworkers are integrated into her personal and professional lives. She lives and works in an area called Center City in downtown Orangetown where, like her friends and coworkers, gays and straights interact regularly. Second, in public Erica regularly holds her straight, lesbian, and bisexual female friends' hands and often greets them with a kiss on the lips. She says that she hugs, kisses, and holds the hands of both her male and female friends in public, and she makes no distinction between whether the women are straight, lesbian, or bi.

As a result of her intimate and affectionate practices in public that blur sexual identity boundaries, some of Erica's acquaintances jokingly and nonjokingly question her heterosexuality. However, even in these situations, Erica avoids disclosing that she's straight and allows others to assume that she might be lesbian or bisexual. Erica tells me about a situation where this happened:

An example of a situation would be me sitting in public with a friend and a girlfriend of mine coming over and greeting me. We greet each other with hugs and kisses and maybe even her sitting on my lap while I'm having a conversation with somebody else. And the other person that I'm with, if they're not aware of the relationships that exist between me and these other people, might make a joke, "I didn't know you liked girls," "I didn't know you had a girlfriend," or "I didn't know that you were on that side of the fence." Some kind of lame, silly statement like that, which I usually chuckle at. I like the fact that people are confused or they don't know; because I think it's silly to try to put everybody in a box. I guess part of that ambiguity . . . I must push it. I think I push it sometimes. I think I allow for people to question it. I don't snap back and say, "I'm a heterosexual! What are you talking about?" So, I don't defend it.

Instead of becoming defensive by suggestions that her physical intimacy with other women identifies her as seemingly lesbian, Erica courts the ambiguity and plays with lesbian/straight identity codes. Her antihomophobia rebukes coding identity and intimacy practices as uniformly heterosexual or homosexual, challenging both heterosexual privilege and binary constructions of heterosexual/homosexual identities as mutually exclusive.

It is, perhaps, not surprising that Erica openly discusses her own same-sex encounter without a sense of shame. Growing up post-Stonewall and in contexts of LGBTQ cultural visibility seems to have laid the groundwork for her to feel comfortable talking about the encounter without much anxiety.

I'm the kind of person who's willing to try anything and again try to not box everything into this is the way it is. This is the way it should be. This is the way it's gonna be. I'm able to be malleable, and I'm also somebody who does not view same-sex relationships as wrong. What I did was fine. It's a piece of my life story now.

As well, she says that this experience caused her to rethink her own straight identity and how an identity category reduces the complicated and messy nature of one's experiences. Erica describes sexual identities as fluid, contextual, and dependent on the circumstances one finds oneself in:

I consider myself heterosexual. Just the same way, like I said before, politically, I consider myself black. But I'm more than that in terms of my ethnic makeup. Just as in sexuality, I'm more than just a straight female. I'm attracted to different things. I don't make myself any promises that I'll never change. I believe that a lot of things are based on the individual person. Give me a woman who does everything right for me and we'll see. This particular woman did not.

Erica's antihomophobia extends beyond blurring sexual identity practices and giving up her heterosexual privilege: her identity practices demonstrate a queering of straight femininity. A queered heterosexual identification contests essentialist and unified conceptions of heterosexuality and replaces them with a fluid, contextual, and dynamic conception of sexualities. (Chapter 5 provides a fuller discussion of women's queered straight identifications.) Erica's antihomophobic practices are also aimed at changing the worldview of her unenlightened acquaintances and friends. For example, she takes some of her homophobic straight male friends to gay bars to show them that gays are just as diverse, "normal," and often unremarkably ordinary as heterosexuals:

ERICA: For example, going to a place like The Pub [a gay bar on Main Street], some friends, if I even bring that up, they're like, "What am I? Fresh meat?" I'm like, "Honey, you're not that cute." And I think it's that they are not able to understand that there's not one kind of gay person. Not everybody is going to be threatening to you. That threatening persona, that threatening gay man [who's effeminate and aggressively flirtatious]. . . . That's what my friends think they are going to encounter anytime they go into a place that is not completely heterosexual, which is unbelievable to me. So, what do I do? I drag them in there anyway.

JAMES: And will they go?

ERICA: Most of the time, yes. Because it's either that or we're not hanging out anymore, I'm pretty, I do what I want to do. It's part of my personality.

JAMES: So you've made people—[Erica interjects]

ERICA: I've absolutely made people go into The Pub.

JAMES: And what do they do?

ERICA: They end up loving the music and playing pool and ordering a
    bunch of drinks and realizing that it wasn't that bad.

In short, Erica attempts to replace her homophobic friends' stereotypical perceptions of gay individuals and spaces with lived interactional
experiences, hoping that experiential reality corrects homophobic
prejudice.

Like Erica, Maureen O'Conner, a thirty-nine-year-old white woman,
who is a small business owner in Orangetown, identifies strongly with
the gay and lesbian community. Having worked in downtown Orangetown since the late 1980s, Maureen has witnessed significant changes
in the local lesbian and gay community over that time. From her active
participation in AIDS fundraising to her vigilance in observing the
interactions of the police with the local gay establishments over the
years, Maureen takes an activist stance in supporting the gay community in Orangetown.

> I think that I've always been supportive of the gay community. And
> when there was discrimination, even with the police department when
> I managed Michael's [a restaurant across the street from The Pub] and
> there was a problem at The Pub, my waitresses were always there. The
> cops were really homophobic back then. I always wanted one of my girls
> there just to make sure there was a woman in the bar when the cop came
> in. Just always to show support. I don't even think about that anymore,
> but from '89 to probably '94, '95, I thought about it. As soon as I saw a
> cop car, I sent one of my waitresses over. I thought that they [the police]
> would be like, "This is a gay thing. I don't want to deal with it." And that
> pissed me off. So I always made sure one of my waitresses was over there.

Straight women like Maureen actively create communities that support
and demand respect and rights for lesbian and gay individuals and their
lives, creating the social conditions that have given rise to and sustain
the lives of lesbian and gay people and a post-closeted culture.

When I ask Maureen how she defines her sexual identity, she says,
"Heterosexual, but I would be open. I wish, I wouldn't mind meeting
a woman if it happens, but I'm pushing forty and it hasn't really happened." Maureen, for example, recently tried to have a relationship with

a woman but did not enjoy being sexually intimate with her. This is how she explains her same-sex experience:

> I tried to go out on a couple dates with a woman, but I wasn't very good at it. I was open-minded. I liked the person a lot. It wasn't natural. It wasn't a natural thing for me. I did have feelings for her, but I just couldn't go through with it. I felt uncomfortable. Like it was unnatural for me, but I did have strong feelings for her.

One might say Maureen wanted to be tempted and to feel a desire for this woman but didn't. This is strikingly different from Martha's nail technician, whose daughter felt sexual desire for another woman but didn't continue the same-sex relationship due to her Christian beliefs against it.

Although Maureen has led a conventionally straight life by many standards, having been married and divorced and raising a daughter on her own, her political identifications are with gay men and lesbians. For instance, Maureen expresses her own identification with the gay community while discussing the importance of the upcoming election. For her, being straight is about dating and relationships, while her social and political identifications position her as a member of the LGBTQ community,

> I'm hoping that the gay community gets out and votes because I think there's a huge voting situation in the gay community and we have a lot of power. You notice when I talk I include myself in [the gay community]. It's kind of fucked up, but I feel that [way]. You know what I mean? And I feel that we have more power and I think that, I think that you're going to see government notice that the minorities have a lot of power in this country and there's a lot of high officials in our country that are gay, that carry a lot of influence.

From her flirting with lesbian customers to her active participation in lesbian and gay social events to her openness in dating women in the past, Maureen's straight femininity blurs boundaries between straight and lesbian identity practices in various situations. Maureen identifies with gay political concerns and the community in general, and she not only criticizes straights' homophobic prejudices but also criticizes gays who label individuals as "closet cases" for not being "out." This is how she explains it:

Sometimes gay people say to me, "I think he's a closet case." And I'd be like, "You wouldn't want people, it took you years to come out of the closet and it was a painful experience for you to come out. Why are doing that to someone else?" If somebody tells me they're gay, then it's on them, not me. It's not for me to say because it's painful for, I find, gay men to come out of the closet. This generation has it a little bit easier. It's not as big a deal, but the judgments that I see go back and forth bother me. Because I think it's a process for a lot of young men and I think they have a difficult time without being labeled if they're not. Why do that? Why even think about it? What if he got labeled and he wasn't gay or if he was struggling with his sexuality and people put more pressure on him and he felt bad about himself over something that he hasn't dealt with and that can be more painful. And the gay community needs to be more sensitive about it. That bothers me. I always tell the gay men about it.

Maureen's antihomophobia is situated from a position *within* the LGBTQ community. She not only stands up for gays and counters heterosexuals' homophobia, but also underscores the difficulty of coming out in a heterosexually dominant society and takes issue with the intolerance of gay men who circulate rumors about other men's sexualities. It is not that Maureen thinks that there is anything wrong with being gay, but rather she focuses on how arduous a process it can be to come out.

Sociologists distinguish between the terms "identity" and "identification." Identification is defined as an attachment to a group of people, while identity indicates a central aspect of one's self-definition. This is a useful distinction for understanding individuals like Jennifer, Erica, and Maureen who self-identify as heterosexual but have strong identifications with gay and lesbian friends and the larger gay community they belong to as allies and friends.

Furthermore, each of these straight women not only blurs boundaries of normative heterosexuality but also recognizes straight privilege as part of a culture that aims to value heterosexuality over homosexuality. While each woman will disclose her straight status at various times to signal her interest in men or to decline someone's interest in her, they each practice an antihomophobia that challenges binary sexual identity categories, and in doing so they carve out space for lesbian, gay, bisexual, and queer people and subcultures through their own identity practices.

The Continuum and the Limits of Compulsory Heterosexuality

Compulsory heterosexuality remains central to the contemporary social organization of straight women's identity practices, particularly straight women who use homophobic practices based in religious views of homosexuality as a sin, but even pro-gay straight women who subtly maintain straight privilege and naturalize the homo/heterosexual binary enact it as well. The continuum provides insight into how straight women and their recurrent identity practices resist, incorporate, and reconfigure the homophobic and antihomophobic dynamics present in the complicated contexts of post-closeted culture. Table 4.1 provides a visual representation of the entire continuum and where each individual woman falls on it.

On one end, even the most homophobic straight women illustrate a degree of tolerance toward lesbian and gay individuals, and some were even comfortable socializing in lesbian and gay spaces. However, this tolerance belies their homophobic prejudices, which were often based in religious worldviews, but also social ones, that judge homosexual identities as abnormal, gay relationships as inferior, and marriage as the exclusive privilege and legal right of straight women and men. Although their Christian moral beliefs appear genuine, they also seem to feel compelled to offer a legitimizing rationale for their homophobic prejudices, one that would be seen as beyond criticism, and even beyond their own personal choice. Religious beliefs often invoke the discourses of piety and tradition to that effect, aiming to seem as if they are unchangeable and thus beyond criticism. Consequently, these straight women's choices to invoke religious rationales to validate their opinions of homosexual identities and relations as inferior make sense given that religious discourses provide cover and lend authority to one's beliefs.

Table 4.1. Continuum of Straight Boundaries of Social Distance (Women)

Strongly Aversive Boundaries	Weak Boundaries	Blurred Boundaries
Martha Louise Ghanima Sandra Patricia Kelly Beth Nia	Dionne Nina Cheryl Margaret Stephanie Jan Nicole Alicia Eileen Kathy Eve Jody Vera Vanessa	Maya Jennifer Susan Denise Kim Erica Maureen

With the exception of Martha, the other four black straight women did not want to be viewed as entirely unsupportive or intolerant of lesbian and gay identities, relations, and same-sex marriage. Still, four out of five black women cited their Christian faith as their justification for opposing gay identities and rights. Only one of the white women, Beth, invoked her Christian faith in disapproving of gay marriage, while the other two white women and Nia, the remaining black woman, adopted social views of homosexuality as deviant and abnormal to substantiate their homophobic attitudes.

Overall, the eight straight women in this category displayed weaker homophobic practices than their straight male counterparts in the previous chapter. For instance, looking at the cases of the most homophobic straight women respondents, I noted that several of them have socialized in gay bars and dance clubs without a sense of anxiety. This was not the case for the homophobic straight men, who generally would not enter a gay bar, for instance. Unlike the men, the straight women respondents did not express a preoccupation with or anxiousness about being potentially perceived as lesbian or bisexual in gay spaces in particular, or more generally in their everyday lives. Generally, even the homophobic straight women exhibited a sense of self that was less defensive about their own styles of dress, bodily comportment, and general appearance being perceived as possibly homosexual in everyday interactions, although there were exceptions to this, as we saw in the case of Nia.

The issue of same-sex relationships and marriages provoked prejudicial responses from all eight straight women in this category. All of these women viewed the idea of same-sex marriage as either violating Christian scripture (Braumbaugh, Nock, and White 2008; Finlay and Walther 2003; Fisher et al. 1994; Olson, Cadge, and Harrison 2006) or as socially deviant and thus culturally illegitimate. Their disapprobation of lesbian and gay relationships and same-sex marriages evidences their wish to maintain the exclusivity of these roles, statuses, and institutions as strictly heterosexual privileges. In effect, they do this by imposing a second-class status on lesbian and gay relations and by denying them the civil right to marry. These straight women, then, illustrate their possessive investment in straight identity as the superior sexuality by marking homosexual relations and same-sex marriages as inferior.

Further, I suggest that these women's investment in heterosexual marriage preservation makes sociological sense, due to the social capital straight women accrue by entering into matrimony and motherhood (Bourdieu 2001; di Leonardo 1987). The social statuses of wife and mother are traditional routes to prestige and power in society, and they remain culturally normative roles and ideals, even when contemporary American society is experiencing marriage deinstitutionalization, with increasing rates of cohabitation and with over a third of all births to unmarried women today (Cherlin 2004).

The middle spectrum of the continuum includes straight women, some strongly religious and others less so, who embrace lesbians and gay men as trusted friends, fellow church members, and valued coworkers. These fourteen straight women's pro-gay practices, unlike those of the straight men in this middle position in chapter 3, embrace both the conventional and the unconventional gender expressions of their lesbian and gay friends, workmates, and kin. However, by retaining their straight status and privilege through the avoidance of practices that would make indistinct their straight sexuality, as well as their view of gay and lesbian sexualities as the identity of a fixed minority, these straight women promote lesbian and gay equality while simultaneously naturalizing the homo/heterosexual division.

In the weak boundaries category of the continuum, three of the six black women reported strong Christian faiths, but they did not use their religious beliefs to condemn homosexuality; rather, they sought to embrace lesbian and gay individuals as members of their religious communities and as intimate friends, as did the three white women who defined their religious beliefs and church membership as key parts of their self-identities. In addition, the black straight women on this side of the continuum, regardless of whether they were religious or not, generally drew on their experiences with racism in understanding the homophobic prejudice lesbian women and gay men negotiate in American society.[12]

The seven straight women in the third category, who blur identity practices of homo/heterosexuality and enact sexuality as fluid, challenge gender and sexual institutional orders through their micro-practices, and demonstrate the socially constructed character of the institutional orders as well. Significantly, these straight women document the ability of individuals to variably reconfigure institutional orders through micro–identity practices of sexuality and gender. At various times and places these women's identity performances and antihomophobic stances reject straight privilege, making sexually fluid experiences part of their straight femininities and illustrating the development of queered identifications among some straight women today.

A comparison of the data in this chapter and the last reveals the paradox that antihomophobic straight women negotiate compulsory heterosexuality differently than their pro-gay straight male counterparts. That is, these antihomophobic straight women reported engaging in practices of sexual fluidity as based in part on their affirmation of lesbian and gay life. In contrast, the antihomophobic straight men in chapter 3 neither reported engaging in sexual fluidity nor made the idea of fluidity a part of their antihomophobic practices. Perhaps, then, the compulsory nature of heterosexuality is now more applicable to straight men than women. The composition of this blurring boundaries category is also revealing, as only four straight men constituted this end of the continuum in the last chapter, while seven straight women constitute it in this chapter. (Again, see the appendix for tables A.1 and A.2 on the complete compositions of both the straight men's and women's continuums.)

In sum, the continuum serves to link straight women's identity practices and perspectives to the constitution, maintenance, and transformation of the social institutions of sexualities and gender. The continuum also documents the role race plays in shaping the straight identity practices of black and white women. That is, on one hand, the continuum shows how some practices and stances construct and reproduce compulsory heterosexuality, homophobias, and gender normativity. On the other hand, it documents how some antihomophobic practices, queered straight identifications, and practices of sexual fluidity constitute and create a post-closeted culture where the discourse and regulatory norm of compulsory heterosexuality is withering in the lives of straight women who consider themselves allies, activists, and members of lesbian, gay, and queer communities today.

5

Queering Heterosexualities?

Metrosexuals and Sexually Fluid Straight Women

Matt Becker told me that on his drive over to my office, his girlfriend asked whether he was going to come out to me as a "metrosexual." I thought to myself, "When did metrosexuality become part of Americans' discourse around straight masculinities? And what does it mean to the straight men who embrace the term as well as those who don't?" Similarly, new terms like "heteroflexible" signal that some straight women now define their sexualities to include same-sex experiences. Although my interviews predate the rise of this neologism, why did ten of twenty-nine straight women I interviewed think of their sexuality as fluid? Some researchers think of sexual fluidity as a practice confined to lesbian, bisexual, or nonheterosexual women (see Diamond 2008), but I explore straight women's experiences of same-sex desire, fantasy, and intercourse.

By exploring these changes and shifts in gender and sexualities in contemporary American society, this chapter looks at the meanings and practices of queered and nonnormative heterosexualities through the narrative accounts of the black and white straight men and women I interviewed. The rise of a post-closeted culture has meant the uneven and complicated normalization of conventional gay men and lesbians by heterosexuals and the broader culture. And as the normalization of homosexuality has diffused into the larger culture, the boundaries between straights and gays have shifted in relation to the social construction of straights' dynamics of desire, behavior, and practices of identity. In arguing that the development of queered and nonnormative heterosexualities must be analyzed in relation to the rise of a post-closeted culture, I examine what it means to enact metrosexual masculinities for straight men and what it means to incorporate experiences of sexual fluidity into definitions of straight femininity for straight women.

By queered heterosexualities, I mean identifications that contest uniform and essentialist understandings of heterosexuality and include some form of sexual fluidity in their self-experience, whether it is dreams, waking fantasies, kissing, or sexual intercourse with a person of the same sex.[1] Queered heterosexualities show that sexual categories do not predetermine or prescribe the sexual desires, behaviors, or identity practices that are assumed under the identity category of heterosexuality. Moreover, queered heterosexual identifications can challenge identity categories themselves, calling into question a normative order premised on supposedly clearly defined sexual desires and behaviors that align with static sexual identities.

However, I do not reduce all nonnormative heterosexual practices to a queered heterosexual position; rather, I draw an analytical distinction between nonnormative heterosexualities and queered heterosexualities.[2] By nonnormative heterosexualities I mean practices that negotiate less conventional gender and heterosexual practices, not gender-bending or queered ones. For example, heterosexual couples who cohabit but do not marry may be seen as demonstrating a nonnormative heterosexual practice in regard to the traditional conventions of marriage and matrimonialism, but they do not necessarily occupy queered heterosexual identifications.

In narrowing down the concept of nonnormative heterosexualities and making it of analytical use, this chapter focuses on metrosexual masculinities as a gender strategy that negotiates normative conventions of gender and sexuality that both contest and reconstruct hegemonic masculinity. The development of nonnormative heterosexual masculine identifications applies to the metrosexual male respondents in the study.

Whereas the adoption of queered straight identifications pertains to the straight women I interviewed and who enact their sexuality as fluid. I categorize as "queered" those heterosexual feminine identifications that negotiate variable kinds of sexually fluid experiences, ranging from fantasies to sexualized and sexual encounters with other women. Queered straight women are allies to queer people and members of queer subcultures. While this positioning is based in part on their enactment of sexuality as fluid, it also emerges from their antihomophobic political ideologies. But, like metrosexual men, these queered straight women challenge the conventional sexual order through their practices of sexual fluidity and antihomophobia, while at other times reconstructing it by enacting binary constructions of sexuality as heterosexual or homosexual, or in making claims to heterosexual privilege instead of contesting its establishment.

In understanding the rise of metrosexual masculinities and their relation to the context of a post-closeted culture, we need to bring economic and cultural shifts into view to grasp the contours of the present conditions of contemporary masculinities. Since the middle of the twentieth century, middle-class men, historically white males, have been increasingly employed by corporations and other similar workplaces where self-presentation became pivotal to the role of the worker. These white-collar workplaces emphasize, then and now, the importance of communicative skills, a "good" personality, and an "attractive" appearance in projecting the interpersonal and professional qualities needed to succeed in these environments (Faludi 1999; Goffman 1959; Luciano 2001). In white-collar employment, appearance has taken on a heightened importance as one's clothes, grooming habits, and bodily capital have become part of the package in performing the role of a "successful" middle-class professional (Salzman, Matathia, and O'Reilly 2005). White middle-class heterosexual male workers consequently signal their professionalism by being au courant, well-coiffed (Barber 2008), and variably stylish—adopting styles associated with gay men, who are stereotypically associated with practices such as being well-dressed, well-groomed, and body-conscious. By hybridizing gay masculine styles and practices into their heterosexual masculinities, heterosexual men have been noticed for the seemingly gay male appeal or metrosexual masculine performances they enact in various contexts (Demetriou 2001; Connell and Messerschmidt 2005). Paradoxically, metrosexual masculinities are hybridized masculinities that both contest and reinforce hegemonic masculinity. In other words, metrosexual performances can be read as nonnormative masculinities that in some cases challenge gender and sexual binaries and hierarchies while in other cases shore them up.

Simultaneously, on the cultural landscape, the change in American media depictions of gay men and lesbians in the 1990s marked an unprecedented turning point, as both the quantity and the quality of gay characters represented in the mass media increased (Chauncey 2004; Dean 2007; Gamson 2002, 2005; Gross 2001; Seidman 2002; Walters 2001). For example, the TV show *Will & Grace*, which ran from 1998 to 2006 and is in rerun syndication, not only captured America's fascination with gay male characters and their relations with straight women friends, "counting 17.3 million views each week" at the height of its popularity in 2000 (Linneman 2008, 586), but also, as the masculinity scholar Michael Kimmel (2012) suggests, broadcasted to straight men a suggestive, self-interested message regarding why they might do well to model themselves after the practices and styles of gay male characters like Will Truman. "The message was simple: Gay men know what straight women want. And if straight men could just be 'a little bit gay,' they'd do very well among women," Kimmel contends (248). If a post-closeted culture has made the adoption of gay masculine practices and styles available to some heterosexual men, then what role has it played in the rise of queer practices of sexual fluidity among heterosexual women?

The sociohistorical context for the rise of queered heterosexualities and acts of sexual fluidity among straight women is the development of post-closeted lesbian and gay enclaves and subcultures in the 1970s and 1980s across urban centers in America (Castells 1983; Davis 1994; Levine 1979). Simultaneously, lesbian and gay studies, particularly in courses, curriculums, and departments of women's and gender studies and other disciplines, became a part of American universities' scholarship and curricula at this time as well (Berger and Radeloff 2011).

That is, in the 1990s, a queer politics and cultural movement became a new organizing force within both lesbian and gay communities and scholarly communities (Chee 1991; Epstein 1996, 1999; Fuss 1991; Seidman 1996). Reacting partly to the entrenchment of identity politics and the renewed homophobia generated by the AIDS epidemic, queer people, activists, and scholars alike sought to disrupt monolithic conceptions of gay and lesbian sexualities, expand the borders of the community to include bisexual and transgender persons, and protest normalizing discourses, identities, and practices that inscribed binary conceptions of sexualities and gender.

Queered straight women, then, negotiate a sociohistorical context where sexual and gender practices, desires, and identities have been renegotiated through the lens of queer culture in the communities of lesbian, gay, and queer people. Against the sexual and gender binaries that maintain normative heterosexuality and gender normativity, queered practices of sexual fluidity, as well as a relational conception of identities as socially constructed, negotiated, and changeable, made sense to heterosexual women who socially and politically identified with lesbian, gay, and queer subcultures. It is in the context of a post-closeted culture after the queer cultural turn that I explore straight women's enactment of sexuality as fluid, their practices of antihomophobia, and their political commitments to queer friends, communities, and culture.

Metrosexual: A New Type of Straight Man?

The term "metrosexual" was first coined by the British journalist Mark Simpson in a 1994 newspaper article on urban men's consumerist practices. Simpson defined a metrosexual as "a young man with money to spend, living in or within easy reach of a metropolis—because that's where all the best shops, clubs, gyms and hairdressers are. He might be officially gay, straight or bisexual, but this is utterly immaterial because he has clearly taken himself as his own love object and pleasure as his sexual preference." Although the term here emphasizes urban men who make consumption a key social identity practice, Simpson does not specify that these are straight men who are perceived as gay. However, this is the key distinction made in the term's definition and circulation in US media between 2002 and 2003 (Ghaziani 2010). From the *New York Times* to *Merriam-Webster's Collegiate Dictionary*, the term in its American reception means something like the following: "a usually urban heterosexual male given to enhancing his personal appearance by fastidious grooming, beauty treatments, and fashionable clothes" (Merriam-Webster 2008). Further, a metrosexual is often mistaken for embodying the stereotypical style and fashion practices of a gay man, partly taking his cues from gay male styles that incorporate less conventional and more feminine style and beauty practices into his appearance.

For example, the much-talked-about Bravo Channel reality TV show *Queer Eye for the Straight Guy*, which ran from 2003 to 2007, exemplified the willingness of straight men to have their grooming, clothing, and etiquette practices made over by a group of urban gay men with high-class taste (Kaye 2009; Miller 2005). *Queer Eye for the Straight Guy* highlights a key aspect of metrosexuality: the development and emphasis placed on the conspicuous consumption practices of straight men who are to now ape gay men and women who ostensibly make practices of style, taste, and appearance central to who they are. Metrosexuals are straight men who shop for designer clothes, purchase expensive hair and skin care products, and enjoy being admired for their sense of fashion, taste, and beauty.

Perhaps metrosexuality's best representatives are straight male celebrities idolized for their beauty, muscular bodies, fashion sense, and the women they date or marry. For example, David Beckham, the former professional British soccer player, married to Victoria Beckham, formerly Posh Spice of the pop music group Spice Girls (Coad 2008), and Brad Pitt, the American actor involved with the actress Angelina Jolie, are exemplars of metrosexual masculinity. These metrosexual celebrities demonstrate the premium put on appearance, beauty, and fashion in projecting an idealized version of contemporary straight masculinity. As celebrities, they highlight cultural goods and distinctions of taste as focal points of their images in the media. On one hand, metrosexual men make straight masculinity nonnormative, associating it with the style and appearance practices of a stereotyped gay male sensibility. Metrosexuality is a hybridization of gay and straight men's styles and identity practices that reinforces stereotypes of gay men as fashion-conscious, well-groomed, and narcissistically focused on their appearances while also celebrating these qualities and the gay men who embody them. On the other hand, other identity markers aim to recuperate the nonnormative gay and feminine coding that metrosexual styles implicate and open up. For example, David Beckham's occupation as a former professional soccer player and his marital status partially recuperate his metrosexual refraction of straight masculinity, marking his straight masculine style practices as perhaps a new hegemonic form in consumer capitalist discourses of masculinity (Rahman 2004). Beckham's performance as a male icon who embraces feminized practices—he wears painted nails and long hair with a short ponytail; he is photographed for gay male magazines; and he comments to reporters on being flattered by his gay male fans' adoration—is indicative of a refiguring of hegemonic masculinity (Coad 2008). From his modeling of underwear for the retail giant H&M to an ad for Breitling watches (figure 5.1), Beckham's metrosexuality is a key part of his success as an icon for contemporary "gay straight" masculinities.

Metrosexuality, or The Stigmatizing of Gay-Friendly Straight Men's Style Practices

Sociologically, I view the term "metrosexual" less as a well-defined concept and more as a point of entry into the meanings, experiences, and micro-practices that surround definitions of contemporary straight masculinities. Exploring the term "metrosexual" with the straight men in my sample proved empirically productive. Metrosexual men are straight men who choose to adopt style, beauty, and appearance practices associated with femininity and gay masculinities, and, in doing so, they challenge hegemonic masculine constructions and embrace antihomophobic stances that contest the stigmatizing of gay men's identity practices in some cases. However, as I will show in the interviews, some of the straight men invoke the term "metrosexual" as a homophobic insult against masculinity practices they view as feminine and seemingly gay.

Perhaps it is not surprising that "metrosexual" is an ambivalent term for the straight men who fit its description in my sample. On the one hand, the term points to a less defensive heterosexual masculinity and to straight men who comfortably socialize with women and gays in settings where straights and gays mix together as part of downtown Orangetown's social scene. On the other hand, the term is part of the production of normative heterosexual discourses that aim to stigmatize nonhegemonic masculinities. Consequently, I argue that the labeling of heterosexual men as metrosexual is a way to contain, variably degrade,

Figure 5.1. David Beckham, metrosexual icon.

and stigmatize their style practices that contest identity codes between straight and gay presentations of self as well as an attempt to devalue the antihomophobic values they represent. Some might think that the label metrosexual is just an innocuous joke to give well-dressed heterosexual men some flak for their style and the time they spend primping. This is, I'm sure, part of the phenomenon, but this facile interpretation misses how hegemonic gender and sexual orders aim to recuperate metrosexual masculinity into another quasi-hegemonic masculine form, blunting a post-closeted dynamic that is reshaping and creating more expansive heterosexual masculine practices and the shifts that condition the rise of antihomophobic attitudes, actions, and subcultures (Rahman 2005).

Further, metrosexual men take up styles and practices of gay masculinities while often relying on the embodiment of conventional masculinities to project their straight status. Thus metrosexual masculinities are a hybridization of multiple patterns of masculinity that are increasingly salient in particular urban contexts. Contradictions around metrosexual masculinities abound. And even if this consumptive masculinity of style becomes a new form of hegemonic masculinity on a local and contextual level, this local position of dominance doesn't necessarily mean it will find its way into national or international forms of hegemonic masculinity, such as in the worlds of politics, athletics, and military forces (Connell and Messerschmidt 2005).

Defining and Stigmatizing Metrosexual Masculinities

First, I provide a sense of how the seven out of twenty-nine heterosexual men in my sample who fit the profile of being metrosexual define the term. I then contrast their descriptions with those of nine out of the twenty-nine heterosexual men who use the term to degrade heterosexual men they view as lacking masculine traits and appear to be quasi-gay or queer. Like high school heterosexual boys who use the word "faggot" against other heterosexual boys to mark them as unmasculine, feminine, and unworthy of respect (Pascoe 2007), adult heterosexual men draw on the discourse of metrosexuality for similar ends. Drawing on a homophobic discourse, some straight men use the label metrosexual to make fun of other straight men, deriding them as feminine, lacking masculinity, or associating them with a host of gay manners, styles, and appearance markers. Unsurprisingly, these nine straight men were the same men who constituted the homophobic end of the continuum. However, not all of the men who blurred boundaries were metrosexual.

After this brief preview, I explore in detail the social contexts of the metrosexual men I interviewed as well as other gay-friendly but non-metrosexual straight men. These exploratory accounts of gay-friendly metrosexual and nonmetrosexual straight men provide a sense of the ways straight men negotiate and variably embrace antihomophobic practices while living in a normative heterosexual society. The majority of the men I interviewed were neither metrosexual nor strongly homophobic in their construction of boundaries of social distance. Rather, the majority of straight men (thirteen out of twenty-nine) men fall into a broad category I call gay-friendly but nonmetrosexual. Not surprisingly, more black men fell into this category, as their style practices did not embody metrosexual masculinities.

None of the straight men I interviewed, however, could be categorized as metrosexual and homophobic. Although I'm sure there are exceptions to this empirically, I also suggest that a pattern among straight men who embrace metrosexual styles is the sense of confidence they exhibit about being straight while also being pro-gay. That is, the social contexts of metrosexual masculinities are associated with urban living, and its cosmopolitan ethos encourages city dwellers to project a sense of ease with openly gay men and women. Table 5.1 provides a cross-classification of the straight male respondents according to whether they are metrosexual or nonmetrosexual and homophobic or antihomophobic. This table, though, does not capture the nuances of homophobias/antihomophobias nor how homophobic and anti-homophobic stances are at times mixed together in the same man.

Table 5.1. Cross-Classification of Straight Men Respondents

Cross-Classification	Metrosexual	Nonmetrosexual
Antihomophobic	7	13
Homophobic	0	9

Nonetheless, it does give a rough sense of how the issue of metrosexual masculinity elicits straight men's varied and complicated negotiation of less-conventional masculine styles, associated with femininity and gay masculinities.

Gay-Friendly Metrosexual Men's Definitions of Metrosexuality

Matt Becker, a thirty-year-old white advertising representative, defines a metrosexual as a "heterosexual male who has a lot of the perceived characteristics of a homosexual male—tidiness, neatness, style with their dress or a flare for fashion, a flare for design coordinated things. Things like that." Similarly, Jason Robson, a twenty-six-year-old black administrative assistant, defines the term as a "guy that dresses nice, gets his hair done, and gets manicures." Echoing this, Nick Lynch, a twenty-two-year-old white waiter, says a metrosexual is "a heterosexual male who's on the cusp of fashion and who can sometimes possibly be construed as gay, exhibits a little bit more fashion savvy, has hair products, skin products, that kind of stuff." Michael Gates, a twenty-two-year-old black college student, adds, "It's a person who is comfortable with his [straight] sexuality. They don't hate on gays or anybody. They might have some feminine attributes, like getting their nails done and stuff like that."

Each of these definitions captures the spirit with which the term is used among my respondents and resonates with its general popular cultural connotations as well. Metrosexual men mix gay/straight identity practices as a consequence of their fashionable styles of dress, grooming habits, and consumption of beauty products or services. A metrosexual masculinity, though, is not a hegemonic masculinity in any simple way. Rather, as a hybrid form of masculinity, the social context of metrosexual men involves socializing with gays and viewing heterosexual women as not just sexual partners but also as simply friends. Before I elaborate on the environment of the metrosexual men in my study, I turn to the definitions of metrosexuality given by straight men who use the term to stigmatize and derisively label a straight masculinity they disassociated themselves from and stigmatized as an unmanly type of straight masculinity.

Stigmatizing Metrosexuality: Homophobic, Nonmetrosexual Men's Responses

In contrast to the metrosexual men who call gays friends and display antihomophobic and antisexist attitudes, homophobic straight men, who establish strong and weak normative heterosexual boundaries of social distance between themselves and gays, are the same heterosexual men who stigmatize and eschew a metrosexual masculinity. For instance, Eric Ward, a twenty-six-year-old white teacher, says,

> To me that's someone, one of those skinny guys. Maybe they swing kind of both ways. But they're very city like. More feminine. I think their ways as far as carrying their body, things that we classify [as feminine] if you're too concerned with your hair. Something like that.

Metrosexual identity practices raise doubts about these men's heterosexual status. As Eric notes, "Maybe they swing kind of both ways."

Similarly, Jerome Gordon, a twenty-two-year-old black college student, defines metrosexual men as feminine and seemingly gay, although they're not. He elaborates on the class and consumption associations of metrosexual men:

> Men that do feminine type things but they're not gay. I think it's the funniest thing I've ever heard. We used to call them pretty boys, guys who took more care of themselves, used to put more care, more manicured, we would call it. Their hair was always perfect, slicked down to the sides. Their nails were always nice. Clothes are always clean. They usually weren't athletes in school.

Metrosexuals are labeled "pretty boys" by Jerome. The adjective "pretty" seems meant to demean attractive men, diminishing their male beauty through a feminine descriptor. Others like William Russo, a thirty-eight-year-old white financial analyst, emphasize the consumption behaviors associated with these kinds of men. In defining the term, William describes how his administrative assistant told him that his expensive designer dress shoes were indicative of metrosexuality. However, he downplays his own conspicuous consumption habits and instead emphasizes the comparatively excessive shopping practices of a male friend:

> I think it's basically a term for guys that are straight that dress well, that are well groomed, but not gay. I don't think of myself as a metrosexual. I kind of think of myself as almost. I'm kind of a redneck that's been around if you think about it because I like living in the city. I like the urban thing, but I don't really obsess that much on myself. My friend is metrosexual. He's married, he's got an expensive house; he's got his wife, but this dude is fucking crazy. He'll spend so much goddamn money on clothes. He'll go to Neiman Marcus and drop thousands of fucking dollars on clothes. I mean that's a metrosexual. I don't consider myself that.

Distinguishing other men's consumption practices as excessive while disavowing his own similar practices, which in actuality are different only in degree, William demonstrates an othering process that codes metrosexuality as an excessive shopping and spending habit. Furthermore, conspicuous consumption is key to metrosexual masculinity, as style is based in the purchase of particular styles of clothing, a certain kind of hairstyle, and one's overall appearance. As Thorstein Veblen (1899) argued, expensive clothes are typically assumed to indicate not only good taste and high quality, but also one's own social class standing to others in a glance. Consumption, then, is tied to style and social class but also identity markers as well. From the subcultural identity styles of the 1970s gay clones (Levine 1998) to generational punks, consumption style practices partly construct social identities. In the case of metrosexuals, designer clothes (or their knockoff versions), along with a fitted to the body and tailored look, are coded as a new style pattern for straight men.

Similarly, Heath Anderson, a twenty-one-year-old college student, emphasizes that metrosexuals deviate from normative masculinity by taking their appearances as something to be attentive to, emphasized, and worked on. A straight man's interest in his appearance associates him with feminine-gay practices and diminishes his straight masculinity.

> I think a metrosexual is someone who is still heterosexual but may tend to, like, for instance, Ben Affleck is metrosexual because he dresses very

proper. He goes to spas, gets manicures, and things like that. They are very into their physical appearance. A man is supposed to say, "I'm done in a T-shirt and jeans and I don't care." Metrosexuals don't think that way. They are almost like models in a way.

For Heath, a heterosexual man constructs his masculinity as hegemonic by viewing himself as "I'm done in a T-shirt and jeans and I don't care." That is, acting "naturally" or "authentically" masculine means that by implication a man who has to try hard to be a man is less a man. However, as we know, the effort to project an attitude of apathy toward one's appearance is an active accomplishment of self-presentation, as all presentations are accomplishments in sociological terms. Further, a metrosexual masculinity is stigmatized due to the care and concern it shows toward appearances, as if the stance of effecting a careless disposition and practice toward one's appearance isn't one of cynical concern and defensiveness, perhaps worrying that one might be viewed as sharing the ostensible values of women and gay men.

Again, these straight men do not identify as metrosexual, but each defines the term as indicative of straight men who exhibit stereotypically feminine-gay identity practices due to their preoccupation with their appearances, fashionable styles of dress, and purchase of beauty products or services. Each definition captures the characteristics of metrosexual masculinity, but only to stigmatize it. For these straight men, metrosexuality is a polluted cultural embodiment of masculinity, and it represents a contestation of straight masculinity that they variably deride, stigmatize, and distance themselves from (Douglas [1966] 1970; Durkheim [1915] 1995). As I showed in chapter 3, straight masculine practices use boundaries of social distance from gay individuals, spaces, and signifiers to signal a pure straight masculinity; these same straight men distance themselves from metrosexual masculinities as well. In short, homophobic straight men stigmatize metrosexual men for embracing nonnormative identity practices.

The Social Context of Metrosexual Masculinities

For these respondents, metrosexual men represent a nonnormative straight masculinity, and their hybrid styles and antihomophobic attitudes are to be avoided due to their polluting associations and the potential loss of a clear straight status. Further, their descriptions of metrosexuality reveal their anxieties about being perceived as possibly gay, and how threatening the potential loss of their heterosexual status and privilege is for their sense of self.

The straight men in my sample who (1) exhibit fashionable styles and an emphasized set of male beauty practices around their clothing and grooming, (2) socialize in mixed gay/straight and predominantly gay settings; and (3) vocalize pro-gay values were ambivalent at times about embracing and identifying as metrosexual. Seven (five white and two black) of the twenty-nine heterosexual men fit the above profile of metrosexual masculinity in my sample. However, only two of the seven men self-identified as metrosexual (Matt Becker and Michael Gates), while the other five men acknowledged how they fit the description, but were ambivalent about embracing the label (see table A.1). In part, the term not only represents a labeling and stigmatizing of their identity practices, but also codes their heterosexual masculine styles as unmanly and not legibly heterosexual. Hence, the ambivalence of the term for straight men who are attempting to carve out a sense of self that is not a normative masculinity but still garners them basic masculine respect.

Further, in a society that disciplines and normalizes straight masculine practices for seemingly every bodily gesture, clothing choice, hairstyle, vocal intonation, and so on, it makes sense that straight men who are labeled by others as illustrative of this new trend and term feel at times uncertain and apprehensive about its application to them. The term, in short, illustrates the normalizing effort to contain a nonhegemonic masculinity, as hegemonic masculine constructions view an interest in fashion, beauty, and appearance as the concerns of women and gay men. For some straight men, this feminine-gay concern must be repudiated in order to maintain a clear straight masculine status. A hegemonic division and hierarchy of straight masculinities marks a metrosexual masculinity as inferior, feminine, and nonnormative.

Each of the metrosexual men in my sample recounted a similar story of someone telling them they were metrosexual due to their fashionable style practices, and further, these individuals suggested that their style marks their straight masculinity as dubious. For example, I asked Nick Lynch what he thought of the term "metrosexual."

NICK: I really don't see the need for identification. It just seems to be a trend that's been popular over the past couple of years in this area and among everywhere, TV news, that kind of stuff. But as far as identity, it's just, if you're into fashion, that's cool. If you like putting gel in your hair at night, that's cool. Sometimes I use hair products, sometimes I don't. I mean I definitely care about how I look when I go out at night. So I dress in clothes that I would find attractive. There are things that I feel comfortable in, but I really think the term "metrosexual" is completely unnecessary. It's categorizing people that don't need to be categorized.

JAMES: Because you?

NICK: The way I dress or they said I had good fashion sense. So I was like, "Oh, so that makes me metrosexual?" And they're just like, "Well, yeah." I was like, "All right, then like half the guys I know are metrosexual," because I appreciate a lot of my friends' sense of style, but I don't think that that's really something; it just seems so insignificant. Before two or three years ago I never heard the term. It was just people who were into fashion. Cool, that's their thing. But now there's, all of a sudden there's a term, there's a label for it. . . . I think it's negative.

JAMES: Do you think it's sort of stereotyping in the way that it's like, "Oh, well . . . "

NICK: He could be gay?

JAMES: Right, yeah.

NICK: I put it along the same lines as that.

Similarly, Jason Robson also voices apprehension. He says, "I guess we just needed a name to come up with. A lot of guys were doing that before that term even came about. So why does it need to be labeled? It just bothers me that they have to label it." Likewise, Derek Perry, a twenty-seven-year-old hotel staff member, says, "I don't put much stock in it. I don't really use the term. It just seemed more like a joke to me."

Metrosexual men in my sample negotiate this stigma by acknowledging the way they embody a fashion-forward style, use beauty products, and call lesbians and gay men friends while being apprehensive of letting others label them metrosexual. While the definition fits, the label can be constraining or simply feel unnecessary. Normative gender and sexual orders and identity formations are tightly co-constructed in everyday life, as the identity practices of metrosexual men simultaneously invoke both feminine and homosexual associations. Further, normative gender and sexual orders work to stigmatize not only gay identity practices but also those of metrosexual or nonnormative heterosexual men. These normative orders and discursive discourses aim to narrow and circumscribe the range of masculinities that can claim value, respect, and recognition. However, within the social circles of these metrosexual men, their metrosexual style and identity practices are already valued, respected, and esteemed. I now turn to an exploration of how individual men negotiate the meanings of a metrosexual masculinity.

"I've Had a Number of People Say to Me That They Thought [I Was Gay]" (Matt Becker)

Matt Becker, a thirty-year-old white male, was well-dressed in a casual suit with a button-down shirt when I interviewed him. An amiable individual who is gregarious and thoughtful in conversation, Matt grew up and currently lives in Orangetown but went to college in the South. He currently works in advertising, but most of his past work experiences have been in restaurants and bars.

Matt's metrosexual masculinity illustrates how some heterosexual men refashion straight masculinities to embrace many of the practices hegemonic masculinity aims to stigmatize, disassociate from, and deny as part of men's behaviors. He takes pleasure in ostensibly feminine-gay preoccupations, such as wearing fashionable clothes, buying beauty and hair care products, and taking an interest in interior design aesthetics.

He also has many women and gay friends he socializes with, and he values these friendships for the rich emotional intimacy they provide. Conscious that many men neither elaborately express their emotions nor feel comfortable being the only man among a group of women, Matt says,

> I think I'm more, I'm more emotional. I think I'm more in tune with my emotions than I think most guys are, or especially most guys would probably be willing to admit. . . . I've always been a guy who's had a lot of

friends who were female, especially when I was younger, but even now. I have a number of friends who are female and exclusively friends and plenty of times going out with them. I mean I go out with four, five, six girls, which is a little abnormal in the sense of what [straight] guys think is typical.

Not surprisingly, Matt says that women tell him he is a metrosexual and make jokes questioning whether he might be gay or not. He says that these jokes are due to his fashionable style of dress, his close friendships with women, and his comfort in being the only man among a group of women. Matt says, "I've had straight women jokingly say it to me, but they always say there's that old cliché there's always something behind a joke. There's always 10 percent of a joke that's true. I've had women in the past make comments that there's been a question [about my heterosexuality], but it was always more of like a bustin' my balls type situation."

Matt's ease with gay friends and gay life comes from having worked in the service industry since he was a teenager. During college he worked in restaurants and bars and later bartended in Orangetown after college. Consequently, he has worked with and befriended many gay individuals over the years.

The society that we live in today, the jobs that I have had, the people that I've come in contact with from the age of fifteen, sixteen up until now, thirty, I've come across such a number of people who were homosexual, bisexual, etc. that I've gotten past the point of assuming everybody I meet is heterosexual. . . . Most of the people that I have known who have been gay I've worked with in restaurants. It seems like there's a lot of gay waiters. . . . When I lived on Main Street [in downtown Orangetown], I just knew the gay community there. When I lived down in North Carolina, the town I lived in, Wilmington, there was a gay community there that frequented one of my bars [where I worked] and they weren't exclusively gay bars.

Due partly to working in service positions with gay coworkers, serving gay customers, and socializing with gay friends/coworkers over the years, Matt takes jokes about him being gay due to his stylish dress and appearance in stride. For instance, he recalls a situation where some gay male coworkers joked about his appearance and followed up with a flirtatious come-on.

> I've had a number of people say to me that they thought, "I would have thought you were gay." I've met more gay guys who gave me a hard time about it. I don't know if they were just hitting on me or that was just the way about them. Maybe they weren't hitting on me. Maybe they were just joking around, welcoming me into the new group, the friendship, whatever, but I have gotten that. I've heard, "You're too clean, you're too neat, you're too. . . . " I've always gotten a big one about the way that I dress. I'm somewhat particular about the way that I dress and that's always been one, and then I've got that look. I don't know, other people's terminology. I'm not using mine. I've had that said to me.

When I ask him whether he remembers a particular situation when the jokes or flirting happened, he says,

> But as far as a particular situation, I don't remember [an] exact particular situation, exactly what was said, but it's usually more in a crowd, one guy will make a joke and it'll be, you know, it'll be full of humor and kind of, like I said again, joking around in front of people, you know, "I'm taking you home tonight." Ha ha. Everyone gets a laugh out of it. That carries over into more kind of joking around and more in a sense of that.

In contrast to straight men who avoided gay individuals and gay bars in particular, worrying about having a gay man flirt with them, Matt is comfortable with these flirtatious overtures and acknowledges that his attention to clothes, fashionable styles, and well-groomed appearance often prompt women, gay men, and other acquaintances to question his heterosexuality. Both his ability to remain nondefensive in the face of questions about his sexual identity and his nonchalant attitude in response to gay men joking that they are going to have sex with him indicate that Matt's antihomophobic metrosexual masculinity demonstrates an ease in mixing and blurring sexual identity codes and that he doesn't view gay and feminine associations as demeaning of his personal worth or masculine character. Further, these women and gay men are friends of his and he takes their questions and jokes as part of the pleasure of their friendship and social company. It is also generally easier to handle sexual flirtations in a crowd of people who act as an audience and establish a sense of safety in numbers, as opposed to one-on-one, where the joking might feel and be meant more seriously and aggressively.

In fact, Matt consciously reflected on why he enjoys being friends with gays and lesbians, remarking on their sense of openness to differences and diversities of all kinds:

> I actually enjoy spending time around gay women and men because, and I'm gonna get into a generality here and I don't care because I've experienced it to be true, they're so much more open and out there and in a number of different senses. I don't mean just about their sexuality. I mean their attitudes toward life and their attitude, I get back to the laid-back thing, that's where I've seen a lot of homosexual people be very laid-back, very open, probably because, I would assume, because they're forced to be if they're living their life. It can't be an easy thing from my assumption, maybe I shouldn't do that, to come out in our society.

From being comfortable as the only man among a group of women to his ease in socializing in gay settings as well as the pride he takes in his stylish appearance, Matt illustrates how straight men value metrosexual practices as ones that enhance their status among their social circles, which include many women and gay individuals.

"I Think Because I Know Gay People, They're More Visible" (Jason Robson)

Like Matt, Jason is often told by female friends that he has a metrosexual style. He recently graduated from college and works as an administrative assistant. Although younger black straight masculine styles are often associated with urban styles of oversized clothing, Jason's style of dress takes on a metrosexual or gay aesthetic. Eschewing baggy jeans, Jason wears jeans that are more fitted but not tight. His shirts, however, are generally tight-fitting and emphasize his lean, muscular build. He says, "Well, I don't wear tight jeans because they're not too comfortable.

Tight shirts I do wear, but the first thing that people think is, 'Oh, he has a good body. So he can't really be gay,' probably something like that. I don't know what they're thinking."

Further, Jason displays feminine mannerisms and beauty practices, such as crossing his legs when sitting and having manicured nails. Yet, again, he does not think people view him as gay as a result of these feminine practices. He says, "I'll sit with my legs crossed like this, like a woman normally sits, but no one would be like, 'Hey, you're gay.' I do my nails. Guys wouldn't notice that anyway."

Due partly, it seems, to Jason's conventional masculine comportment and partly to ideological constructions that position black straight masculinities as exaggeratedly heterosexual and masculine, Jason's "feminine" identity practices are not coded, he says, by others as indicating a gay identity or creating homosexual suspicion of himself. However, he says women tell him he's metrosexual due to his stylish way of dressing and manicured nails. Furthermore, when I ask Jason whether he thinks of himself as a "typical guy," he says no.

> A typical guy's [interest] where they're supposed to live [for] sports, especially football. I hate watching football. It's the most boring thing. I don't mind playing it; it's still boring. Drink beer. Beer tastes like crap to me. Hang around with guys. I don't like doing that. I'd rather hang around with all girls. When you hang around with just guys all the time, all they're talking about are girls. There's only, how long can you talk about something like that for every single day, all the time? So with girls, you don't have to talk about that all the time and you can talk about that with them too. Some of them would mind, some of them won't.

Although Jason prefers women as friends to men, this preference is also motivated by sexual self-interest, as he explains: "One reason why I do it, hang around girls a lot, because I started to notice that they're wrong. The more girls you hang around with, the more girls you get."

Whereas other heterosexual men, he says, are jealous of his numerous "friendships" with heterosexual women, other heterosexual women, he says, find his many female friends to be a source of curiosity. Jason realizes that socializing with only women is coded as a gay identity practice, but he also knows that straight women often enjoy being friends with gay men and consequently they often wonder whether he is gay due to his many female friendships. He uses this stereotype of gay identity to his advantage in pursuing women for sexual relations.

> Even girls that aren't associated with them [his women friends]. They'll wonder why you are hanging around with those girls. Actually, why would those girls hang around with you if they find out that you're not gay? They'll wonder why all these girls are hanging around with you, then you have another girl. . . . No girl's ever asked me if I was gay or anything that sees me associating with a lot of girls. They've never asked me that, but it does attract them more.

Metrosexual men risk being perceived as gay due to not only their style and beauty practices but also the composition of their friendship circles that include groups of women. Jason, however, indicates that a preference for female friends has its benefits as well. Other women, he observes, are curious about him due to his female friends, wondering whether he's gay or not, and as he puts it, "then you have another girl." Also I met Jason's current girlfriend once out at a gay bar and noted that his gay friends introduced them. It seems, then, that Jason's gay friends facilitate him meeting women as well.

However, after a series of questions about whether Jason has ever found himself attracted to men, in which he says that he never has, he becomes defensive in answering questions about his masculinity. For example, knowing from earlier in the interview that his East-Indian Jamaican mother raised him, I ask him, "How do you think your mother shaped your sense of masculinity?" He says,

> Well, I grew up with her. So I was around her all the time and I didn't turn out feminine. I grew up with my cousin, who's a girl. So I pretty much grew up around women my whole life and I never turned out acting feminine in any way. I guess just the way she [my mother] acted and the way she portrayed herself. She never really acted like a girl. She never acted sappy. She didn't show that much emotion to a lot of things.

Jason's defensiveness can be seen in how he emphasizes that even though he grew up around his mother, aunts, and female cousin, he doesn't demonstrate feminine manners associated with women. He then affirms his straight masculine status by not "acting feminine." While he is able to befriend gays and lesbians and admit to me that he has some nonconventional masculine practices that others might see as possibly gay, he aims to maintain his heterosexual privilege by repudiating feminine bodily gestures and comportment. In contrast to Matt, Jason endeavors to maintain his heterosexual status and privilege while embracing antihomophobic values, even when socializing with gay men in gay spaces. However, lacking racial privilege like Matt, Jason does not aim or consciously allow himself to blur boundaries between heterosexuality and homosexuality. Rather, by maintaining straight masculine privilege, Jason makes up for the inequalities of race, class, and color. Although Jason variably embraces an antihomophobic practice, he maintains his heterosexual privilege by assuming that others view him as straight, even in gay bars. For example, when Jason has gone to gay bars, he didn't think that other patrons assumed he was gay, as men neither flirted with him nor asked him about his sexuality. He says, "No one talks to me. No one tries to hit on me or anything. . . . If they asked me [whether I was gay], I would correct it. No, I'm not gay, whatever."

Although Jason's statement that he does not think others view him as gay when he's socializing in gay bars seems dubious to me, his development of an antihomophobic attitude partly comes out of his experiences as a black man dealing with racism in American society. When I asked him why he was supportive of gays, he explained his support by drawing an analogy to being black:

> Because I'm black and if you look at it from the standpoint of the one time black people were discriminated against by everyone. Why would you discriminate against somebody else? Just put yourself in their shoes because you actually can because black people are still discriminated against. So just go to someplace else and see how a gay person feels. It's that they can hide it and a lot of times they do hide it and that messes them up inside. So just let them be who they are because you can't hide who you are.

For him, being antihomophobic is analogous to being antiracist, as he empathizes with the discrimination that gays experience as similar to discrimination against himself and blacks in general.

Further, Jason's pro-gay values are illustrated by his active choice to befriend gay individuals. In college, for example, he chose to live in a dorm suite with a gay student, Adam Atwood, and his boyfriend, Diego Garcia. He recalls the situation:

> I mean he [Adam] kind of tried to hide it [being gay] at first. I did see that they [Adam and Diego] were going to try to hide at first and I was like, "I know Greg," the person that they lived with before; so they must have known that I knew that he [Greg] was gay. By associating with him [Greg], then I [think they thought I] would be friends with them.

As a result of being friends with Adam and Diego, Jason started going more often to gay bars in Orangetown and becoming friendly with other gay individuals.

> I think because I know gay people, they're more visible. When I didn't really, before I met Adam and Diego, they weren't so visible, but now that I know them, they're a lot more visible. . . . Then I met more gay people and then they become more visible. So now I see more gay people. . . . Plus, because of where I am in Orangetown I just see more gay people around. I live around the corner from The Pub [a gay bar].

A post-closeted dynamic conditions the normalization of homosexuality not only for gays but for straights as well. Moreover, this dynamic creates gay and straight friendships and a gay cultural competence for straight men like Jason. However, in a post-closeted dynamic, the integration and routinization of gays and lesbians are not so much institutional as informal and interpersonal.

"If Some Gay Guy Comes On to Me I Think That's Flattering" (Nick Lynch)

Nick lives and works in Center City in Orangetown, an area of the city where local residents, college students, and others patronize a variety of restaurants, bars, and small shops. A couple of blocks down the street from the restaurant-bar Nick works at is one of the five gay bars in Orangetown; the other four are in the vicinity as well. Nick's restaurant-bar, like the other ones in the area, is patronized by straight and gay individuals who comfortably mix together.

For gay-friendly metrosexual men, the dynamics of a post-closeted culture are increasingly routinized by where they socialize and whom they call their friends. That is, the bars and restaurants where they drink and eat, along with the people they know and meet, include out gay men and lesbian women. Consequently, the fact that other individuals they meet are gay and lesbian is taken-for-granted and a normalized facet of their social milieu. Although his experiences are not reflective of the majority of my heterosexual male respondents, Nick nonetheless illustrates the integration and normalization of gays and lesbians as part of America's post-closeted cultural dynamics. Nick's post-closeted context demonstrates a pattern of gay visibility and integration that captures the new kinds of social interactions, interpersonal relationships, and spaces some straight Americans experience as day-to-day life. However, before Nick moved to downtown Orangetown, he says, he held stereotypical views of gay individuals.

> I'd say the initial year I worked and lived down here that I had some pre-conceived notions—all lesbians are fat and ugly and dress like men; gay guys all act like women and are extremely effeminate. But I mean after working down here, after a while I knew that there was no way in hell just by looking at a person that you could tell. I met a lot of guys that I thought were straight turned out to be gay [and] the other way around. Same thing with women.

Living and working in downtown Orangetown changed Nick's stereo-typical perceptions of gays *and* straights. The ideological construc-tions that associate gay men with femininity and straight men with masculinity were challenged by his experiences of living in downtown Orangetown, where a diversity of gay and straight individuals' gender performances are evident. These gay and straight men's masculine per-formances overlap in their embodiment of gender, challenging the nor-mative expectation that men's masculinities indicate their sexual identi-ties. As Nick observes, "I mean I've met gay men who were more butch than I am and they're muscular; they're like manly manly. They've got deep voices; they play sports. They just happen to be sexually and romantically attracted to men." As a result of his experiences, Nick now tries not to assume that gender practices indicate one's sexual identity. His past homophobic stereotyping of all gay men as feminine and all lesbians as masculine is replaced by an antihomophobic practice that is now critical of those gender and sexual normative constructions.

A recent incident demonstrates his antihomophobia and how it shapes his interpersonal relationships with male friends who he thinks might be gay but doesn't know for sure. In this case, Nick explains that he disclosed his sexual identity to his new friend, Ryan Caputo, only after finding out that Ryan had a crush on him. He recounts the incident:

NICK: Something happened a couple of weeks ago where I had a regular customer who said he wanted to hang out some time. After we hung out, his female roommate asked me why I hadn't made a move on him and I was just like, "What are you talking about?" We were hanging out in a crowd—sometimes we hang out at his house, but there are other people there. I'm not gay. I mean, I kind of had an intention to tell him [that I'm straight], but he had never broached the subject. So I was just gonna leave it be until he did. So I mean he knows now that I'm not interested in him like that, but . . . I didn't know right away whether or not he was gay or straight. He exuded some stereotypical gay qualities at times, but he had never mentioned it to me. I mean he's nineteen years old. I'm twenty-two. He told me he had girlfriends in the past. So I wasn't gonna assume anything until I knew for sure, and then I found out by his female roommate telling me that he had a crush on me.

JAMES: So what did you think was gay about him?

NICK: I don't know. It's just kind of like a feeling.

JAMES: But you said there were some stereotypical things. Like what?

NICK: He's quite effeminate, the way he dressed—very tight designer clothes. I don't know, just having these words come out of my mouth almost sounds like stereotyping.

Nick's antihomophobic stance problematizes the coding of masculinity practices as indicative of a heterosexual or a homosexual identity. He understands the subtle normative heterosexual practice enacted by labeling sexual identity through masculine conventionality or lack thereof. Also, his desire to not label masculine practices as indicating a straight status is also representative of his own experiences in being misperceived as gay. By being friends with many gay men, Nick has been exposed to a diversity of masculine and feminine gay male styles and knows that gay men sometimes fit stereotypes and sometimes don't.

Sexual fluidity and the exploration of sexual desires and identities are also things Nick is familiar with as a result of being part of this post-closeted culture. He recounts how his best friend recently started to date a woman:

> I've had friends who in the process of the past few years have ques-
> tioned their own sexual identities, have gone from straight to gay or
> went from straight, gay, then straight again, just experimenting. . . . Up
> until recently, I thought, well, we both thought, she [my best friend] was
> straight, but she just recently started dating a girl and is giving that a
> chance because she's starting to question her own sexuality. She's my best
> friend. Like two months ago, I would have said she was straight and now
> I have no idea where it's going.

Sexual desire and identities escape rigid classifications like gay and straight among Nick's circle of friends. Sexually fluid desires and identities also represent an anti-normalizing or queer politics and ethics of everyday life, where new identities, identifications, and relations emerge and resist the constrictions of normalization and its reduction of sexual desire to an identity category (see Meeks 2002, 327–32; Seidman 1997, 212–36; and Ward 2008b, 147–49).

Although none of the straight men I interviewed discussed practices of sexual fluidity as part of their sense of sexual identification,[3] Nick's response to the question of whether he could imagine himself having sexual desires for another man in the future illustrates his own sense of heterosexual subjectivity while reflecting his experience of his best friend having engaged in same-sex practices unexpectedly. He explains,

> Well, I mean it's hard to tell. Like I said, I've had friends who have
> changed their sexual identity. I mean at this point in time I've never had
> a sexual fantasy, I've never had a daydream about dating a guy. I've never

thought of a male friend like that in any way, shape, or form. So I really, like right now as a person, I'm saying no for the future, but there's no way to tell how you change as life progresses.

Hegemonic masculinity is defined in part by defensiveness in being viewed as feminine or homosexual; Nick's metrosexual masculinity counters this, replacing defensiveness with a relational openness. We can further see this lack of defensiveness in the fact that Nick does not feel compelled to disclose his heterosexual status in everyday conversation. For example, when I ask, "Do you ever let people know you're a hetero-sexual by talking about girls or someone you dated? Do you say, 'Oh my girlfriend or ex-girlfriend,' or something like that?" Nick responds,

Not in initial conversation. I don't think it makes that big a difference. Like I'm not guarded about my heterosexuality. If some gay guy comes on to me I think that's flattering. If he finds me attractive, it's a self-esteem booster, whatever, but I'm not gonna lead him on. But I also don't like talking to somebody for the first time and just being like, throw[ing] out all these cues and making sure they know I'm straight. Somebody who knows me and has spent enough time with me they know that I'm straight; I've only dated girls. It's not something that I feel needs to be said.

In contrast to the straight men who reacted homophobically when viewed as gay, as discussed in chapter 3, Nick is flattered when a man flirts with him, taking it as a compliment that this man found him attractive. For Nick, being taken as gay is not an insult, nor does this compliment imply a loss or assault on his masculinity. He does not aim to signal his straight status in a defensive or anxious manner, as people who know him would already know he's straight. Nick's social contexts and the makeup of his groups of friends matter as well. By being exposed to a diversity of gender displays among gay men and calling many gay, lesbian, and bisexual individuals friends, he gains prestige among them as well as among his gay-friendly straight friends for having a "secure" heteromasculinity. Nick and his social world, then, represent a significant shift in the social construction of straight masculinities and a serious challenge to its hegemonic order.

Gay-Friendly, but Not Metrosexual: Chris Savage and
Variations in Heterosexual Masculine Styles

Chris Savage is a thirty-three-year-old black man who grew up in Orangetown. Wearing his hair in corn rows, he is direct during our interview. Unlike the men discussed previously, Chris is not metrosexual, and his style practices do not blur gay and straight identity codes. Rather, due to racial and racist codes of black heterosexual masculine styles as markers of potential aggression, violence, and danger, Chris recounts how people, mostly white people, react to him and his urban dress style when he is walking on the streets of downtown Orangetown:

> [I]f I wear a coat that has sort of an urban look, I could be on my way anywhere, I think that people automatically assume, "Here's some thug," "Here's some street kid," or whatever. Sometimes I appear to look younger than I actually am. So that also takes into effect and I just think that I start seeing people grabbing, if I'm walking by a kid, grab their kid or grab their pocketbook. "Are you serious?" There are other times, if I have a shirt and a tie on and some khakis, people speak to me, they smile at me. . . . You get perceived in a better light when you do have on khakis, not necessarily a tie but a collared shirt, a leather jacket, as opposed to some designer jacket by some rap group or whatever.

Similar to many of the black straight men I interviewed, Chris dresses in an urban style that does not mark him as potentially gay. Rather, black urban styles code these men as hypermasculine and, by extension, exaggerate their straight virility in America's popular culture imaginary. However, he says that due to working at a local gym in Orangetown known for its gay membership and as a gay cruising space, some of the black women he has dated questioned his heterosexuality:

> I've actually dated several women that thought I was gay. Mainly because I work at the Orangetown Gym. The Orangetown Gym has sometimes, it's characterized as a pickup place for people who are homosexual. I never. It doesn't apply to me. I think she [my girlfriend] was just pretty shallow and just generalizing to everybody.

I asked Chris whether he thought that this perception of him as possibly gay was also due to recent media coverage last year of the down low phenomenon that his girlfriend might have heard about, especially because of the *Oprah Winfrey Show*'s broadcast in April 2004, which featured the author J. L. King talking about his controversial book *On the Down Low* (2004).[4] I interviewed Chris in March 2005. I asked, "Do you think it's the idea that there are people who are on the down low and that's why she's so doubtful?" He said,

> Well, I did I have an incident where I was in jail briefly and so people always correlate bad, you know, sexual abuse in jail and I don't know. I'm a short guy in stature or whatever and I don't really act tough. I don't run around threatening people, cursing at them. I try to talk to people with respect. She was probably thinking how could this guy make it in such a ruthless place with these types of mannerisms. I can be, I can defend myself basically. I can adjust to whatever environment you put me in. If I need to be more assertive or aggressive, I can be. But it's not necessarily something I do naturally.

Prisons are a place where men have sex with other men for a variety of reasons, from being coerced and raped to choosing to temporarily engage in homosexual sex while incarcerated to identifying as bisexual or gay and desiring to have sex with men (see Rust 2000). It is also well documented that one in nine black men between the ages of twenty and thirty-four are incarcerated, and that overall one in fifteen black adults is in jail (Liptak 2008). This high and disproportional rate of black male incarceration, then, showed up in my sample through interviews with black straight men like Chris. For these black straight men, the discourse of the down low and homosexual sex practices were associated with experiences of incarceration, leading some respondents and their social circles to associate prison with homosexuality.

Chris describes himself as having been homophobic for most of his life, explaining that he did not associate with lesbian and gay individuals until somewhat recently. This change occurred in 2000. After he was released from prison that year, Chris decided to volunteer at the Orangetown Gym. As a volunteer there, Chris met his current coworker, Henry Merchant, a black gay personal trainer, who took

Chris under his wing and taught him how to be a fitness instructor. Chris says,

> I wasn't trying to hang out with them [gays]. I wasn't trying to do nothing with them. After meeting Henry, his generosity as far as just trying to teach me different things. . . . I had just got out [of prison]; I was in a halfway house. And I just wanted to help people. And I decided I would volunteer at the Orangetown Gym. So I volunteered there and wasn't sure what I was going to do. Henry [said,] "Why don't you be my assistant fitness person. I'm going to show you what to do." He took me around. Taught me how to teach aerobics classes, taught me how to do step moves, and stuff like that. Once I started getting used to these things, I was like, "Man, this is a honor. I really appreciate this guy taking the time out. From this point on, I will not judge anyone based on their sexuality." And between that time, 2000 and now, I also found out from my kids' mother that she was sort of having these bisexual encounters and it just made, it all hit me around the same time from two different angles.

Chris's friendship with Henry caused him to reflect on his own stance toward homosexuality and his disrespect of gay people. As a result of this transformative friendship, Chris now embraces pro-gay values and calls several lesbian and gay individuals friends. His stance toward same-sex marriage and lesbian and gay families is illustrative of this.

> First of all, from my experience the people who I know are gay are good people. So good people, great character, good jobs, that leaves room for good upbringing and stability. The only thing they may have. Their children, whether they adopt or whatever, will have to learn how to deal [with them being gay]. But I think that the love that will be expressed in that household will overcome any joke or threat that may be made to the child about the parents, about their parents being lesbian or gay. So I support it [same-sex marriage] 100 percent, and plus it's another tax bracket. Overall, I think it can help the state of the economy, but people have to be more willing to hear [gay] folks' side, from the lesbian, from the homosexual, not so much about why they are [gay] but what they bring to the table. Then I think it will be a little bit easier for us to start moving forward.

Having grown up and lived in Orangetown his whole life, Chris invariably encounters acquaintances who inquire about Keyshia Baldwin, the mother of his three children, and her sexual involvement with women over the last couple of years. As a result of being friends with gay individuals and no longer viewing homosexuality as morally wrong and shameful, Chris is now less perturbed by questions regarding Keyshia's sexuality.

> It just put it into perspective for me. With regards to what is going on that you're going to have friends regardless of what their sexuality is. It's not going to be a problem. I'm not concerned about what people may say about me. So once I got that part down, it helped me become friends with Henry; it helped me with my kids' mother. Because now I occasionally may see somebody [who asks], "Is your kids' mother gay?" I'm like, "I'm not really sure. You'll have to ask her." It prepared [me] to answer questions that usually I might have in the past, I would have been offended, like, "Who you talking to? You talkin' to me? About my kids' mother? Don't be talking in a disrespectin' manner when she's not here." I'm a little more at ease with it. I can talk about it without getting all ruffled and things. It's not that serious.

Reflecting on homophobia in the black community, Chris says that the association of homosexuality with HIV/AIDS continues to be one impetus in the stigmatization of gay people.

> I know that in the African American community it's like we don't even want to deal with [homosexuality] because it automatically put us into that helpless category of now we are going to be perceived, even though the numbers are already there as far as HIV and AIDS. I think it will just even heighten that awareness and I think that it will just kind of cut us off from maybe having relationships with other races. So I definitely think that's an issue.

Insightfully, Chris explains that the silence and invisibility around homosexuality in Orangetown's black community are partly due to the black community's reluctance to negotiate the stigma of homosexuality and HIV/AIDS in addition to the racial and racist attitudes and discourses they must already manage.

Although Chris's urban, nonmetrosexual style of dress marks him as embodying a conventional black straight masculinity, his antihomophobic values are partly the result of his friendship with Henry, a black gay coworker who went out of his way to train Chris as a fitness instructor. Moreover, this friendship's transformative power extends beyond his comfort in having gay friends or his political support of same-sex marriage, but also helps him to manage questions about the sexuality of the mother of his children from inquisitive acquaintances.

"I'm Just a Sloppy Heterosexual-Looking Kind of Guy" (Ken Stacey)

Ken Stacey is a thirty-three-year-old white male who works as a research scientist in the larger Orangetown metropolitan area. Ken is a tall man with a closely shaved haircut who appears intimidating due to his large stature and masculine appearance. However, he has a kind demeanor and is a strong advocate for gays with his friends and family. Both he and his wife consider some of their closest friends to be lesbians and gay men whom they have known for over a decade.

Like Chris, Ken does not blur gay and straight identity codes in his style practices, nor does anyone associate him with a gay or metrosexual style. Rather, Ken illustrates how some heterosexual men paradoxically experience their lack of an ostensibly gay or metrosexual style as a sense of exclusion from being perceived as fashionable, attractive, and valued for their appearance. Instead, these heterosexual men view their nonmetrosexual masculinity as a mark of their inability to exhibit "good" taste, male beauty, and verbal acumen. Voicing a sense of low self-esteem regarding his appearance, style, and self-presentation, Ken says,

> Gay men are usually better-looking, have better hair, better clothes, more articulate. That type of thing. You know almost like a metrosexual. [They have] some kind of treatment to their hair. But just in general care a lot about their appearance, good-looking, in good shape. I'm bald, overweight. I usually don't dress well unless my wife helps me. I'm just a sloppy heterosexual-looking kind of guy; someone that you definitely wouldn't think of as looking gay. Maybe I'm just not attractive enough [laughs].

Although some straight men deride gay and metrosexual style practices for their association with femininity and for blurring the identity markers of gays and straights, other straight men, like Ken, expressed a sense of shame and envy due to their nonfashionable styles, larger body sizes, and presentation of self.

Perhaps not surprisingly, Ken uses the term "metrosexual" to jokingly refer to other heterosexual men who dress well, like his sister's boyfriend, Walter Close. In his interactions with Walter, who dresses stylishly, Ken makes Walter uncomfortable by calling him a "metrosexual." He says,

> Everyone [in my family] kind of jokes once in a while that he [Walter] looks, that he is metrosexual. It's kind of a running joke. He is definitely uncomfortable with the idea of being gay or gay people. So it's kind of a running joke on him that he looks metrosexual.

Even though Ken is overall quite strong in his support of lesbians and gays, there is a subtle homophobic implication in this labeling of Walter as metrosexual. By jokingly calling Walter a metrosexual, Ken reinforces and plays on an emasculating, normative heterosexual discourse by implying that Walter enacts gay/metrosexual style practices, which bring into question Walter's heterosexual masculine status. However, in the context of knowing that Ken feels devalued for his lack of a gay/metrosexual masculine style, this joke perhaps indicates feelings of envy of Walter's style as well.

That practices of sexual fluidity were absent among my straight male respondents illustrates gender differences between men's and women's sexual subjectivities, as some scholars note (Diamond 2008). The disciplinary norms that construct and constrain straight masculinities often posit the lack of homosexual desires and behaviors as the basis of a straight identity (Anderson 2008), whereas same-sex practices among straight-identified women are often condoned. Same-sex behaviors often lack the same cultural weight of stigma when enacted by "straight" women than when practiced by men.

However, what I did find among the straight men in my sample is the development of conscious fantasies of homosexual desires and identities; something scholars have noted as constitutive of the unconscious psyches and fantasies of heterosexuals in general (Butler 1990; Chodorow 1998; Kimmel and Messner 2010, 371). Ken, for example, discusses conscious fantasies of same-sex desire in relation to gay media images and asserts that they have caused him to think about his own sexual identity. He talks in particular about *Kinsey*, a film about the life and work of the pioneering sexuality scholar Alfred Kinsey:

> I would say I'm heterosexual. But I'm just thinking of the movie *Kinsey*. I remember him saying in the movie that no one's 100 percent gay or 100 percent straight. We're all somewhere in the middle, whether it's 99 percent straight or 97 percent gay or whatever it is. And I'd say I'm, I'm really not sure I'd say 95 percent straight. I always think that there is a little piece of me that is, I don't know what the word is, possibly gay or at least open to that idea. And I don't mean to say I'm attracted to men or anything like that. Of course, the ideas cross your mind; they definitely don't repulse me so. There's always a little piece of me that considers it.

Ken's antihomophobia means the ability to think about his own homosexual fantasies, and it also demonstrates his view of gay and straight men as moral equals. Although Ken relies on his marital status and conventional masculine practices to project a clear straight masculinity, he openly discusses the idea of gay sex, the type of men he is attracted to, and how gay media visibility in movies such as *Kinsey* and TV shows like *Queer as Folk* and *Sex and the City* have encouraged him to think about his own homosexual desires, even though he tells me he has not had sex with a man.

> KEN: The gayest thing that ever happen to me, I would watch *Sex and the City* with my wife. And I don't consider myself gay and I'm not attracted to men, but I was saying to her if I was gay the guy that I would fall in love with is one of the guys on there, it's Mr. Big. It's, I don't know if you've seen the show?
>
> JAMES: Yeah, [the actress] Sarah Jessica's?
>
> KEN: Her boyfriend and because I like to smoke cigars and he does. His apartment, just his mannerisms. The fact that he's funny just attracted me to him, and I would say that to my wife and we would just laugh. When I say attracted, I like him as a person. I think he's

funny. If he's standing in front of me, I don't think I would want to kiss him or anything. But it was one of those things, where if I was gay that'd be my first choice for a man to be with [*laughs*].

Ken is confiding in me something that he's talked about privately with his wife. His hedges and qualifications suggest that this expression of sexual fluidity is a delicate issue for him, and it is opened up in part by my interview's line of questioning. It is a living example, happening or emerging in the interview as we speak. Analytically, his narrative demonstrates that close friendships with gay men as well as lesbian and gay media images have created the psychological and social space for him to imagine what it would be like to be gay and the type of man he would be attracted to. However, it is also convenient for Ken to name a male actor as the man he finds sexually attractive. In comparison to those gay individuals Ken actually knows and interacts with, a well-known actor is a *safe* fantasy male to name, due to the very fact that ever meeting, let alone being sexually involved with, the actor who plays Mr. Big is exceedingly far-fetched and unattainable for most Americans. Nonetheless, Ken's antihomophobic practices entail not only the condemnation of prejudice and discrimination toward gays but also something not openly talked about by married heterosexual men—that is, a comfort in imagining what it would be like to be gay and thus a queering of straight masculinity to a limited extent.

In conclusion, metrosexual masculinities lie between hegemonic masculine constructions and subordinated gay masculinities. They negotiate the relationships among conventional masculine behaviors, sexual identities, and the accompanying privilege or subordination of those identity statuses. That metrosexual men blur gay and straight identity codes and variably embrace "feminine" practices of style, taste, and fashion speaks to the normalization of feminine-gay associations among heterosexual men (and women).

The metrosexual men I interviewed blurred normative heterosexual boundaries and made nonnormative their own straight heterosexual masculine identity practices at various times. Moreover, it is the mixing and making indistinct of the straight/gay identity practices that illustrate how counterhegemonic discourses and practices enter into heterosexual masculinities, demonstrating their gay-affirmative values and antihomophobia. The limit or danger of metrosexuality is its potential to be recoded into another type of dominant masculinity, its potential to recuperate straight privilege by coding metrosexual behaviors, styles, and fashions into a strictly straight identity practice, repudiating its gay associations. This potential for the recuperation of metrosexual masculinities points to both the homogenizing, blunting force of normative heterosexuality and the constant limits nonnormative heterosexual masculinities negotiate in everyday life. Metrosexual masculinity may end up presenting no threat to hegemonic masculinity, and instead may become part of a new constellation of dominant masculinities.

It is important to note that nonnormative practices also take a back seat at various times in everyday life. Each of these straight men aimed at various times to project an unambiguous heterosexual masculine identity by showing interest in women. While showing interest in women may be done in conscious or even strategic ways, a claim to heterosexual privilege is often an unconscious action. In other words, the ability to "do" heterosexual masculinity without knowing it is part of what constitutes its status as privilege. The assumption of heterosexual status and its accompanying privilege is central to how men achieve respect in everyday life and of course accurately reflects and defines their sense of self as well. Consequently, it is accurate to argue that metrosexual men both contest and reinforce hegemonic masculinity through their gender practices and strategies in everyday life. This notwithstanding, metrosexual men typically projected their straight masculinity through antihomophobic practices that problematized the stigmatization of lesbians and gays, and they thus serve as models of respect, equality, and justice in a society where differences of sexuality continue to matter in everyday life and in political battles for rights and recognition.

Queered Straight Femininities and Sexual Fluidity

In her book *Sexual Fluidity: Understanding Women's Love and Desire*, the psychologist Lisa Diamond (2008) demonstrates that sexual fluidity, defined as "situation-dependent flexibility in women's sexual responsiveness," ranging from desires and fantasies to actual sexual behaviors, is a central facet of nonheterosexual women's sexualities (4). Using longitudinal data over a ten-year period to track seventy-nine lesbian, bisexual, and unlabeled but nonheterosexual-identified women, Diamond finds that sexual fluidity is a central social-psychological organizing principle in these women's sexual desires and identities (56–59). For instance, she states,

> among the two-thirds of women who changed their identities over the ten-year period of the study, most undertook changes that accommodated a broadening of their attractions rather than increased exclusivity. Specifically, women were more likely to switch to unlabeled and bisexual identities than to heterosexual or lesbian identities over the ten years of the study. In fact, by 2005 [when the study ended] fully 80 percent of the sample had identified as bisexual or unlabeled for at least some period of time. (105)

This study systematically documents the relative expansiveness of sexual desire among women, but its findings are based on a sample of *nonheterosexual women*, and an emphasis on sociological forces such as normative heterosexuality are often absent from its analysis. Further, the social contexts in which these women broadened their attractions are not explored, nor are the meanings they gave to these shifts in their sexual experiences and behaviors.

This notwithstanding, Diamond also interviewed eleven heterosexual women as a comparison group to the seventy-nine nonheterosexual women. She recruited these heterosexual women from a college class on sexuality, which, she suggests, conditioned their ability and openness to discuss the dynamics of sexual fluidity:

> Of course, the very fact that these women were willing to sit down and talk to me about why they considered themselves heterosexual, and whether that might ever change, makes them unrepresentative of the average heterosexual woman! Most heterosexual women never even think about their sexual identity; *the presumption of universal heterosexuality is so strong that they never have to question it*. (58; italics mine)

Although this statement captures the status of heterosexuality as a norm, it overstates its current compulsory power (Seidman 2002;

Walters 2001) as well as underplays sexual fluidity as a central part of *all* women's sexualities, which is the central argument Diamond puts forth more generally.[5]

Prior research by the psychologist Carla Golden (1996) with college-educated and non–college-educated heterosexual women shows that sexual fluidity is evidenced by straight women and their imagining of the possibilities of being in lesbian relationships. Golden notes that the concept of sexual fluidity was encountered by her sample of college heterosexual women when they enrolled in women's studies courses, joined feminist groups with lesbian members, and engaged with other materials that discussed sexual fluidity. For some of these heterosexual college women, thinking of sexuality as situational, person-dependent, and fluid confirmed their sense of heterosexuality as an unchanging, "primary" part of their self. However, others agreed that their sexuality was fluid but "thinking about sexuality, however, had led them to make a conscious choice *not* to explore their lesbian or bisexual potential" (Golden 1996, 237). For these straight women, the stigma of homosexuality was too powerful a barrier for them in exploring nonheterosexual relationships and identities. Golden also interviewed a group of feminist women between the ages of twenty-eight and forty-five who experienced their sexuality as fluid but were heterosexually identified or partnered. In contrast, these feminist women said they could imagine themselves being in relationships with women in the future if their current heterosexual relationships ended.

Golden's research highlights two important sociological conditions in heterosexual women's adoption and understandings of sexual fluidity. First and foremost, women must simply be exposed to the notion of sexual fluidity, and, second, this exposure to and thinking about sexual fluidity must occur in contexts that support critical thought and experimentation with one's sexuality, and affirm the lives of lesbian, bisexual, and queer women.

The sociologist Arlene Stein (1997), in her book *Sex and Sensibility: Stories of a Lesbian Generation*, explains that 1970s lesbian feminism created a sociohistorical context that conceptualized lesbian identity to be as much a political commitment to other women as a sexual desire for them. If political solidarity—not sexual desire—defined lesbian identity in the 1970s, the late 1980s and 1990s witnessed the queering or decentering of lesbian feminism from within, Stein argues (1992, 1997). This process of decentering lesbian feminism included increased recognition for, among others, former or ex-lesbians, whose sexual fluidity led them to ambivalently leave behind their lesbian identifications and form relationships with men.

Focusing on formerly identified lesbians, Stein charts variations in how these women negotiated the process of leaving behind their lesbian identity and points out that unlike most heterosexual women who do not have a highly developed sense of sexuality as a socially constructed process, ex-lesbians did. Additionally, she notes, "They were often highly aware of 'heterosexual privilege,' recognizing that the greater the number of individuals who came out as lesbians, the more powerful and less stigmatized lesbians in general would be" (172).

Keeping these insights about sexual fluidity and ex-lesbians' recognition of straight privilege in mind, we can see that a queered heterosexual feminine identification similarly recognizes straight privilege and homophobia as social forces that stigmatize same-sex desire and aim to divide sexuality into discrete identity categories (e.g., straight or lesbian), thus locating queer sexuality within a polluted minority group. However, queered straight femininities counter normative heterosexuality through their antihomophobic practices that affirm queer persons and same-sex desires. These women enact same-sex desires through their own adoption of sexual fluidity, making same-sex desire a part of their own queered identifications. In their everyday lives, queered straight women embrace identity practices that blur lesbian/straight boundaries by flirting with women, by refusing to disclose their straight identity when homosexual suspicion arises, and by integrating sexual desires for women into their own self-experiences.

Following Stein's historical outline, the period 1990–2010 is not only a time of the decentering of lesbian identity, but also a time when the normalization and integration of lesbians and gay men into mainstream American life takes an upward turn (Loftus 2001; Stein 2010). As a result of a post-closeted dynamic, straight Americans experience the efflorescence of lesbian, gay, and queer cultural practices that condition and support straights who contest and oppose straight privilege and homophobia. Queered heterosexualities are part of both the normalization of lesbian and gay sexualities and the persistence of antinormalizing queer practices and discourses that circulate in LGBT subcultures.

The queered straight feminine identifications in my sample emerged out of the friendships between these straight women and their lesbian, gay, and queer friends. Ten (six white and four black women) of the twenty-nine heterosexual women discussed fantasies and experiences of sexual fluidity with me during the interview (see table A.2 in the appendix for the demographic characteristics of these women). The ten women who embraced sexually fluid practices are indicated by the number sign (#) after their name in table A.2.

These queered straight women's experiences of sexual fluidity grew out of queer-affirmative contexts that supported their fantasies and experiences of same-sex sexuality. These contexts ranged from having an older sister who identified as bisexual or sexually fluid to forming friendships with lesbians and gay men or being part of social circles in college where there was an active lesbian and gay student body. For instance, some recall attending gay events like popular dances sponsored by their college's gay/queer student union. Other women talked about feminist, lesbian, and gay subject materials being part of their college curriculum, along with queer students who lived the curriculum. Some women identify living and working in downtown Orangetown's mixed gay/straight neighborhood as crucial to developing their political identification with lesbian, gay, and bisexual friends. Regardless of the particular context in which these women were introduced to queer persons and culture, what they have in common is the set of queer-affirmative values they experienced, fostered by spaces for exploring sexual difference and the communities of queer people.

Of the ten women who discussed their experiences of sexual fluidity with me, only seven of them blurred boundaries between heterosexual and homosexual identity practices. For these seven straight women, their insistence on contesting boundaries is connected to their political identification with queer friends and the larger queer community. Although I do not argue that these heterosexual women's pro-gay political stances caused them to engage in same-sex intimacy, I do suggest that their willingness to blur lesbian/straight boundaries and engage in sexualized and sexual encounters with women does develop out of their membership in lesbian, gay, and queer subcultures; moreover, their experiences of sexual fluidity are made meaningful in relationship to their queer friends who have come out and processed the normative status of heterosexuality and its stigmatizing of homosexuality. For these seven straight women, being strongly antihomophobic means at times taking on lesbian and queer labels to combat homophobia, including experiencing same-sex sexuality. Their acts of sexual fluidity are embodied expressions of their belief in the equivalent standing of homosexuality and heterosexuality. By labeling these seven straight women "queered straight women," I mean to capture their boundary-blurring practices, antihomophobic politics, and various acts of sexual fluidity. These seven straight women are positioned as blurring boundaries on the continuum.

Before I discuss the seven straight women with queered identifications, I briefly elaborate on the three straight women who enact their sexuality as fluid but establish weak, as opposed to blurred, boundaries. Table 5.2 is a cross-classification of the straight women respondents by whether they experienced their sexuality as fluid or not, crossed by their position on the continuum as blurring boundaries or not. If they did not blur boundaries between gay and straight identity practices, then they fell on either the weak or strong end of the continuum's spectrum. (Again, table A.2 in the appendix provides an overview of the women respondents' position on the continuum and their demographics; the ten women who embraced sexually fluid practices are indicated by the number sign after their name.)

Sexually Fluid but Not Queered: Straight Women and Private Same-Sex Experiences

In contrast to the seven queered straight women, there were three other straight women who enacted their sexuality as fluid to varying degrees. But these three women neither blurred boundaries between heterosexual and homosexual identity practices nor took on at any point the label of bisexual, lesbian, or queer; they thus cannot be thought of as "queered" in their heterosexual identity perspectives. Rather, their experience of same-sex sexuality was more of a private experience, whether as evidenced in a fantasy of another woman or in an actual relationship with one. A key characteristic of these three straight women is that

Table 5.2. Cross-Classification of Straight Women Respondents

Cross-Classification	Sexually Fluid	Not Sexually Fluid
Blurred Boundaries	7	0
Weak or Strong Boundaries	3	19

they do not incorporate their experiences of sexual fluidity into their straight feminine identities. As we will see, unlike the queered straight women, these three women do not express strong political identifications with lesbian, gay, or queer friends and subcultures. While they have gay friends, support the right to same-sex marriage, and view gays and straights as equals, they define their sexual identities as narrowly heterosexual.

Consider Eve Donegal. Eve is a fifty-nine-year-old white mother of three daughters, who has been separated from her second husband for over a year now. She has shortly cropped hair and speaks in a pleasant, matter-of-fact tone, but seems a little distracted, as her twenty-one-year-old daughter, her youngest, is supposed to call her for directions at some point during our interview. Sitting in front of her work desk, after work hours, when nobody else is around, I ask Eve to define her sexual identity and to tell me what it means to her. She replies, "straight. I have a preference to have physical, sexual contact with people of the opposite sex."

Regarding sexual identity practices that perform a gay identity, Eve explains that she's not a good reader of those kinds of interactional cues. "Well, I hear people talk about gaydar and stuff like that and I really don't have a clue when I first meet somebody. . . . Actually, I think people tell me someone is gay and I'm surprised." Although she's not quick to pick up on expressions of sexual identity, Eve tells me she is close to several lesbian and gay friends. For instance, a lesbian coworker of hers came out to her over a decade ago, and this made them closer friends. Besides her gay friends, she is also friends with her eldest daughter's best friend, who happens to be a gay male, and has hosted him at her home and visited with him and her daughter in New York City, where they live.

Although Eve is supportive of gay friends, she says she purposefully avoids blurring some gay/straight boundaries. She tells me, "I don't put a rainbow sticker on the car. I know that that's definitely a symbol of sexual preference. I wouldn't do that because I'm not gay and because I'm thinking that people who do do it are saying that they are that." Of course, it isn't homophobic to not put a rainbow sticker on one's car's bumper, but it does show how Eve is conscious of negotiating gay/ straight identity symbols to indicate her straight status.

Regarding whether her own appearance performs a clear straight femininity, Eve recalls a friend of hers who thought she might have been a lesbian due to her short hair, but otherwise she says most people who know her would identify her as straight due to her having been married for most of her adult life. However, when I asked, "Besides the woman who commented on your short hair, has anyone else ever thought you were gay?" Eve says, "No, but I do know, I have a friend who would think that I was bisexual. I did have a woman lover at one point. Back in the '60s."

As this same-sex relationship occurred before her first marriage, when Eve was in her early twenties, I asked whether it had changed her sense of her sexual identity. She explains, "I think it made me realize that you can have sexual pleasure regardless of gender. It made me far more understanding of where those energies come from." I ask whether she would be open to having another sexual relationship with a woman today. "I'm not closing the door to it," she says, "but really know at this point in my life that I am far more attracted to men than women, physically."

During the interview Eve confided that she recently posted an Internet dating profile on a popular website, where she defined herself as heterosexual by stating that she was looking for a long-term relationship with a man. In Eve's case, it seems that her sexual fluidity is a thing of the past, as she has been married twice and finds herself to prefer sexual relationships with men. Indeed, she neither connects this past experience of sexual fluidity to her current sexual identity status nor expresses a sense of it directly informing her own pro-gay stances. Rather, her same-sex relationship of over thirty years ago seems to be more of a private experience that she shared with me in being candid about her own sexual life journey and its complexity.

Like Eve, Vera Godina, a twenty-year-old white ethnically Russian college student, shyly tells me that she has found herself attracted to women while still self-identifying as heterosexual. I ask her who she found attractive. Hesitantly she replies, "It was like people in movies. Like whatever. She's really pretty." "Like who?" I ask. "Angelina Jolie," she says. However, Vera confides to me that she hasn't had a sexual encounter with another woman. Asked whether she would be interested in one, she explains, "I don't know. I'm not sure I would want to and I'm not sure how it would feel in the future."

In contrast to Eve, who is almost sixty, Vera has her whole life ahead of her. Both her age and her expected college degree position Vera with a wide set of possibilities and life paths. However, at this point in time, Vera's straight status remains unchallenged by an actual sexual experience with another woman. Besides telling me about her attraction to women, she says she's disclosed this only to her past summer female roommates, who confided to her first about their bisexuality and interest in women, too. Unlike the queered straight women and their social circles of openly lesbian and gay friends, neither Vera nor her bisexual female friends are out and open about their same-sex attractions.

In short, Vera and Eve neither consider themselves members of a larger queer community nor think of their sexual fluidity as part of their antihomophobia. Rather, their experiences and thoughts of sexual fluidity are private feelings that they shared with me in their willingness to be interviewed about straight identities and the complex nature of sexual desires.

Maya Gaines and the Social Context of Queered Heterosexual Women

Maya, a nineteen-year-old black college student, says that since high school she has had lesbian classmates and friends who she knew growing up. She moved to Orangetown to go to college and has become friendly with some of her sister's lesbian and gay friends. Commenting on what she thinks of as the state of gay life and its integration into the fabric of day-to-day existence in downtown Orangetown, Maya explains,

> If I saw two gay guys kissing or holding hands, I would just walk by just
> as if it was a guy and a girl, but I think some people would maybe walk

by, not now, but a couple years ago, would have been like, "Why are they doing that, especially in public?" "That's disgusting" type of thing.

For Maya, lesbians' and gay men's public displays of affection are normal and unremarkable. She thinks that attitudes like hers are a growing trend, and she takes the lack of others' negative reactions toward lesbian and gay displays of public affection as illustrative of this trend toward tolerance.

In her short dating history, Maya has dated only men. Although she says she is quite affectionate toward her female friends, from holding their hands in public to kissing them on the lips or sitting in each other's laps, she views her physical affection toward her female friends as demonstrative of feelings of friendship, platonic love, and not sexual interest. These same-sex displays, though, might be read as a strategy that indicates sexual openness to potential male mates. Like Jason Robson's strategy of associating with groups of women in meeting potential sexual partners, Maya's strategy might be a heterosexual feminine equivalent for attracting heterosexual male partners.

Subjectively, however, Maya does draw a boundary between these affectionate displays and being sexually intimate with a woman as the difference between being straight and being lesbian. When I ask Maya how she defines her sexual identity and what it means to her, her response indicates this:

> As straight. . . . To me it means that if a girl approached me at a bar, I would turn her down, you know. I don't, I think girls are attractive and, like I don't judge girls, but if I see a girl, I'll say, "Oh, she's a good-looking one." Like I have a friend, I always say she's beautiful, and she thinks she's ugly. Like I have no problem telling a female they're [sic] attractive, but if one made a move on me, I wouldn't, as far as I know, I wouldn't go for it. So, that's straight to me.

If Maya had sexual encounters with women, then according to her self-definition she would not be straight, but since she does not have sex with women, she is straight. Clear enough. However, when I ask whether she has ever been aware of sexual feelings for a person of the same sex, she explains,

Not really. No, except Angelina Jolie. Like if she called me up and was like, "Hey, let's make out," I'd make out with her, but I think she's absolutely beautiful, the most gorgeous, hottest person on earth.

The interesting subtext of Maya's response to this question is that in her everyday life she does not think of women as potentially sexual or romantic partners, but when asked to imagine a woman who might change her mind, she thinks of a famous actress known for her beauty and strong sex appeal and also importantly *unavailable* as a potential sexual partner. The beautiful actress Angelina Jolie compensates for or rationalizes Maya's fantasized same-sex desire and behavior. Still, it bears notice that expressions of same-sex desire, even just fantasies like Maya's, illustrate not only the declining stigma of homosexuality, but also the conscious embracing of queer practices of sexual fluidity to a certain extent.

"I Think It's a Fluid Kind of Thing" (Susan Van Dam)

Interviewing Susan Van Dam, a thirty-eight-year-old white married woman with two kids, at her large government office, proved to be clarifying, if not a little surprising, for me. My first impressions of Susan were that she seemed congenial and conventional, but when I asked her how she defined her sexual identity she surprised me by saying,

Heterosexual, but I think I could be bi. Just haven't had the right woman. [*She laughs at her play on this popular cliché.*] I think sexuality is sometimes circumstantial. . . . I think it's a fluid kind of thing.

However, due to the fact that she's married with children, Susan acknowledges that most people assume she's straight:

I'm married and have kids. People, I think the majority of people would just say, "There's an indication that she's straight." . . . But maybe my closest friends like might have said, "I wonder if she ever took a ride on the wild side." You know what I mean? Just because they know me as liberal. . . . My close friends might think that I've had other [nonheterosexual] experiences.

On one hand, Susan identifies herself as politically liberal, and this partly explains her expressions of sexual fluidity and the possibility that she could be bisexual, even though she has dated only men and is now married. On the other hand, when Susan was a teenager in high school, her sister Angela came out to her as bisexual, and among their family members confided only in Susan about her bisexuality and girlfriend. As a result, they became even closer, and Susan would accompany Angela to lesbian and gay establishments at that time. Susan recalls these outings and her impressions of Angela's sexuality at that point:

> When I went to gay bars, it was with my sister. . . . My sister was bisexual. She was gay and then in her younger years, throughout her twenties, then she went straight. I still think she's bi but then again, especially in her case I think she's one of the people who it is kind of circumstantial. She's searching for a soul mate. I think she has personal issues that need to be satisfied by the right person. . . . Now she's married with kids.

Susan's statements about her own sexual fluidity seem to be partly informed by her sister's experiences of being involved with women, although her sister is now married to a man as well. Reflecting on this and her parents' liberal values, Susan explains,

> I've had my own experiences where I think I could take a walk on the wild side, so to speak. And I wonder was that my conditioning too? Because I was a teenager when I was exposed to homosexuality, a lesbian community, or does it have to do with the fact that my parents are from Holland and they are really tolerant?

Susan's bisexual sister, her participation in and involvement with lesbian and gay life, and her social and political upbringing have all most likely played a role in her pro-gay practices and her own sense of sexual desire as a shifting, circumstantial, and fluid component of oneself. That is, cultural practices and identities come from, to invoke Ann Swidler's (1986) popular metaphor, a toolkit of culture writ large, which individuals use to understand and make sense of the world. In combating antigay attitudes, Susan referenced her sister's and her own experiences after her sister came out:

I would speak openly about it [her sister's bisexuality] if the discussion came up. Because I guess I feel this need to show how normal it is. You know what I mean? Just because socially and politically I want there to be tolerance, so if I felt like people wanted to discuss homosexuality, I would give me as an example or my sister, my relationship with my sister as an example.

If Susan's adoption of antihomophobic practices is sincere and her own self-identification as bisexual or not exclusively heterosexual real, then it makes sense that she's unafraid of embracing accusations that she's a lesbian herself. Recalling a situation where rumors were circulating about her own sexuality, she explains,

Well, I was in a band and some people concluded that since I was the lead singer in a rap band that I must be gay. And then the funny thing is that I wrote a song about a friend of mine who was a woman, they were like, "There's proof." It was a song about being best friends, me admiring this woman, who I had no attraction to and it was just like we were best buddies. She traveled a lot and was very adventurous. So I needed to write a song about something, so I wrote a song about her, and then this individual said, "Oh, that's proof." And so I combated that by saying, "Yeah, I am."

Susan's reaction to rumors that she was a lesbian indicate her antihomophobic stance and her willingness to take on a lesbian identity to counter rumormongering about her own sexuality.

Reflecting on American society today and the status of lesbians and gay men as now more tolerated and accepted, Susan believes that lesbians and gays are more visible and have gained more rights and recognition, and she hopes that being gay will become less and less an issue of prejudice and discrimination.

Yes, I think there's more tolerance. It's episodic. You know what I mean? If you were to look at society as a whole you'd probably come up with a lot of examples of gay intolerance and hate crimes and everything like that, but gay intolerance and hatred is doomed to failure, I think. Whereas fifty years ago you wouldn't be able to conclude such a thing. . . . I think just like the civil rights era in the late '60s and '70s, I think people were getting over the hump of being able to at least talk about it, ask for rights. But right now, people are becoming more like me and that it's not that big of a deal anymore if you're gay or straight anymore. I would be really happy if people who were gay aren't afraid or are like me: I don't care whether you think I'm gay or straight.

I ask Susan whether she had ever had any sexual feelings for another woman. She recounts her feelings for her best friend, Samantha Reich:

> I thought she [Samantha] had feelings for me and so then I always thought she likes me. Because she had been in a relationship with a woman and now she's married too. 'Cause one time when we were out partying, she took my hand and I . . . But she was just trying to help me walk and I . . . She was just a little worried about me and so I was just like, "She likes me." And I found that very flattering and so then I fell in love with her and it was just, we were both in heterosexual relationships and we're very close friends. I consider her my best friend. And the one time we went to go see the Buena Vista Social Club at the Concert Hall, she broke it to me gently, "Susan, I don't have any feelings for you." She's just like, "I always kind of got the impression that you thought I had a crush on you but I just love you as a friend." And I just laughed really hard and "Oh, man." I kind of liked the idea of somebody being attracted to me who was gay. You know what I mean? It just proves to me that my belief is that sexuality is fluid. That sometimes it can be biological, but also circumstantial.

Although Susan did have sexual feelings for Samantha, they were never sexually involved and they were both in relationships with men. Susan's story illustrates that sexuality includes not just sexual desire but also feelings of affection and attachment, emotions often associated with friendship as well as romantic love. In other words, sexuality is not reducible to sexual desire alone; it is also about feelings of intimacy, affects of attachment to another, and connection through expressions of affection. For me, Susan's expressions of sexual fluidity seem at times to be as much about her affirmative lesbian, gay, and queer political views as about her sexual desire for women. Ironically, for some straight women, sexual fluidity or identifications as bisexual or not being exclusively straight are as much about their pro-queer politics as actual same-sex desires. This is ironic, since it recalls Arlene Stein's (1997) observations of lesbian feminists in the 1970s who were in committed relationships with women due more to their feminist politics than their actual sexual desires.

"The Joke about [My Women's College] Was You Sort of Had to . . . Sleep with a Woman" (Denise Lee)

Denise Lee is a married twenty-nine-year-old black woman who recently finished her graduate degree. Sitting in her living room in a house in a suburb of Orangetown, I ask Denise how she defines her sexual identity. She explains that it has shifted since she married.

> I think it also changed when I got married. Because my sexual identity is in a formal sort of sense, I'm in a lifetime relationship with my husband. And I guess the way that would be defined by me and other folks is as a relationship with a man, a monogamous relationship with a man. But before I got married, I dated men exclusively. So that's at least how I would define my sexual orientation, sexual identity.

Growing up in the greater Washington, DC, metropolitan area, Denise started going to gay bars and clubs soon after she turned twenty-one. She says that she enjoyed the difference and energy of gay venues and that it was natural for her to feel friendly toward gay people in those places, similar to the way she felt close to her high school gay friends. Regarding this time in her life, she says, "It was mostly gay men. In DC when I would go [to gay bars] I had a very good friend, a gay man and most of the bars and clubs that we would go to were gay, were gay men's [bars and clubs]. I got tons of attention, but not because I was gay."

Many of the queered straight women I interviewed described deep and strong attachments to their gay male friends, if not presently, then in the past. In gay slang, these straight women are referred to as "fag hags," a problematic, variably offensive, ugly-sounding term, but nonetheless one that points to the deep friendship, emotional closeness, and often the romantic-like intimacy that develop between

straight women and gay men (see Muraco 2012). During her soph-
omore year in college, Denise lived with Ben Ivins, a gay male she
had befriended her first year. Reflecting on her gay male friends who
have come out to her and her involvement in gay life during college,
Denise says,

> Ben came out my, our, freshman year in college. My first boyfriend Rick
> came out to me, I dated him when I was sixteen. He came out, I don't
> know, at some point when we were in college, but you kind of always
> knew that he was gay. I mean I knew he was gay when I was dating him.
> He wasn't my first boyfriend. He was the first guy that I slept with. . . . I
> lived with Ben in college my sophomore year, then we lived off campus
> together our summer after our sophomore year. And other people I
> met . . . one of the things that was pretty big on campus was the lesbian,
> gay, bisexual alliance dances. They threw the best dances on campus and
> probably actually the only dances. So I went to a bunch of those dances
> and events, partially to support Ben, but also partially because the music
> was really good. So I meet a lot of people there and they didn't come out
> to me. I just knew that they were gay.

Due to her close friendships with gay men and lesbians as well as
attending a women's college that normalized sexual experimentation
and fluidity as part of its culture and college lore, it's not surprising that
Denise and her other women friends discussed whether they had, were
having, or wanted to have sex with women. Sexual fluidity and talking about same-sex encounters were part of their casual conversations
and even a hallmark of their college's reputation. With a sense of levity,
Denise recalls her college's reputation:

> The joke about [my women's college] was you sort of had to do two
> things before you graduated: One was sleep with a professor and another
> one was sleep with a woman. It was like did you do either one of those
> things. I think that people were open to that possibility. And often there's
> a lot of experimentation going on amongst my friends. Not necessarily
> whether or not I was a lesbian but questions about whether or not I had
> slept with a woman, or whether I was thinking of sleeping with a woman
> or open to it or what have you. There were lots of questions about that.

Not surprisingly, Denise did end up flirting with and kissing several different women while she was in college.

> Yeah, in college I kissed a couple of women to sort of see what the experience was like and stuff like that. . . . I never dated a woman. Yeah, no, it was more like you, it was sort of I was drunk at a bar, OK, we're flirting, then we're going to make out kind of thing. . . . If I continued to date women, I don't think I would identify as heterosexual. Because I never, I never identified as bisexual. I didn't identify as a lesbian. So it definitely could have [affected my sexual identity]. It [these sexual experiences] didn't.

Lesbian, gay, and queer classmates, same-sex practices, and discourses of fluidity were part of her college's social milieu, and thus her practices of sexual fluidity gain meaning in that context. When I ask Denise whether she would have had a sexual experience with a woman, she says,

> Yeah. I thought that was a possibility. I was open to it. If I had met someone who I really, really liked and I was attracted to them, I probably would have done it but I didn't. And so it didn't seem like something that I needed to experience in order to be sure that I was straight, you know. And even sort of kissing women wasn't something that I needed to do to prove that I was straight or to make sure. It was just something that I was open to doing, if that makes sense.

From her friendships with lesbians and gay men to her own sexual experiences, Denise's antihomophobic practices affirm lesbian and gay life and counter homophobic prejudice. Antihomophobic practices develop in a context where gay individuals and their subcultural practices and discourses are integrated and routinized as part of the social fabric of some colleges' liberal environments in particular. That is, straight women who have lesbian and gay friends and participate or have participated in lesbian and gay subcultural life illustrate these experiences in their queer-affirmative politics and solidarity with LGBTQ individuals. Remarking on this phenomenon, Denise says, "I was going to say that I would like to think I'm just a tolerant person but I think, yes, most certainly, having friends who were gay and sort of exploring issues has made me more aware of gay rights and better in line to support them and be an advocate for them."

Thinking about the issue of same-sex marriage and how it elicits homophobic responses from friends she talks to about it, Denise says that while "stereotypes are less severe of gay men and gay women," people have also learned how to avoid appearing homophobic by trying to embrace more tolerant-sounding speech when it comes to lesbian and gay issues.

> I think that people are sort of better about talking about it [homophobia], though, but I think it's still common. . . . I think when I have a conversation with a good friend of mine and she says, "If gays want to define their marriage differently than heterosexuals, but I don't think they can have the same kind of marriage that we do." I mean, I think that's bullshit. I think that's part of homophobia. I think those are negative stereotypes most certainly. I think in some ways it's become OK to say stuff like that. It's become less OK within mainstream society or at least when people are talking to me to use words like "faggot." I think that words used for lesbians, using the word "dyke," that people can pretty much agree I'm not going to do that because I understand that I could offend someone. But I think that people have different ways of talking about it.

As we have seen, from Denise's strong antihomophobic stances to her ability to openly discuss her own sexual experience with women, her queered straight identification is based on her affirmation of lesbians and gays as social and moral equals to straights. Although Denise's experiences of kissing other women didn't lead to further intimate acts or changes in her perception of her own straight identity, these same-sex experiences take on meaning in the context of her long history of social and political support of her gay friends since high school, and then their further development by her attending a women's college that made same-sex experimentation part of its social milieu.

"I Have Had Experiences outside Heterosexuality" (Kim Masterson)

Dressed in blue jeans and a fashionable top that wraps around her waist, Kim Masterson is a twenty-four-year-old white woman who grew up in a middle-class suburb bordering Orangetown. Although gender-conventional in appearance and personality, Kim tells me that while she considers herself heterosexual and has a boyfriend, she has had sexual experiences with women. She explains, "If I had to define my sexuality, it would be that I'm heterosexual." I ask her what that means to her. She says, "That I'm not close-minded about anything. I have had experiences outside heterosexuality and I would again probably. If I had to define it, I would say that I'm heterosexual but I wouldn't limit it to that necessarily."

Kim tells me she is not ashamed of having had sex with a woman in high school or her attraction to other women she liked in college. She says her close friends from high school and her current boyfriend know of her sexual interest in women. Although Kim knew women in college who used same-sex acts to get male attention, she is adamant that her attraction to women is based neither on dismissive notions that it's "trendy" to be bi or gay nor on a desire to titillate college men at parties by kissing another woman in front of them. She says that her boyfriend is bothered, for example, by her attraction to women and does not view it in a joking manner.

> It makes my boyfriend nervous. I'm pretty honest with my thoughts and feelings. He's not the type to find that amusing or attractive. He was kind of put off by it. I think it's 'cause he knows that it's an actual possibility and stuff. It's not like something I would do for him. He was confused and probably a little bit nervous, but he's also very old-fashioned and Catholic.

However, Kim does not consider her sexual attraction or experience with a woman to entail a loss in her status as a heterosexual woman. She says, for instance, that her older sister has had sexual experiences with women and that it was not unusual in her circles for girls to have had a sexual experience with another girl in high school. Kim explains, "I think that it was almost a common occurrence. Well, maybe not common. But in high school it was known for girls to sorta explore each other. I know my sister did."

Noting the strength of conventional feminine appearance norms for straight women, Kim says that if she dressed less conventionally feminine or dressed like Melissa Bradley, a lesbian friend she had a crush on in college, then other people would be more likely to suspect or wonder whether she is bisexual or lesbian.

> For Melissa, for instance, who's very original in every aspect, even her clothing, she didn't care. It wasn't like it was for anybody else, which I believe is how a lot of women dress, which is for men. I guess that would be one thing that would give it away. That would make me second-guess if somebody was straight or not if they had no regard for their attraction towards men among clothing.

Kim, then, shows a conscious awareness of her flirtatious behaviors toward men and that in part she dresses in ways that she thinks men find attractive. Her straight feminine practices create a clear script of what is expected of her: she should be "accommodating," should avoid being aggressive, and should postpone having sex until she is married. She elaborates on this:

> Just the little things that people teach boys versus girls from day one, I wonder how that affected me. What would be different about me? What might I be doing right now if I weren't told to be seen and not heard, or to be polite? I feel like most women are taught to be accommodating. I think it would be just a very different life if I was encouraged to be outgoing and aggressive, and sexual, basically. I think I was taught to equate sexuality with marriage and there was nothing outside of it. Sexuality, I think what I say about white women is pretty in general, I think we were taught to stifle it and wait until marriage for the sake of morality and religion and remaining a virgin.

Moreover, she says sex with men has a scripted quality as well.

> [I]f you think about sex itself, for [heterosexual] men it's like the best, that's like their goal. For [heterosexual] women, it's kinda like on the way to something better, it's not necessarily the end-all for women. So it's kinda like they [heterosexual men] get what they want and you end up feeling kind of, not empty but kind of, just this weird dynamic, which I would imagine isn't there if it was two women. I would imagine it being more mutual, probably satisfying.

Here Kim implies that heterosexual sex makes her feel emotionally empty and unsatisfied. In contrast, she has a romanticized view of lesbian sex as mutually satisfying. In a telling contrast, she describes her own sexual experience with a woman in high school at age seventeen this way: "It was freeing. It was the first time that I thought outside the box. I was not trying to impress anybody with anything. I was just fully being myself, fully relaxed. I'll never forget it." Kim's conventional straight femininity is rebellious, in that she has explored sexual feelings for women. Homosexuality is "outside the box" of conventionality for her, and this represents a rebellion against normative heterosexuality's foreclosure of same-sex desires among straight-identified women.

Although Kim supports gay marriage and gay and lesbian rights, her own imagined comfort level in being in a lesbian relationship is illustrative of her feelings about homosexuality. Kim explains, "I was kinda like I wonder if I could be happy with that [a lesbian relationship], or if it would be weird for me. If that's even an option for me, or the second that I became involved, I would realize that it's not for me and freak out or something."

The limit of Kim's antihomophobia and comfort with homosexuality is illustrated by her own fantasy of whether she would feel comfortable in a relationship with a woman. She wonders whether she could surrender her heterosexual status and privilege and deal with the stigma of homosexuality. For her, homosexual desire and sex do not make her question her primary identity as a straight woman, but a lesbian relationship would, as it would most likely entail significant changes in how she self-identifies and how others identify and think of her.

Kim's queered straight femininity is based on her experiences with sexual fluidity, her identification with lesbian friends, and the readings in her women's studies classes, all of which form and give meaning to her antihomophobic beliefs and awareness of straight privilege. When I ask Kim what it means to her to be a white heterosexual woman, we have the following exchange:

KIM: I feel like I have two out of three things going for me, as far as having walls up against me or obstacles in my way. We would talk in my class [in women's studies] a lot about, I can't remember the term but it was almost like double or triple negation.

JAMES: Oppression?

KIM: Yeah. Being African American and a woman and gay, their writ-
ings, they're always like very angry. I mean it was just kind of like:
can there be any other obstacle in front of them? I was just always
fascinated by that. And so my feelings as a woman, feeling oppressed,
were kind of alleviated when I realized that I am white and I am
middle-class and I'm straight, so I'm not constantly dealing with
things that other people are every day.

Here Kim draws an analogy between race and social class privileges as
similar to heterosexual privilege. Being part of antihomophobic circles
and learning about queer women of color in women's studies courses
have given Kim a knowledge base from which to view her own identity
and position within hierarchies of privilege and subordination.

From her high school sexual experience with a girl to her attraction
to women in college to the women's studies classes she took, Kim's and
other queered straight women's sexual fluidity is conditioned by and a
consequence of an acknowledgment of same-sex desires as part of their
own subjectivities, and a resistance to identity labels as limiting their
own range of sexual desire and identity.

"I Don't Consider Myself to Be Gay, but It's a Subculture That I Feel Like I'm Included In" (Erica Harris)

Erica Harris, a young black woman whom we met in chapter 4, recently
graduated from college and has been living and working in downtown
Orangetown for the last three years. By working and living downtown,
Erica has become friends with even more lesbians, bisexual women,
and gay men than when she was in college. Erica's identification with
Orangetown's lesbian and gay community has grown as a result of her
living situation.

I don't consider myself to be gay, but it's a subculture that I feel like I'm
included in. It's like my white friends who agree with me on a lot of
things feel they're a part of the black power movement because they're
embracing these ideologies and they're sharing them with the rest of the
world. I feel the same way about gay culture as a culture of people I have

affection for. It's important to me that everyone's on the same page, and I have a hard time tolerating people who are intolerant. I just really do. Having gay people who I'm so close to, it's changed [me]. Maybe where I would have chuckled off at a [gay] joke, now I stop it in its path. That's not cool, don't do it again.

Drawing a parallel to white friends who share her understanding of black racial politics, Erica opposes sexual intolerance in the same way that she opposes racial intolerance; in both cases she aims to promote justice for minority groups.

Even though she isn't gay, Erica considers herself a part of Orangetown's gay subculture. Her sense of membership in the gay and queer community compels her to be a strong advocate for lesbians and gay men. For her, being a queer ally entails promoting tolerance and acceptance. As she commented, she is now even more adamant in countering mundane gay jokes that she would have laughed at in the past.

Her straight male college friends are at times uncomfortable with her strong solidarity with the gay community and at times express their opinions about her numerous friendships with gay men by calling her a "fag hag."

[W]hen I've been called a fag hag by friends of mine, which drives me crazy because I don't like the way it sounds. It's not a very aesthetic phrase anyway. I'm not a hag at all, but I have many friends with different sexual orientations—gay, straight, bisexual. A friend of mine said less than two weeks ago, "You're the perfect fag hag," and tried to yuk it up like it's a joke, which again I tolerate to a certain degree, they're saying it to me. Had they said it in front of somebody else who might have been like, "I'm gay and she's my best friend, why would you say something like that," I might have been a little bit more quick to reprimand this person, but instead it was, "Please don't ever say that to me again." I tried to laugh it off and act like I wasn't hurt by it.

Here Erica offers us a brief insight into a straight male friend's reactions to her many friendships with gays, lesbians, and bisexuals. Her straight male friend's discomfort with gay individuals seems to lead him to deride Erica as a "fag hag," and by extension to devalue her gay friends.

It was not surprising to me when Erica told me that she had recently been sexually intimate with a woman for the first time in her life. She says that the experience brought up a host of issues for her, from how she thinks about her own sexual identity to feelings of being uncomfortable in a sexual, as opposed to affectionate, interaction with another woman. Regarding this experience, Erica explains,

> There was one woman in my life recently, within the past year, a girlfriend of mine who everybody assumed there was something going on between the two of us. We were very close. After a bottle of wine, we'd be holding hands on the table and be intimately laughing and whispering to each other. We went home together and it was very interesting. I found that for me, being with another woman, the aspect of kissing and holding one another was what I enjoyed. The more sexualized aspect of it I wasn't as comfortable with. And it was interesting because I found, like I said, to a certain degree it was stimulating and interesting and then it wasn't. It was almost uncomfortable for me and it didn't feel comfortable for me, which again could have been my own pretenses, my own prejudices about whether or not it should feel comfortable for me, which is something else that I still think about. . . . For a few months if somebody asked me, "Are you straight or gay?" I probably would have been like, "I don't know. I can't answer your question right now." And I'm lucky enough to be in the position I am where I have friends who I was able to explore these ideas. I was able to say this is how I felt; this is how I feel about myself and they were very receptive to me figuring it out.

Erica says that exploring her sexual feelings and desire for a woman caused her to question her own straight identity. Through the experience she reflects that she was less comfortable being sexually intimate with a woman, realizing that this might be partly her own absorption of the stigma attached to same-sex sexuality. Erica enjoys more the affectionate, as opposed to sexual, aspect of intimacy with women. She also notes her good fortune to be able to discuss and process this experience with supportive queer friends who understand the delicacy of sexual exploration.

Discussing the lesbian, gay, and queer subculture she belongs to in Orangetown, Erica explains that her own experiences of sexual fluidity are emblematic of the experiences of her friends.

One of my very good friends, Matt, who's gay, we went to Montreal together and went to the Black and Blue Party, [which is] just like a huge gay rave. I didn't even know it was gay orientation until we got there, and I was like, "All these beautiful men and no clothes. What's going on?" We had a fantastic time, but by the end of the night, he [Matt] was trying to convince this girl to go home with him and his friend and it was kind of strange. I'm like, "What are you doing? I've never seen this side of you before." He said, "I don't know. I've never been in this situation. I'm kind of curious." But he's dated men for the past ten years. He's openly gay. He's comfortable with that, but he has this curiosity about women, which is just very interesting to me because it's on both sides [straight and gay]. Everybody's kind of questioning what is sexuality even? I think everybody's trying to play with the definitions. Everyone's changing it. But again, this is my, this is my small world, which combines just recently being a college student with a subculture of downtown.

I underscore the importance of sexual context in understanding Erica's and her gay friend Matt's practices of sexual fluidity. Erica's same-sex experience occurred after she had moved to downtown Orangetown and been immersed in its queer subculture. Her experience of sexual fluidity is a situation that her queer friends are used to hearing and comfortable talking about in detail. That is, sexual fluidity is part of queered straight women's experiences, the experiences of their lesbian and gay friends, and the queer subculture they belong to and constitute in Orangetown.

"I Like Cher . . . We're Pretty Similar in a Lot of Ways" (Maureen O'Conner)

Maureen, who was introduced in chapter 4, is one of the most queer-identified straight women I interviewed. For example, she tells me that over half of her friends are gay men and lesbians, that she prefers to vacation in gay resort towns like Provincetown, Massachusetts, and that she introduced her gay brother to his current partner of ten years. Maureen's solidarity with lesbians and gay men has been a lifelong practice. Starting in high school, when she first began working in the restaurant and bar industry, she says, gay men often sought her friendship and support. Recalling this period in her life, she explains,

Some of the gay men, they were young and the guys in the kitchen [at the restaurant] would make fun of them and I would yell at them, and they [the gay men] would be like, "I'm telling Maureen when she comes in." And when I would come in, I'd be like, "You what? You're saying these comments?" And so now when these guys grew up and they were out of high school, they were my loyal customers on Main Street because I was always good to them when they were in high school. So I guess when I was in high school I was good too.

Like the sexual fluidity of many of the other queered straight women, Maureen's sexual fluidity seems to be as much about her political commitment to affirming lesbian and gay life as her actual sexual desires. Recall Maureen's definition of her own sexual identity: "Heterosexual, but I would be open. I wish, I wouldn't mind meeting a woman if it happens, but I'm pushing forty and it hasn't really happened." She did date and attempt to have a sexual relationship with a woman in the past, but says, "It wasn't a natural thing for me. I did have feelings for her, but I just couldn't go through with it. I felt uncomfortable. Like it was unnatural for me, but I did have strong feelings for her." Nonetheless, in the context of Maureen's social circles and given the fact that she has worked and lived in downtown Orangetown for over fifteen years, it makes sense that she has seriously considered being in a relationship with various women over the years, as she so strongly identifies with its gay, lesbian, and queer subculture and is surrounded by LGBT individuals in both her workplace and interpersonal circles.

Also, like the majority of queered straight women I interviewed, Maureen has a gender-conventional self-presentation. With her shoulder-length red hair, pale skin, and preference for dark shades of lipstick and red velvet dresses, Maureen's appearance and style are decidedly feminine. As well, Maureen observes that gay men often compliment her taste in fashion: "I love clothes. I like fashion. I've always been that way. I like lipstick. . . . Gay men like me because I'm open and they like the way I dress and I attract them. They [gay men] come up to me in the mall and they like what I have on and they start talking to me."

Maureen, like many of the other queered straight women, performs a conventional straight femininity. Even though she flirts with women and has dated and tried being sexually intimate with one in the past, her boundary-blurring sexual identity practices are counteracted partly by her traditional feminine self-presentation. Moreover, queered straight women, like Maureen, are routinized figures in lesbian, gay, and queer communities (Mock 2003) and in American popular culture as well (Winkler 2000). From celebrities like Bette Midler, who started her career singing in gay New York bathhouses in the 1970s, to current ones like Lady Gaga, who is a pastiche of Madonna, Grace Jones, and Liza Minnelli, queered straight women embrace and support lesbian and gay life through their antihomophobic practices, boundary-blurring sexual behaviors, and public embracing of same-sex desire. For instance, when I asked Maureen how she would hypothetically feel about her teenage daughter being a lesbian, she responded by referencing an interview with Cher, identifying with Cher's response to the same question:

> Actually, I've thought about it. You know why? Because Cher gave an interview and I like Cher, and we're pretty similar in a lot of ways, and I saw her being interviewed about her daughter coming out and they said that she was very un-Cher like. But she said it wasn't about her [daughter]. . . . It was about protecting her from the media and protecting her from the world. Because the world isn't as open-minded as her and when I heard her say that, I said, "I wonder if I would be the same way."

Maureen says of course she would support her daughter's lesbian identity. She and the other straight women I have discussed are queer allies. Part of their sense of solidarity is illustrated by their openness to engage in acts of sexual fluidity as part of their political and social identification with queer subculture. Although they often embody and project conventional straight feminine styles of appearance and dress, they represent the decentering of queer culture from within straight life. No longer is queer culture just centered on the experiences of lesbians and gays; it now includes queered straight women who identify with the subculture and affirm queer life.

These queered straight women's identifications illustrate that women's sexual feelings and desires are fluid, contextual, and changeable. From their expressions of same-sex fantasies to their actual sexual experiences with other women, queered straight women demonstrate their own investment in queer politics and culture. In an American cultural climate where same-sex expressions between women are often read through the lens of a heterosexual male fantasy of sexual titillation, these straight women counter this homophobic and sexist reduction as antithetical to their own sexual subjectivities and queer-affirmative values.

Metrosexuals, Queered Straight Women, and Post-Closeted Culture

Queered and nonnormative heterosexualities are an important development in sexual politics and queer cultural life. Decades of lesbian, gay, and queer political activism should be understood as conditioned by the struggles of not only lesbian, gay, and queer people but also their straight friends and allies. In the context of lesbian and gay social and political integration in America, we are witnessing queered straight women who socially and politically identify with lesbian, gay, and queer people and culture and metrosexual men who embrace less conventional practices and styles associated with gay masculinities. The identity practices of metrosexual men, gay-friendly nonmetrosexual men, and queered straight women demonstrate the multiple and varied identifications they have with lesbian, gay, and queer people and culture. They signal the complexity of straight identifications and the constantly transforming boundaries between heterosexualities and homosexualities in post-closeted contexts today.

In American society's kaleidoscope of multiple masculinities, from queered straight masculinities (Heasley 2005) and homophobic dudes who have sex with dudes (Ward 2008a) to "alpha" males who aim to be hegemonic, there are also metrosexual men who aim to reject the values and prescriptions of hegemonic masculinity and variably embrace "feminine-gay" styles, fashions, and practices while being antihomophobic. Metrosexual masculinities, though, are not queered straight masculinities. Rather, the men, who variably identify themselves and are thought of by others as metrosexual do not adopt practices of sexual fluidity, but they do think of themselves as gay-friendly and as contesting norms that construct sex/gender divisions as associating masculinity with only heterosexuality. By viewing their own masculinities as well as those of other gay and straight men as more diverse, multifaceted, and fluid than the normative stereotype of gay men as effeminate and straight men as masculine, metrosexual men aim to construct an environment where gender and sexual identity practices are not reduced to the reproduction of male and heterosexual privilege and power.

While being nonnormative in some respects, metrosexual masculinities also employ a gender strategy that performs a heterosexual masculinity that aims to claim status for its fashionable styles and practices, its enlightened values of antihomophobia and antisexism, and a recognized position within circles of urban cosmopolitanism. Metrosexual men can and do reinforce hegemonic masculine norms through subtle claims of heterosexual status and privilege at various times, even if they do this more for personal than social and political reasons.

In thinking about queer culture and conceptions of heterosexuality, some scholars view the two as diametrically opposed. For instance, in her book *In a Queer Time and Place*, the queer theorist Judith Halberstam (2005) defines her focus on queer culture's spaces and temporal constructions as excluding heterosexual formations, arguing, "Queer uses of time and space develop, at least in part, in opposition to the institutions of family, heterosexuality, and reproduction" (1). However, as I've shown, straight feminine identifications can be queered and subversive of binary conceptions of sexuality as fixed and defined as either heterosexual or homosexual. Indeed, by investigating queered identifications among straight women, I show that their practices reconstruct sex/gender norms by aiming to resignify feminine conventions as escaping solely heterosexual practices and including same-sex desires and experiences as well.

Terms for queered straight women include "fag hag," "LUG" (lesbian until graduation), "hasbian" (a woman who has been in a lesbian relationship but is now in a heterosexual one; see Stein 2010), and more recently "heteroflexible" (vaguely used to refer to straight women who engage in same-sex experimentation for male attention and/or out of a "bi-curious" sensibility; see Rupp and Taylor 2010). Regardless of the term, but like the ex-lesbians in Arlene Stein's study, queered straight women define their sense of self in relation to lesbian, bisexual, and gay individuals, demonstrating that expressions of sexual fluidity are part of their political solidarity with lesbian, gay, and queer people and cultures (see also Knox, Beaver, and Kriskute 2011; Vrangalova and Savin-Williams 2010). Indeed,

metrosexual men and queered straight women, among others, are helping to constitute the spaces, practices, and beliefs that make up, affirm,
and encourage lesbian, gay, and queer people and post-closeted culture
today.

6

Conclusion

Straights, Post-Closeted Culture, and the Continuum of Identity Practices

Since the Stonewall riots of 1969, significant changes have occurred in the lives of gay and lesbian Americans—from their increasing local, state, and federal enfranchisement to their unprecedented normalization in popular culture. But, just as emphatically, patterns of normative heterosexuality have changed significantly over the last four decades. Although straight identities and practices are still normative and enforced in seemingly every institution, from the family and mass media to religion and the government, the increase in the visibility and social incorporation of gays and lesbians, no matter how uneven and unequal, underscores the decline of the centrality of the closet in American life.

In post-closeted contexts, straights can neither assume the invisibility of gays and lesbians nor count on others to always assume their heterosexuality. Straights also cannot assume that other straight individuals are homophobic or intolerant of gays and lesbians. And, even if a straight person is intolerant, there is less tolerance for public displays of homophobia. In America today, in a way scarcely imaginable just two decades ago, tolerance for gay and lesbian Americans is conditioned by the formation of a straight culture that appeals to its antihomophobia to claim an enlightened status.

I argue that a post-closeted dynamic, which is marked by the pervasive presence of openly gay and lesbian individuals and a pattern of cultural normalization, is increasingly common in core areas of social life, and is thus refashioning sexual identity performances, normative hetero-sexuality, and homophobias. Today nonheterosexuals have more options regarding the association of sexual desire, behavior, and identity; and het-erosexuals are often more deliberate and reflective about establishing a heterosexual identity. To be clear, I am not claiming the end of the closet; rather, though the conditions of the closet persist, the chief patterns of sexual and gender disadvantage in the core institutions of American soci-ety are decreasingly a product of compulsory heterosexuality.

That is, if the concept of a post-closeted dynamic seems to overstate the increasing tolerance, cultural normalization, and social integration of gay men and lesbians, it is due to the contradiction between everyday and institutional life in America. Gay cultural normalization and social integration form an uneven pattern that is most salient in everyday life and interpersonal relationships. A post-closeted dynamic represents more of a micro-sociological phenomenon, and it doesn't capture as well the experiences of gay men and lesbians in many social institu-tions, regions, and places (Barton 2012; Seidman 2002; Williams, Giuf-fre, and Dellinger 2009).

Normative heterosexuality, to be sure, remains a dominant principle of organization in the state, health care agencies, private industries, and even popular culture. But a post-closeted cultural dynamic is still a sig-nificant pattern in these spheres as well. From the demedicalization of homosexuality to important legal changes decriminalizing sodomy and promulgating gay marriage, domestic partner benefits, adoption rights, and antidiscrimination ordinances, gays and lesbians are a visible and growing minority presence in America's social institutions. Heterosex-uality may still be normatively and institutionally enforced, but it is no longer compulsorily maintained by criminalization, medical sanctions of homosexual pathology, or governmental policies and agencies that make it a requirement for institutional participation.

Moreover, everyday life is not without its homophobic pitfalls and heterosexist traps. On the contrary, gays' social integration in daily life doesn't mean the end of sexual identity or everyday self-management practices. Rather, it means that gays' self-management decisions of dis-closure are now more often about situation-specific contexts, not life-shaping patterns of concealment, filled with shame and fear.

If everyday gay existence is increasingly "beyond the closet," then straights are faced with a new set of social identity dynamics. Gay visibility and integration mitigate the power of the discourse of compulsory heterosexuality, making straight identity practices less taken for granted and now more conscious, deliberate, and purposeful. Furthermore, straights encounter a society that increasingly disapproves of public homophobia and homosexual intolerance. Therefore, in place of overt acts of homophobic prejudice, straight men and women employ normative gender practices to indicate their heterosexuality. Gender identity practices, then, have taken on a renewed importance in sexual identity practices and politics. Since gender identity practices are the grid for a heterosexual/homosexual sign system that is overlaid on them, masculine/feminine practices have become a key site and structure for the performance of sexual identity and straight and gay identity politics.

Complicating the matter, though, is that straights and gays now often look and act alike. In other words, gay integration is in part conditioned by gay men and lesbians who embody conventional, even normative, gender self-presentations. While straights attempt to use gender-normative practices to recuperate straight privilege, gender-conventional gay men and lesbians undercut this strategy. As a result, if gender-normative practices fail to project a clear heterosexual identity, then resorting to normative heterosexual boundary practices, which put social distance between oneself as straight and gay individuals, signifiers, and spaces, makes sociological sense in post-closeted contexts. Normative heterosexual boundary practices are subtle and include soft homophobic forms of informal exclusion, nonrecognition, and disrespect. On the other hand, tolerant attitudes and gay-affirmative values encourage the blurring of heterosexual/homosexual identity practices, a lessening of boundaries of social distance, efforts to not claim heterosexual privilege, and general attitudes that condemn practices of exclusion and disrespect.

Polling data show that young Americans are increasingly supportive of gay and lesbian relationships at higher rates than older Americans. For example, in 2012, 65 percent of young Americans, ages eighteen to thirty-four, stated that lesbian and gay relationships were morally acceptable, while 55 percent of Americans ages thirty-five to fifty-four found them so, and for those fifty-five and older, support dropped another nine points to 46 percent (Gallup 2012). Still, it's hard to disentangle age, social context, and other demographic variables in accounting for the newfound support of lesbian and gay life.

For example, the survey researcher Jeni Loftus (2001) finds that while older Americans are more likely to disapprove of homosexuality, Americans' more liberal attitudes toward homosexuality are "not due to the aging of the population" (769). In her study, the most significant demographic variable is the increasing rates of educational attainment, which account for one-third of the increase in Americans' positive attitudes toward homosexuality. However, that leaves another one-third of the change unaccounted for, and, tellingly, Loftus concludes by stating, "It is possible that these changes in attitudes are due largely to the gay and lesbian liberation movements" (780).

While the post-closeted contexts created by lesbian and gay social movements, along with their unprecedented representations in the mass media, have affected all Americans, they most likely matter most for young Americans, whose formative years have been most profoundly shaped by them. This notwithstanding, normative heterosexuality and gender normativity, then, continue to shape and condition the expression of gay and straight identities. But in the context of a post-closeted cultural dynamic, straight individuals are more intentional, calculated, and careful in how they establish and perform their heterosexualities. Similarly, in this context, some gays and lesbians are living fuller lives, but it's often at the cost of excluding nonnormative gender expressions and queer individuals who complicate or contest gays' claims to minority rights and cultural normalization.

Historical Shifts in the Closet

The analyses of the previous empirical chapters, along with the synthesis of the extant historiographical work on heterosexualities, documented social and historical shifts in the social construction of heterosexual masculinities and femininities. These shifts represent broad and historically significant reconfigurations in the closet, gender, and the homo/heterosexual division since the 1890s.[1]

Between the 1930s and 1950s in America, the closet of antihomosexual discrimination was built—homosexuals were prohibited from being served in bars and restaurants and were fired from federal government jobs, and Hollywood films were forbidden to portray homosexual characters or even mention their existence (Chauncey 2004, 5–22; D'Emilio 1983, 2002). Historians, legal scholars, and sociologists have documented the dismantling of the various parts of the closet and its repressive practices of oppression over the course of the thirty-year period from the 1960s to the 1990s (Adam 1995; Chauncey 2004, 2008; D'Emilio 2002; Epstein 1999; Eskridge 1999; Gamson 1998; Seidman 2002; Walters 2001; Weeks 2007; Yoshino 2006).

Following their lead, I have claimed that a post-closeted culture has arisen under conditions of unprecedented popular cultural visibility and social and legal enfranchisement in the mid-1990s and the first decade of the twenty-first century. From the rise of *Ellen*, *Will & Grace*, and *Queer Eye for the Straight Guy* to widely acclaimed and blockbuster movies such as *Philadelphia*, *Brokeback Mountain*, and *The Kids Are All Right* to the 2003 landmark US Supreme Court case *Lawrence v. Texas*, which overturned the Court's 1986 ruling in *Bowers v. Hardwick* that maintained state sodomy laws as constitutional (Chauncey 2001) to the 2013 decision that declared the Defense of Marriage Act (DOMA) unconstitutional in denying federal benefits to married same-sex couples, we have witnessed dramatic shifts in the cultural, social, and legal standing of lesbians and gay men in America in ways unimaginable to the Stonewall generation of out gay men and lesbian women.

In table 6.1, I offer a typology of what I call "historical shifts in the closet," using both the research in this book and the historical scholarship to date, to understand the present period and its historical antecedents. This typological table is meant to capture broad and historically overlapping social changes in synoptic form. The time periods overlap, indicating the uneven quality of the social and historical changes occurring during the evolving formations of the closet. My designation of four historical shifts in the closet—the pre-closet period, 1890–1930s; the rise of the closet, 1930s–1960s; the decline of the closet, 1960s–1990s; and the rise of a post-closeted culture, 1990s–present—is a heuristic device for describing key historical changes along three dimensions of sexual life in America: heterosexual identities, homosexual oppression, and the status of homosexual men and women. Of course, the historical configurations and social realities of these periods are more complicated than what

Table 6.1. Historical Shifts in the Closet

	The Pre-Closet Period, 1890–1930s	The Rise of the Closet, 1930s–1960s	The Decline of the Closet, 1960s–1990s	The Rise of a Post-Closeted Culture, 1990s–Present
Heterosexual Identities	"Normal" men and women	Shift from "normal" to heterosexual	Less assumed, but strongly normative	Increasingly defensive, conscious, and deliberate
Homosexual Oppression	Not state-sponsored, but still socially repressive and polluting	State-sponsored and repressive of an everyday public gay life	Declining state-sponsored practices; preponderance of normalization; term "homophobia" is coined	Legal enfranchisement; increasingly informal and variable boundaries of social distance; institutional, regional, and place variances
Status of Homosexual Men and Women	Fairies as publicly visible homosexual men, along with nonvisible queers; a double life is the dominant pattern; homosexual women are in "romantic friendships" or pass as men and "female" husbands to female wives	Hidden and leading double lives as publicly heterosexual but privately homosexual; rise of homophile political groups in 1950s: Daughters of Bilitis and Mattachine Society	Increasingly visible; the personal and interpersonal normalization of lesbian/gay identities; Stonewall riots and the rise of lesbian feminism and gay liberation	Normalization and significant increases in cultural visibility; social and political gains; growth in attitudes of tolerance/acceptance; queer political and cultural turn: ACT UP, Queer Nation, Lesbian Avengers, Transgender Menace

these analytical categories can capture. Nonetheless, the table serves as a visual summary of my study and the social and historical changes that have made it possible in the twenty-first century.

Understanding Straight Identity Practices and the Reproduction of Heteronormativity

In this study, I talked with black and white straight men and women to understand the meanings they attached to being straight, to analyze the interactions they reported with lesbians and gay men, and to document the variety of homophobic and antihomophobic stances (as well as the mixture of the two) that were found among their conventional ways of speaking and acting in everyday life. Based on the data collected, I claimed that straight identities were socially constructed through the boundaries of social distance that the respondents enacted

Table 6.2. Continuum of Social Distance and Straight Identity Practices

	Straight Men	Straight Women
Strongly Aversive Boundaries of Social Distance	• Homophobic talk based on social and religious beliefs of gays as deviant and/or sinful • Strong disassociation from gay spaces, persons, and symbols • Gays' gender nonconformity is stigmatized • Highly anxious about being perceived as possibly gay themselves • Vigilant in maintaining straight privilege	• Homophobic talk often based on religious beliefs of gays as sinful • Weak disassociation from gay spaces, persons, and symbols • Gays' gender nonconformity is stigmatized • Aim to maintain straight privilege
Weak Boundaries of Social Distance	• Associate with gay friends but often use women (friends, girlfriends, or wives) to signal their straight identity • Subtly aim to maintain straight privilege • Gays' gender nonconformity is still stigmatized • Social order is based on a straight majority/gay minority discourse • Metrosexual identifications but no practices of sexual fluidity	• Associate with gay friends alone and less anxious about being thought of as gay • Subtly aim to maintain straight privilege • Gays' gender nonconformity is variably nonstigmatized • Social order is based on a straight majority/gay minority discourse • Variably embrace cultural roles such as gay men's close friends or "fag hags" • Sexual fluidity without queered identifications
Blurred Boundaries of Social Distance	• Performances of sexual-gender identities of gays and straights are viewed as socially constructed and fluid • Contest boundaries between gay and straight identities • Surrender straight privilege • Metrosexual identifications but no practices of sexual fluidity	• Performances of sexual-gender identities of gays and straights are viewed as socially constructed and fluid • Contest boundaries between gay and straight identities • Surrender straight privilege • Sexual fluidity with queered identifications

Note: I use the term "gays" for the sake of brevity, but I mean it to include both lesbian women and gay men.

in performing their identities in various situations and contexts. By boundaries of social distance, I mean the practices these straight individuals used to associate or disassociate themselves from lesbian and gay symbols, individuals, and spaces. By capturing a range of identity practices and mapping them onto to a continuum, categorized as moving from homophobic practices at one end to antihomophobic practices on the other, I developed three broad categories: strongly aversive, weak, and blurred boundaries of social distance.

The continuum provided a grading of the boundary practices that straight men and women used, and showed how race shaped respondents' positions on it. Table 6.2 summarizes the continuum and provides an overview of the main points of the book. By way of conclusion,

I review the continuum and its categories, discussing the gendered and racial dynamics of each category as I proceed from one end of the continuum to the other. In sum, the continuum is a way of talking about straight identity practices, the different ways black and white straight men and women "do" their sexual-gender performances in certain recurrent contexts. Further, it links (micro) straight masculine and feminine identity practices to the (macro) production of the social orders of sexualities and gender. In other words, some straight individuals created the stabilization of the contemporary order of sexual identities and its accompanying social inequalities, while others promoted social change and supported LGBT equality. Of course, other straight individuals were indifferent or unaware of what their words and deeds did, but they still influenced and shaped sexual identity politics and its social organization in America.

Strongly Aversive Boundaries of Social Distance

Strongly aversive boundaries of social distance are used to construct a sexual institutional order where heterosexuality and homosexuality are hierarchically organized. In this sexual order, heterosexuality is viewed as superior because it is assumed to be normal and natural, while homosexuality is marked as inferior because it is assumed to be abnormal and unnatural. The strong categorical position includes heterosexual identity practices and discourses that in their most hegemonic form aim to return American society to a social order where heterosexuality is repressively dominant and homosexuality is emphatically subordinated. This social institutional order is akin to one of closeted dynamics, where gay identities are made invisible to the public and experienced as privately shameful. A traditional gender institutional order is also reinforced, as straights in this category enact a tight co-construction of gender and sexual norms, asserting that straights are gender-traditional and lesbians and gay men are gender-nontraditional and -nonconformist. Moreover, for these straights, gays' gender nonconventionality adds to their already stigmatized social status. The black and white straight men and women in the strongly aversive category constructed boundaries of strong social distance aimed at contributing to the reproduction of the existing gender and sexual orders, and, in fact, they do so in such a way that the existing orders are, essentially, taken for granted.

Differences between the straight men and women clearly existed within the strong boundaries category. The homophobic talk and attitudes of the nine (six black and three white) straight men were harsher than those of the straight women. Moreover, this harsher tone carried over into differences in the men's interactional practices, as they more strongly disassociated themselves from gay individuals, symbols, and spaces. The straight men were vigilant in aiming to maintain a straight status and its privilege, so much so that some men described an intense social-psychological anxiety when in the presence of gay individuals or, in their worst case, entering a gay space such as a bar, where they would be surrounded by gays. This notwithstanding, I found that in public spaces, such as places of work, restaurants, and other public areas, many of the straight men who expressed homophobic sentiments felt compelled to enact a modicum of tolerance toward lesbians and gay men. This generally included avoiding the use of epithets like "fag" and "dyke," even if these epithets remained part of their private interactional practices with friends and family members.

In contrast, the eight (five black and three white) straight women in the strongly aversive boundaries category reported having lesbian and gay acquaintances and family members whom they cared about, and their identity practices of disassociation from lesbian and gay symbols, persons, and spaces were distinctly less pronounced. Their homophobic practices were often more subtle and nuanced and less vitriolic than the men's. For instance, anxieties of being viewed as lesbian or possibly lesbian were less present among the women.

However, the issue of same-sex marriage provoked the eight straight women to express their disapproval of lesbian and gay people and their relationships, and to reject the idea that gays should be entitled to the right to marry. Most of the women based their disapproval on Christian religious beliefs, which justified their condemnation of homosexuality. At the same time, the salience of their disapproval of gay marriage pointed to their own investment in maintaining their straight privilege by reserving the social status of wife for only other straight women like themselves. They did not want this status and role devalued through the recognition of gays and lesbians as equals in the eyes of state law and American society.

The continuum also showed that black straight men and women (six and five, respectively) were more likely to be in the strong boundaries category than white straight men and women (three and three, respectively). Black straight men and women were also more likely to invoke religious beliefs in disapproving of homosexuality, whereas white straights used both social and religious rationales of gays as deviant and sinful to justify their homophobic stances. However, in the context of a post-closeted cultural dynamic, both black and white straights struggled with notions of being perceived as homophobic and intolerant due to the stigma now attached to being homophobic in America today. But for black straight men and women, even though their Christian religiosity legitimated viewing homosexuality as sinful and the black churches they attended often enforced this belief, they themselves experienced another level of discomfort in being prejudicial against another group of people, in this case gays, as they themselves face prejudice, if not discrimination, by being black in America.

Weak Boundaries of Social Distance

The weak boundaries category or middle group of straights engaged in antihomophobic practices, but they maintained their hetero privilege by taking the homo/heterosexual division for granted. This reinforced an understanding of fixed sexualities that positioned gays as a minority and straights as a majority. Although they aimed to reform negative views of lesbians and gays, they simultaneously reproduced normalizing boundaries by accepting the underlying categories of sexual identities as "natural," and these straight men—but less so the straight women—expected "normal" gays and lesbians to be gender-conventional as a condition for their advocacy of more egalitarian treatment.

To be sure, Michael Kimmel's (2005, 2008) and Raewyn Connell's (1987, 1995) conceptions of normative straight masculinity as constructed through homophobia or the marginalization of gay masculinities continue to be highly relevant in understanding contemporary constructions of straight masculinities. However, as I and other scholars (Anderson 2009; McCormack 2010) have shown, a range of antihomophobic practices have developed in the context of pro-gay views and practices of inclusion. The sixteen (eight black and eight white) straight men who drew weaker boundaries of social distance from gay individuals and symbols, and viewed gays as friends, respected coworkers, or loved family members, enacted practices of antihomophobia and promoted sexual equality. However, a subtle form of privilege was maintained when these men disclosed their straight status to avoid ambiguity or by having their female friends, girlfriends, or wives accompany them to gay and mixed gay/straight events and spaces. And this was a clear gender difference between the straight men and women, as the women did not discuss using male friends, boyfriends, or husbands to project their straight status. Rather, straight women felt comfortable and at ease in gay spaces alone with just other lesbian and gay friends present.

For the fourteen (six black and eight white) straight women in the weak boundaries category, the development of their antihomophobic practices is conditioned by the ways in which American culture is less likely to code women as potentially lesbian or bisexual. Moreover, when cultural codes mark a woman as potentially homosexual, this suspicion is often filtered through a heterosexist lens that constructs sexual intimacy between two women as open to or aimed at straight men's gazes and desires (Hamilton 2007; Rupp and Taylor 2010). There seemed to be more latitude given to women's identity practices, and, overall, the straight women reported less surveillance by others regarding their straight identity performances than the men.

Furthermore, many of these women described deep, intimate, and close friendships with lesbians and gay men. These friendships served as an important basis and development for their gay-affirmative values and practices. For example, some of the religious black and white straight women left more conservative faiths and joined more liberal ones that welcomed lesbians and gay men as members, and others maintained their membership in their faith, but personally disavowed its stance against same-sex marriage.

While some straight women I interviewed had mostly lesbian friends, others described close and intimate friendships with mostly gay men. The friendships between straight women and gay men often entailed these women becoming knowledgeable about the rich symbolic world of gay and straight identity codes. And it is worth noting that although arguably a derogatory term, the popular cultural designation of some straight women as "fag hags" denotes straight women's friendships with gay men as a quasi-institutional role patterned in gay culture, and there is no parallel to the relationships between gay men and "fag hags" among straight men and their friendships with gay men or lesbians. The friendships between these gay men and straight women tap into gay male sensibilities, such as melodrama, camp, fashion, and diva worship, that gay male culture cultivates and thrives on (Halperin 2012).

However, a distinction among the antihomophobic practices of the straight men and women in this category versus the next was that while all of them viewed gays and straights as moral and social equals, straights in the weak boundaries category maintained their straight status and privilege by consciously not blurring gay/straight identity practices. That is, these straight men and women did not want to be mistaken as gay or bi, and they subtly reinforced the hetero/homo binary division and by extension retained their straight privilege.

The seven (five white and two black) metrosexual men mostly fell into the weak boundaries category as well. Five were in the weak boundaries category and two were in the blurred boundaries category. These were straight men who exhibited fashionable styles and a set of male beauty practices that ranged from fashion-forward clothes and personal style to fastidious grooming habits. They mixed gay and straight practices and blurred codes of conventional masculinity and heterosexuality. The metrosexual men felt comfortable socializing in gay and mixed gay/straight spaces and described lesbians and gay men as friends and part of their social milieus. Although the metrosexual men I interviewed aimed to be critical of homophobic and sexist practices associated with hegemonic masculinity, they embraced *less conventional* masculine and heterosexual practices, *not gender-bending or queer ones*. That is, they did not report engaging in practices of sexual fluidity and queer sex, but they did display softer forms of masculinity, such as wearing their hair long and sporting "feminine" clothing elements in their styles.

For me, metrosexual masculinity practices were a gender strategy (Hochschild and Machung [1989] 2012) that blurred and contested normative masculine and heterosexual practices, but they also reproduced hegemonic masculine norms. By incorporating less normative gender and/or sexual practices into their presentations of self, the metrosexual men challenged hegemonic masculinities, but at the same time their practices were liable to be recuperated into gender- and sexual-normative orders, where their metrosexuality might be codified as a middle- or upper-class variation on a quasi-hegemonic masculine form.

The contradictions of metrosexual masculinities are unavoidable in a normative heterosexual society. Like gay masculinities, such as being a "bear" (a gay man with a large and hairy body) or any other gay "masculine" type, metrosexual masculinities both contest and reproduce hegemonic masculinities (Hennen 2005). For example, ads for current popular Axe brand deodorants and hair gels are not selling a nonnormative masculine practice. Nor does the celebrity David Beckham's or other men's metrosexual practices of shopping for and wearing designer clothes necessarily mean a simple and uncomplicated resistance to normative masculinities as a hybrid metrosexual form. Rather, these practices of metrosexualities are often recuperated into another derivation of normative masculinity that, if not hegemonic, then, is aimed at approximating middle- or upper-class versions of ones.

Regarding the racial composition of the metrosexual category, only two black men fell into this category, which proved unsurprising as many of the young black straight men in my sample tended toward an urban style of baggy jeans or pants, loose shirts, and oversized hoodies. Further, age seemed to play a factor as well, as older black and white men expressed a certain amount of distance from what they ostensibly viewed as a popular trend for younger men. Older black straight men also said they didn't embrace sagging jeans or oversized shirts, and older white men avoided tight jeans and longer hair, for example, thinking them styles inappropriate for their age. However, even straight men who might have embraced a metrosexual style (like the other two men who blurred boundaries but were not metrosexual-identified) reported feeling unable to do so as a result of having a larger body size or an aging body, which made metrosexual styles unbecoming for them.

Although strong religious beliefs were often a barrier to tolerance and support of gay men and lesbians, several black and white straight women and men in this group expressed moderate or even high levels of religiosity, but their religiosity did not determine their stance on the morality of gay people or their legal right to marry. Further, the black men and women in the weak category linked their experiences with racism in understanding the homophobia gays and lesbians must negotiate in everyday life. This understanding of the link between racial and sexual oppressions conditioned these black straight men's and women's pro-gay stances and their support of lesbian and gay friends, family, and coworkers. The intersections among religious faith, homophobias/antihomophobias, race, and heterosexualities should continue to be examined for the multiple stances straight Americans embrace in post-closeted contexts today.

Blurred Boundaries of Social Distance

The eleven straight men and women who blurred boundaries between heterosexuality and homosexuality at various times through their identity practices enacted antihomophobic practices in their everyday lives, both by challenging the status quo and by drawing attention to the socially constructed character of sexualities and gender. These straight men and women refuse the equation of gender conventionality with a straight identity; conversely, they reject the notion that gender nonconventionality indicates a lesbian and gay identity. They do this to contest stereotypes of gays as gender-nonconformist, and because they know from experience that lesbians' and gays' (and straights') gender presentations are diverse and varied. At this end of the continuum, then, we are witnessing the development of antihomophobic straight masculinities and femininities that aim in their most counterhegemonic forms to contest and subvert the reproduction of normative heterosexuality and gender normativity.

In particular, the four straight men at this end surrendered their straight privilege and blurred boundaries by allowing themselves to be viewed as gay at times. All four of these straight men were white, and they seem to trade on their white privilege to compensate for the loss of a straight status when others viewed them as gay. In contrast, black straight men who went to gay settings with gay friends disclosed their identity to recover straight status and privilege, and thus none of them fell into this category.

Straight men who blurred boundaries would use the word "partner," for example, instead of "wife," as a way to avoid signaling their straight and marital status. Others were part of the lesbian and gay scene and weren't defensive if someone thought they might be gay or if gay men flirted with them. Although they would come out to men who flirted with them to avoid leading them on, these straight men eschewed announcing their straight identity status in an anxious, defensive manner.

The seven straight (three black and four white) women who blurred boundaries of social distance were the ones who displayed the most "activist" set of antihomophobic practices in the study. Their practices included blurring sexual identity practices and consciously letting themselves be viewed as nonheterosexual. These straight women purposefully surrendered straight status and privilege, too. They openly discussed the sexual fantasies they had of other women as well as their sexual experiences with women lovers. Their practices of sexual fluidity were conditioned by their queer-affirmative values. Queered straight identifications were exclusively found among the women, and the central feature of their queered identifications was sexual fluidity. Consequently, their queered straight femininities demonstrated the shifting boundaries between heterosexual and homosexual behaviors, practices, and identities in today's contemporary femininities. The normalization of lesbian and gay identity practices and the development of a post-closeted culture entail shifts and changes in gender and sexual behaviors, statuses, and identities. In part, I argue that like lesbian feminism in the 1970s, which conceptualized lesbian identity to be as much a political commitment to women as a sexual desire for them (Stein 1997), queered straight women's practices of sexual fluidity in the 1990s and early twenty-first century were similarly as much about their political identifications with queer friends and subcultures as their own sexual desires.

Queered heterosexualities show that sexual categories cannot determine sexual desires, behaviors, or the variety of practices that constitute sexual identities today. The category of heterosexuality is shot through with complexities of desire and many kinds of erotic experiences; so much so that for some straight women the category of heterosexuality itself must be rethought, reconfigured, and resisted. The concept of queered heterosexualities captures their experiences and contestations of rigid identifications, which aim to enforce gender and sexual normativity. Identities and identifications that circumscribe sexual desires, behaviors, and practices under a presumably unitary category do not capture these women's political identifications, sexual experiences, and queer solidarity. These women provide a blueprint of a set of queered straight identifications in contemporary American sexual politics and culture. Moreover, they demonstrate that queer culture is no longer the sole province of lesbians, gays, bisexuals, and transgender persons; rather, it now includes queered straights who politically identify with LGBTQ individuals and subcultures.

Regarding the gender differences in the blurred boundaries category, more women (seven) than men (four) fell into this category, demonstrating that being strongly antihomophobic seemed to be a stance women were more able to take on than men. Moreover, only the women engaged in practices of sexual fluidity, partly on the basis of their queer-affirmative stances. The four straight men neither reported engaging in sexual fluidity nor made the idea of being fluid part of their pro-gay practice. In other words, the loss of a straight status seemed weightier for men than for women. And a similar dynamic applied across the two racial groups: blacks, as an already stigmatized racial group, risked more in surrendering straight status and privilege than whites, who can draw on racial privilege, and in many cases class privilege, to compensate for the stigma of a nonheterosexual status (Froyum 2007).

The black and white straights at the antihomophobic end of the continuum tended to be nonreligious, nonpracticing believers, or atheists. This suggested that the lack of a religious faith conditioned their ability to be more activist-like in their solidarity with lesbian, gay, and queer people, as religious teachings against homosexuality were absent from their worldviews.

Conclusion

Growing up in a strongly homophobic town, I sought a college and later a profession where I could be an "out" gay man. In contrast, my straight brother, Gene, did not make his choice regarding what college to attend or his profession as a high school teacher on the basis of being an "out" straight guy. Rather, like most straights, he could take the acceptance, recognition, and respect accorded to heterosexuality for granted. However, his decision to support my gay identity, to befriend openly lesbian women and gay men, and to support a Gay Straight Alliance

(GSA) at his high school are some of the ways by which he enacts a pro-gay stance in his everyday life and at work with his students and fellow teachers. His choices are the same kinds of choices every straight person faces in deciding on the boundaries that he or she will create in interactions with LGBTQ people and in negotiating the countless number of symbols of gay and straight identities that circulate in post-closeted contexts.

I have argued for a social and historical approach to understanding the shifts and changes in the social status of black and white straight men's and women's identities. The concept of a post-closeted culture captures the dismantling of antigay discrimination, the integration of out lesbians and gay men, and the number of vivid LGBTQ representations in American society's diverse media landscape today. In this study I have documented the different ways that straight people, through actions and words, have socially constructed boundaries between heterosexuality and homosexuality. As their interactions with lesbian and gay individuals, symbols, and spaces have become more varied, numerous, and complicated, straights have become more conscious, defensive, and deliberate in establishing their identity status. With the rise of a post-closeted culture, black and white straight men and women have started to rethink what it means to be straight and their place in America in the twenty-first century.

Table A.1. Characteristics of the Straight Men

Pseudonyms of White Straight Men	Age (in 2005)	Marital Status	Highest Educational Degree	Occupation	Religious Affiliation	Boundaries of Social Distance
Eric Ward	26	S	MA	Teacher	Not religious	Strongly aversive
Tom Allen	35	S	BA	Government analyst	Nonpracticing Protestant	Strongly aversive
William Russo	38	S	MA	Financial analyst	Not religious	Strongly aversive
Paul Nelson	56	M	MA	Teacher	Presbyterian	Weak
Milton Elias #	36	S	BA	Small business owner	Greek Orthodox	Weak
Derek Perry #	27	S	AA	Hospitality staff	Spiritual	Weak
Jeff Rapaport	37	M	BA	Accountant	Jewish	Weak
Marvin Silverman	5I	S (D)	BA	Small business owner	Nonpracticing Jew	Weak
Joe Bell #	27	S	HS	Waiter	Agnostic	Weak
Carl Rosenberg	40	S	MS	Graduate student	Jewish	Weak
Robert Simon	34	S	MS	Engineer	Nonpracticing Catholic	Weak
Matt Becker #	30	S	BA	Advertising representative	Agnostic	Blurred
Ken Stacey	33	M	MS	Chemist	Atheist	Blurred
Alan Waters	40	M	PhD expected	Graduate student/ instructor	Nonpracticing Catholic	Blurred
Nick Lynch #	22	S	AA	Waiter	Not religious	Blurred
Pseudonyms of Black Straight Men	Age (in 2005)	Marital Status	Highest Educational Degree	Occupation	Religious Affiliation	Boundaries of Social Distance
Rodney Smith	33	M	MA	Teacher	Raised Baptist/now Muslim	Strongly aversive

Table A.1 *(Continued)*

Pseudonyms of Black Straight Men	Age (in 2005)	Marital Status	Highest Educational Degree	Occupation	Religious Affiliation	Boundaries of Social Distance
Terry Bogan	34	S (D)	BA	Security officer	Assembly of God	Strongly aversive
Martin Alexander	44	M	HS	Energy technician	Christian	Strongly aversive
Jessie Clayton	21	S	AA	Hospital staff	Not religious	Strongly aversive
Jerome Gordon	22	S	BA expected	College student	Pentecostal	Strongly aversive
Heath Anderson	21	S	BA expected	College student	Catholic	Strongly aversive
Richard Barrett	56	M	MSW	Healthcare institute director	Baptist	Weak
Toby Marcus	50	S (D)	BA	HIV coordinator	Christian	Weak
George Nelson	21	S	BA expected	College student	Christian	Weak
John Jordan	54	S (D)	BS	Former nurse/ now on disability	Episcopalian	Weak
Mark Wilson	30	S (D)	BA	Teacher's assistant	Non-practicing Masonic Order	Weak
Michael Gates #	22	S	BS expected	College student	Not religious	Weak
Chris Savage	33	S	BA	Personal trainer	Atheist	Weak
Jason Robson #	26	S	BA	Administrative assistant	Atheist	Weak
Darryl White	42	S	MSW	Government administrator	Baptist	Not included*

Note: S = single; D = divorced; M = married; HS = High School; AA = Associate of Arts; BA = Bachelor of Arts; BS = Bachelor of Science; MA = Master of Arts; MS = Master of Sciences; MSW = Master of Social Work; PhD = Doctor of Philosophy

# indicates a metrosexual identification.

* I have excluded Darryl from the analysis, as he did not identify as heterosexual but as a "sexual being." He reported having relationships with both women and men. Although he is of interest for discussions of sexual fluidity, he remains an outlier in my sample and obfuscates my focus here on heterosexual masculinities.

Table A.2. Characteristics of the Straight Women

Pseudonyms of White Straight Women	Age (in 2005)	Marital Status	Highest Educational Degree	Occupation	Religious Affiliation	Boundaries of Social Distance
Louise Miller	61	S (D)	BA	Retired administrative staff	Catholic	Strongly aversive
Beth Moore	26	M	MHS	Physician's assistant	Episcopalian	Strongly aversive
Patricia Jordan	58	M (D)	HS	Executive at nonprofit	Catholic	Strongly aversive
Margaret O'Riordan	35	M	AA	Administrative staff	Catholic	Weak
Jan Pollan	47	M	BA	Executive at small business	Methodist	Weak
Nicole Carey	26	S	MA	Research analyst	Nonpracticing Catholic	Weak
Alicia Donovan	32	S	PhD expected	Graduate student	Spiritual	Weak
Eileen Mahoney	42	M (D)	PharmD	Pharmacist	Nonpracticing Methodist	Weak
Kathy Murphy	24	S	BA	Retail store manager	Catholic	Weak
Eve Donegal #	59	S (D)	BA	Project manager	Protestant	Weak
Vera Godina #	20	S	BA expected	College student	Jewish	Weak
Jennifer Dowd #	47	S (D)	MA	Occupational safety officer	Nonpracticing Catholic	Blurred
Susan Van Dam #	38	M	MA	Government analyst	Nonpracticing Catholic	Blurred
Kim Masterson #	24	S	BA	Recent college graduate	Nonpracticing Protestant	Blurred
Maureen O'Conner #	39	S (D)	AA	Restaurant/ bar owner	Nonpracticing Catholic	Blurred
Pseudonyms of Black Straight Women	Age (in 2005)	Marital Status	Highest Educational Degree	Occupation	Religious Affiliation	Boundaries of Social Distance
Martha Lewis	54	S (D)	MA	Christian counselor	Christian	Strongly aversive
Ghanima Powell	20	S	BA expected	College student	Methodist	Strongly aversive
Sandra Morgan	43	M	BS	Public health manager	Christian	Strongly aversive
Kelly Jones	33	S	PhD expected	Graduate student	Methodist	Strongly aversive

Table A.2 *(Continued)*

Pseudonyms of Black Straight Women	Age (in 2005)	Marital Status	Highest Educational Degree	Occupation	Religious Affiliation	Boundaries of Social Distance
Nia Gray	21	S	MA expected	Graduate student	Not religious	Strongly aversive
Dionne Watkins	68	S (D)	BA	Retired social worker	Catholic	Weak
Nina Carlisle	23	S	BA	Administrative staff	Baptist	Weak
Cheryl Barksdale	20	S	BA expected	College student	Spiritual	Weak
Stephanie Phillips	Refused	M	MA	AIDS project manager	Raised Baptist, Methodist	Weak
Jody Knight #	20	S	BA expected	College student	Not religious	Weak
Vanessa Marshall	27	S	BA	Retail store manager	Methodist	Weak
Maya Gaines #	19	S	BA expected	College student	Not religious	Blurred
Denise Lee #	29	M	PhD	Professor	Nonpracticing Catholic	Blurred
Erica Harris #	22	S	BA	Restaurant manager	Not religious	Blurred
Naomi Lynch	23	S	HS	Health care assistant	Not religious	Not included*

Note: S = single; D = divorced; M = married; HS = High School; AA = Associate of Arts; BA = Bachelor of Arts; BS = Bachelor of Science; MA = Master of Arts; MS = Master of Sciences; MSW = Master of Social Work; MHS: Master of Health Sciences; PhD = Doctor of Philosophy; PharmD = Doctor of Pharmacy

# indicates a woman who engaged in practices of sexual fluidity.

* I have excluded Naomi Lynch from the analysis, as she did not identify as heterosexual. When asked about her sexual identity, she stated, "I like both men and women, but I don't like to be called bisexual or heterosexual."

NOTES

NOTES TO THE INTRODUCTION

1. My brother and I identify as racially mixed due to the racial identities of our white father and Mexican American mother, but phenotypically, we appear white to others in social interactions due to our light-skinned complexions.
2. Of course, issues of sexualities, gender, and race are as salient for nonblack people of color (see, for example, the excellent collection of essays on Latina/o sexualities edited by Marysol Asencio [2010]; on Asian American sexualities, see Russell Leong's [2011] edited volume).
3. It should be noted that the question was asking whether same-sex relations should be decriminalized, not whether same-sex couples should be allowed to legally marry.
4. I thank Nancy Fischer for suggesting to me the phrase "strongly aversive."
5. However, in order to maintain a sense of place, I have not changed the names of past cities mentioned by the interviewees in their quotes. As most of the interviewees grew up in cities throughout the Northeast, this maintains the study's sense of location in this region without revealing the interviewees' actual identities.

NOTE TO CHAPTER 1

1. Of course, focusing on gay marriage as the most highly esteemed arrangement for queers' intimate relationships means devaluing nonmarried LGBT relationships. At the same time, it is important to sociologically study the shifts in the closet in the historical present to understand the alterations in the homo/heterosexual binary through the new and unprecedented patterns of a post-closeted culture, which should not be taken for granted or rhetorically dismissed as simply homonormative (see Barton 2012; Butler 2004, 5; and Lewin 2009, 7–9).

NOTES TO CHAPTER 2

1. Although I use the term "masculinity," I acknowledge the historian Gail Bederman's (1995) careful historicizing of this term and its emergence in the 1890s in efforts to shore up ideologies of men's status. Bederman's study provides an edifying discussion of the differences between definitions of manliness and masculinity and the sociohistorical reasons for the latter's development in America at this time (see especially pp. 16–20).

2. Of course, this is not the only possible sketch, nor is it even a historically exhaustive one, for it centers on historical scholarship that explicitly analyzes heterosexualities as distinct from gender identities.

3. However, Freud and these sexologists held competing notions over the etiology of same-sex sexuality as congenital or developmental (see Chauncey 1982; Meyerowitz 2010).

NOTE TO CHAPTER 3

1. See Hochschild (2003) on the sociological logic of gratitude and its role in the gender dynamics between straight couples. For her, gratitude means that a person feels that he or she is offering something extra in the emotional exchange between individuals. A common example is a wife who feels grateful for her husband's support of her career or higher earning power.

NOTES TO CHAPTER 4

1. The feminist sex wars of the 1980s and 1990s led to debates over female sexuality (Duggan and Hunter 2006), such as a woman's ability to consent to sex under male domination in a rape- and harassment-prone culture (e.g., MacKinnon 1989; Segal 1994, 1997), and they fomented the growth of work on prostitution and pornography; still, these studies did not analytically focus on heterosexuality's role in shaping these women's femininities (e.g., Burstyn 1985; Vance 1984; Snitow, Stansell, and Thompson 1983).

2. I draw on lesbian and queer theories in this chapter to understand the identity practices of heterosexual women and how they perform their identities while negotiating the systems of normative heterosexuality and male domination (Butler 1990). Judith Butler (1990) argues that Adrienne Rich and Monique Wittig theorize the construction of heterosexuality among women as centrally excluding the existence of nonheterosexuals, especially lesbians as "women." Butler argues that the category "women" has been overdetermined by its relation to men and thus understood in exclusively heterosexual terms. Clearly, historical studies support this claim, and first- and second-wave feminism, along with the general enfranchisement of women as equals and the weakening of male privilege, have been formed in part through the exclusions, denials, or repudiations of lesbianism since at least the 1920s. Historically, if not presently as well, the specter of lesbianism has served as a way to effectively discredit any effort to support women's empowerment (Smith-Rosenberg 1993; Meyerowitz 1994b; Duggan 2000). However, both lesbians' and women's social movements as well as their identity practices and knowledge production have altered the systematic power and enforcement of heterosexual and male domination in America today.

3. As in chapter 3, I define heterosexual femininities as configurations of sexual-gender practice and discourse that refer to the identity categories of heterosexuals and women and are organized in relation to the structures of sexual and gender orders. Heterosexualities generally, but not necessarily, align with sexual

behaviors and desires orientated to the other—as opposed to the same—gender. Femininities are gender practices that generally refer to women and female bodies but may include men and nonfemale bodies as well (Schippers 2007).

4. The queer theorist Steven Seidman (2009), though, does differentiate normative heterosexuality as more sociological in its theorizing of heterosexual domination and homosexual subordination, arguing that normative heterosexuality more clearly links the enforcement of heterosexuality in social institutions and relations than the term "heteronormativity." For him, heteronormativity has been generally used in exclusively cultural critiques and textual analyses, as opposed to empirical analyses of the enforcement of normative heterosexuality. Also see Barry Adam's (1998) discussion of the terms "heteronormativity," "homophobia," and "heterosexism" for a similar position to Seidman's. Other sociologists, like Karin Martin (2009), have bypassed this debate over terminology and empirically embraced "heteronormativity," aiming to spell out its sociological value through research. Seidman also views compulsory heterosexuality as theorizing an overly strong "gender structuralism," one that is no longer sociohistorically accurate in describing many American women's lives. I don't disagree with his assessment of the relations between men and women, but I also don't think we have to relegate compulsory heterosexuality to the decades of the 1970s and 1980s. My usage of "compulsory heterosexuality" embraces a weak notion of gender structure, one meant to understand its shifts historically.

5. Similarly, I think Connell's notion of hegemonic masculinity, while perhaps it does emphasize more the gender order over the sexual order, allows the theorization of gender and sexualities more clearly than simply heteronormativity in understanding the social construction of straight masculinities.

6. The sociologist Patricia Hill Collins ([1990] 2000, 89–90) observes that black women's beauty is devalued in a hierarchy where white features, as represented through lighter skin color, hair texture, and other phenotypical characteristics, are deemed more beautiful and desirable than black ones. Racial and racist discourses, moreover, generally construct black bodies and sexualities as hypersexual (Collins [1990] 2000, 2004; D'Emilio and Freedman 2012). This hypersexual discourse stigmatizes black women's femininities as masculine. The stereotypical images of hypersexual welfare queens with several young children or hypersexed black women dancers in "strip hop" music videos reinforce this point, for example (Collins 2004; Hunter 2010).

7. The women interviewed identified as black or white heterosexual women with the exception of one of the black women, Naomi Lynch. I have excluded her from the analysis, as she did not self-identify as heterosexual, which is the subjective definition I used in my study for both the women and men I interviewed regarding heterosexual identities. Naomi stated, "I like both men and women, but I don't like to be called bisexual or heterosexual." I address this issue again in the third section of the chapter when I discuss sexual fluidity among the straight women I interviewed.

8. See Julie Bettie's (2005) analysis of how white high school girls wouldn't express outright racial prejudice against Chicana girls but instead channeled their racial tensions into opposing affirmative action policies. This is similar to straight women in my study who avoid being explicitly homophobic and instead express their prejudice against gays by opposing same-sex marriage. I thank Nancy Fischer for pointing out this connection to me.

9. It is important to note that many homeless black queer youth have been kicked out of their homes due to their adoption of nonstraight identities. For example, see Aviv 2012.

10. See Dawne Moon's (2004) ethnographic study of a reconciling and nonreconciling Methodist congregation. The former is a trend in the Methodist faith that openly embraces lesbian and gay members as part of their faith's religious community. Thus, within the United Methodist Church, churches that belong to the Reconciling Congregations Program illustrate the post-closeted cultural dynamic I am examining here among straights.

11. Before the Stonewall generation, moreover, these relationships were part of gay men's secret and coded language in public settings, where heterosexual people would not be able to understand the double entendre and subcultural meaning of words like "gay" as indicating homosexuality in the 1920s and 1930s. A famous historical example of the relationship between a straight female celebrity and her gay male fans is the idolization of Judy Garland by gay men in the 1950s and 1960s and their use of the phrase "Are you a friend of Dorothy?" to indicate by way of Garland's role in *The Wizard of Oz* their homosexual identity and interest in knowing whether another man was homosexual as well (Chauncey 1994). After Stonewall, this relationship becomes increasingly part of public knowledge and discourse around gay men and straight women's friendships.

12. For the sake of avoiding repetition between this chapter and the next, I did not present Erica's statement that connects the opposition to racial oppression and the opposition to sexual oppression. This statement from her is included in chapter 5's discussion of straight women's practices of sexual fluidity and their adoption of queered identifications.

NOTES TO CHAPTER 5

1. I use the term "queered heterosexual" instead of "queer heterosexual" to indicate a subject position that is not a total rejection of the identity category of heterosexuality, but rather a contestation of its meanings. Queered heterosexualities incorporate practices of sexual fluidity partly out of antihomophobic stances and partly due to identifications with LGBT people and culture. I thank the anonymous peer reviewer for his/her insightful commentary on this analytical point.

2. Other examples of nonnormative heterosexualities might include those heterosexuals who oppose monogamy, such as lifestylers or swingers (Frank 2008) and individuals involved in polyamorous relationships (Sheff 2006), as well as heterosexuals who engage in non-vanilla sexual practices like BDSM. Whether

the various bisexual identifications and practices of women lifestylers or poly-amorous women may be considered a queered heterosexuality is beyond the scope of this chapter. However, as most lifestyle men claim to be "not gay, but not homophobic," they are better thought of as indicating nonnormative rather than queered heterosexualities, as they exclude sexual fluidity or bisexuality from their self-identification, according to the anthropologist Katherine Frank's (2008) study.

3. There was one exception. Greg, a fifty-six-year-old white heterosexual man, states that he did not connect engaging in sexual behaviors with a boyhood friend as indicating homosexual desires to him at that point in time. In fact, he does not recall the term "homosexual" as part of his vocabulary at the time. He says, "Back in the 1960s the term 'homosexual' never even existed in terms of a twelve-year-old would never even hear the word." Regardless of the accuracy of Greg's statement regarding what adolescent boys in the 1960s heard and said about homosexuality, he does not incorporate sexual fluidity into his sexual identity practices today, nor does he think of this past same-sex experience as shaping his heterosexual self-identity. For these reasons, I do not explore Greg's account of his adolescent same-sex behavior.

4. It is important to note that the rhetoric of the "down low" or "DL" positions black men who have sex with men (MSM) as dissimilar to the white MSM. Both black and white MSM similarly disidentify with gay identity labels, and both often invoke their normative performances of masculinity as partly explaining their rationales for rejecting gay identities and communities. The sociologist Jane Ward's (2008a) analysis of white MSM sex ads on the website Craigslist finds that a set of "white" archetypes, such as surfers, skaters, and frat boys, circulates in the rhetoric of white MSM's self-descriptions for homosexual sex. In part, these "white" archetypes seem to be in keeping with these MSM's het-erosexual identifications that employ misogynist and homophobic stances while simultaneously seeking homosexual sex.

5. See Diamond 2008, 84–90. In thinking about women's sexual fluidity through depth psychology, psychoanalytically, Nancy Chodorow (1978, 1999) argues that one central social-psychological developmental configuration among girls is the making of their mothers as their first love object. Girls' love of their mothers situates them within a homosexual object choice position. Thus, Chodorow's work suggests that sexual fluidity among women, both straight and queer, has psychological underpinnings, which take place early on in girls' social-psycho-logical identity formation.

NOTE TO CHAPTER 6

1. Chauncey (1994) dates the use of the term "closet" by lesbians and gay men to the 1960s (see especially pp. 6 and 9–26). I follow him in using it to character-ize the historical shifts in the development of antihomosexual state-sponsored oppression over the course of the late nineteenth and twentieth centuries.

Adam, Barry. 1995. *The Rise of a Gay and Lesbian Movement*. New York: Twayne.
———. 1998. "Theorizing Homophobia." *Sexualities* 1 (14): 387–404.
Adams, Mary Louise. 1997. *The Trouble with Normal: Postwar Youth and the Making of Heterosexuality*. Toronto: University of Toronto Press.
Alba, Richard. 1999. "Immigration and the American Realities of Assimilation and Multiculturalism." *Sociological Forum* 14 (1): 3–25.
Alexander, Jeffrey. 1988. *Durkheimian Sociology: Cultural Studies*. New York: Cambridge University Press.
Allen, Frederick Lewis. 1931. *Only Yesterday*. New York: Harper and Brothers.
Allen, Paula Gunn. 1993. "Lesbians in American Indian Cultures." In *Hidden from History*, ed. Martin Duberman, Martha Vicinus, and George Chauncey, 106–17. New York: Meridian.
Almaguer, Tomás. 1993a. "Chicano Men: A Cartography of Homosexual Identity and Behavior." In *The Lesbian and Gay Studies Reader*, ed. Henry Abelove, Michèle Aina Barale, and David Halperin, 255–73. New York: Routledge.
———. 1993b. *Racial Fault Lines*. Berkeley: University of California Press.
Altman, Dennis. 1982. *The Homosexualization of America*. Boston: Beacon.
Anderson, Elijah. 1999. *Code of the Street: Decency, Violence, and the Moral Life of the Inner City*. New York: Norton.
Anderson, Eric. 2005. "Orthodox and Inclusive Masculinity: Competing Masculinities among Heterosexual Men in a Feminized Terrain." *Sociological Perspectives* 48 (3): 337–55.
———. 2008. "'Being Masculine Is Not about Who You Sleep With . . .': Heterosexual Athletes Contesting Masculinity and the One-Time Rule of Homosexuality." *Sex Roles* 58: 104–15.
———. 2009. *Inclusive Masculinity: The Changing Nature of Masculinities*. New York: Routledge.
Anderson, Robert, and Tina Fetner. 2008. "Cohort Differences in Tolerance of Homosexuality: Attitudinal Change in Canada and United States, 1981–2000." *Public Opinion Quarterly* 72 (2): 311–30.
Armstrong, Elizabeth. 2002. *Forging Gay Identities: Organizing Sexuality in San Francisco, 1950–1994*. Chicago: University of Chicago Press.
Arnett, Jeffrey Jensen. 1994. "Are College Students Adults? Their Conceptions of the Transition to Adulthood." *Journal of Adult Development* 1 (4): 213–24.

Asencio, Marysol, ed. 2010. *Latina/o Sexualities: Probing Powers, Passions, Practices, and Policies*. New Brunswick: Rutgers University Press.

Atkinson, Ti-Grace. 1974. *Amazon Odyssey*. New York: Links Books.

Aviv, Rachel. 2012. "Netherland: Homeless in New York, a Young Gay Woman Learns to Survive." *New Yorker*, December 10.

Barber, Karen. 2008. "The Well-Coiffed Man: Class, Race, and Heterosexual Masculinity in the Hair Salon." *Gender & Society* 22 (4): 455–76.

Barry, Kathleen. (1979) 1983. *Female Sexual Slavery*. New York: New York University Press.

———. 1995. *The Prostitution of Sexuality*. New York: New York University Press.

Barton, Bernadette. 2012. *Pray the Gay Away: The Extraordinary Lives of Bible Belt Gays*. New York: New York University Press.

Battle, Juan, and Lisa J. Schulte. 2004. "The Relative Importance of Ethnicity and Religion in Predicting Attitudes towards Gays and Lesbians." *Journal of Homosexuality* 47 (2): 127–42.

Bederman, Gail. 1995. *Manliness and Civilization: A Cultural History of Gender and Race in the United States, 1880–1917*. Chicago: University of Chicago Press.

Benhabib, Seyla. 1999. "Civil Society and the Politics of Identity and Difference in a Global Context." In *Diversity and Its Discontents: Cultural Conflict and Common Ground in Contemporary American Society*, ed. Neil J. Smelser and Jeffrey C. Alexander, 293–312. Princeton: Princeton University Press.

Benjamin, Jessica. 1998. *The Bonds of Love: Psychoanalysis, Gender, and the Problem of Domination*. New York: Pantheon.

Berger, Michelle, and Cheryl Radeloff. 2011. *Transforming Scholarship: Why Women's and Gender Studies Are Changing Themselves and the World*. New York: Routledge.

Bernstein, Elizabeth. 2007. *Temporarily Yours: Intimacy, Authenticity, and the Commerce of Sex*. Chicago: University of Chicago Press.

Bérubé, Allan. 1990. *Coming Out under Fire: The History of Gay Men and Women in World War Two*. New York: Free Press.

———. 2001. "How Gay Stays White and What Kind of White It Stays." In *The Making and Unmaking of Whiteness*, ed. Birgit Brander Rasmussen et al., 234–65. Durham: Duke University Press.

Best, Amy L. 2000. *Prom Night: Youth, Schools, and Popular Culture*. New York: Routledge.

Bettie, Julie. 2005. *Women without Class: Gender, Race, and Identity*. Berkeley: University of California Press.

Biblarz, Timothy, and Judith Stacey. 2010. "How Does the Gender of Parents Matter?" *Journal of Marriage and Family* 72 (February): 3–22.

Blow, Charles. 2008. "Gay Marriage and a Moral Minority." *New York Times*, November 29.

Bourdieu, Pierre. 1984. *Distinction*. Palo Alto: Stanford University Press.

———. 2001. *Masculine Domination*. Palo Alto: Stanford University Press.

Boyd, Nan Alamilla. 2003. *Wide-Open Town: A History of Queer San Francisco to 1965*. Berkeley: University of California Press.

Braumbaugh, Stacey, Steven Nock, and James Wright. 2008. "Attitudes toward Gay Marriage in States Undergoing Marriage Law Transformation." *Journal of Marriage and Family* 70 (May): 345–59.

Brekhus, Wayne. 2003. *Peacocks, Chameleons, Centaurs: Gay Suburbia and the Grammar of Social Identity*. Chicago: University of Chicago Press.

Brewer, Paul. 2003. "The Shifting Foundation of Public Opinion about Gay Rights." *Journal of Politics* 65 (4): 1208–20.

Brownmiller, Susan. 1975. *Against Our Will: Men, Women and Rape*. New York: Simon and Schuster.

Bunch, Charlotte. 1975. "Not for Lesbians Only." *Quest: A Feminist Quarterly*, fall.

Burawoy, Michael, Alice Burton, Ann Ferguson, and Kathryn Fox, eds. 1991. *Ethnography Unbound*. Berkeley: University of California Press.

Burstyn, Varda, ed. 1985. *Women against Censorship*. Vancouver: Douglas and McIntyre.

Butler, Judith. 1990. *Gender Trouble: Feminism and the Subversion of Identity*. New York: Routledge.

———. 1992. *Bodies That Matter: On the Discursive Limits of "Sex."* New York: Routledge.

———. 2004. *Undoing Gender*. New York: Routledge.

Cahn, Susan. 2007. *Sexual Reckonings: Southern Girls in a Troubling Age*. Cambridge: Harvard University Press.

Calhoun, Craig, ed. (1992) 1999. *Habermas and the Public Sphere*. Cambridge: MIT Press.

———. 1994. "Social Theory and the Politics of Identity." In *Social Theory and the Politics of Identity*, ed. Craig Calhoun, 9–36. Cambridge, MA: Blackwell.

Califia, Pat. 1994. *Public Sex: The Culture of Radical Sex*. Pittsburgh: Cleis.

Canaday, Margot. 2009. *The Straight State: Sexuality and Citizenship in Twentieth-Century America*. Princeton: Princeton University Press.

Cancian, Francesca. 1987. *Love in America: Gender and Self-Development*. New York: Cambridge University Press.

Cantú, Lionel. 2002. "A Place Called Home: A Queer Political Economy: Mexican Immigrant Men's Family Experiences." In *Sexuality and Gender*, ed. Christine Williams and Arlene Stein, 384–94. Malden, MA: Blackwell.

Carbado, Devon, ed. 1999. *Black Men on Race, Gender, and Sexuality: A Critical Reader*. New York: New York University Press.

Carby, Hazel V. 1986. "It Jus Be's Dat Way Sometime: The Sexual Politics of Women's Blues." *Radical America* 20 (4): 9–22.

———. 1992. "Policing the Black Woman's Body in an Urban Context." *Critical Inquiry* 18 (4): 738–55.

Carrigan, Tim, R. W. Connell, and John Lee. 2002. "Toward a New Sociology of Masculinity." In *The Masculinity Studies Reader*, ed. Rachel Adams and David Savran, 99–118. Malden, MA: Blackwell.

Castells, Manuel. 1983. *The City and the Grass Roots: A Cross-Cultural Theory of Urban Social Movements*. Berkeley: University of California Press.

————. 1996. *The Rise of the Network Society: The Information Age: Economy, Society, and Culture.* Vol. 1. Malden, MA: Blackwell.

Chapkis, Wendy. 1997. *Live Sex Acts: Women Performing Erotic Labor.* New York: Routledge.

Charmaz, Kathy. 2007. *Constructing Grounded Theory.* London: Sage.

Chasin, Alexandra. 2000. *Selling Out: The Gay and Lesbian Movement Goes to the Market.* New York: Palgrave.

Chauncey, George. 1982. "From Sexual Inversion to Homosexuality: Medicine and the Changing Conceptualization of Female Deviance." *Salmagundi* 58–59: 114–46.

————. 1994. *Gay New York: Gender, Urban Culture, and the Making of the Gay Male World, 1890–1940.* New York: Basic Books.

————. 2004. *Why Marriage? The History Shaping Today's Debate over Gay Equality.* Cambridge: Perseus.

————. 2008. "How History Mattered: Sodomy Law and Marriage Reform in the United States." *Public Culture* 20 (1): 27–38.

Chee, Alexander. 1991. "A Queer Nationalism." *Out/Look* (Winter): 15–19.

Cherlin, Andrew. 2004. "The Deinstitutionalization of American Marriage." *Journal of Marriage and Family* 66 (4): 848–61.

————. 2009. *The Marriage-Go-Round: The State of Marriage and Family in America Today.* New York: Knopf.

Chodorow, Nancy. 1978. *The Reproduction of Mothering: Psychoanalysis and the Sociology of Gender.* Berkeley: University of California Press.

————. 1998. "Homophobia: Analysis of a Permissible Prejudice." Presentation at American Psychoanalytic Association Public Forum, New York.

————. 1999. *The Power of Feelings: Personal Meaning in Psychoanalysis, Gender, and Culture.* New Haven: Yale University Press.

Clark, Danae. 1993. "Commodity Lesbianism." In *The Lesbian and Gay Studies Reader,* ed. Henry Abelove, Michèle Aina Barale, and David Halperin, 186–201. New York: Routledge.

Clatterbaugh, Kenneth. 1997. *Contemporary Perspectives on Masculinity: Men, Women, and Politics in Modern Society.* Boulder: Westview.

Clemetson, Lynette. 2004. "Gay Marriage and the Black Church." *New York Times,* March 1, A1, A12.

Coad, David. 2008. *The Metrosexual: Gender, Sexuality, and Sport.* Albany: State University of New York Press.

Cohen, Jean. 1985. "Strategy or Identity: New Theoretical Paradigms and Contemporary Social Movements." *Social Research* 52 (4): 663–716.

————. 2002. *Rethinking Intimacy: A New Legal Paradigm.* Princeton: Princeton University Press.

Cole, David. 2013. "Equality and the Roberts Court: Four Decisions." *New York Review of Books,* August 15, 28–30.

Collins, Gail. 2009. *When Everything Changed: The Amazing Journey of American Women from 1960 to Present.* New York: Little Brown.

Collins, Patricia Hill. (1990) 2000. *Black Feminist Thought: Knowledge, Consciousness, and the Politics of Empowerment.* New York: Routledge.

———. 2004. *Black Sexual Politics: African Americans, Gender, and the New Racism.* New York: Routledge.

Conerly, Gregory. 2000. "Swishing and Swaggering: Homosexuality in Black Magazines during the 1950s." In *The Greatest Taboo: Homosexuality in Black Communities,* ed. Delroy Constantine-Simms, 384–95. Los Angeles: Allyson.

Connell, R. W. 1987. *Gender and Power.* Palo Alto: Stanford University Press.

———. 1995. *Masculinities.* Berkeley: University of California Press.

Connell, R. W., and James Messerschmidt. 2005. "Hegemonic Masculinity: Rethinking the Concept." *Gender & Society* 16 (9): 829–59.

Constantine-Simms, Delroy, ed. 2000. *The Greatest Taboo: Homosexuality in Black Communities.* Los Angeles: Allyson.

Corber, Robert and Stephen Valocchi, eds. 2003. *Queer Studies: An Interdisciplinary Approach.* Malden, MA: Blackwell.

Corbett, Ken. 1993. "Between Fear and Fantasy." *New York Times,* February 3.

———. 2009. *Boyhoods: Rethinking Masculinities.* New Haven: Yale University Press.

Corrado, Carolyn. 2010. "White Noise: Constructing Whiteness in Hip Hop America." Ph.D. diss. proposal, Department of Sociology, State University of New York at Albany.

Dang, Alain, and Somjen Frazer. 2004. *Black Same-Sex Households in the United States.* New York: National Gay and Lesbian Task Force Policy Institute and the National Black Justice Coalition.

Davis, James Earl. 2001. "Black Boys at School: Negotiating Masculinities and Race." In *Black Education Revolution,* ed. Richard Majors, 169–82. London: Taylor and Francis.

Davis, Whitney, ed. 1994. *Gay and Lesbian Studies in Art History.* Binghamton, NY: Haworth.

Dean, James Joseph. 2007. "Gays and Queers: From the Centering to the Decentering of Homosexuality in American Films." *Sexualities* 10 (3): 363–86.

———. 2011. "The Cultural Construction of Heterosexual Identities." *Sociology Compass* 5 (8): 679–87.

———. 2013. "Heterosexual Masculinities, Anti-homophobias, and Shifts in Hegemonic Masculinity: The Identity Practices of Black and White Heterosexual Men." *Sociological Quarterly* 54 (4): 534–60.

Dellinger, Kirsten, and Christine L. Williams. 1997. "Makeup at Work: Negotiating Appearance Rules in the Workplace." *Gender & Society* 11 (2): 151–77.

Demetriou, Demetrakis. 2001. "Connell's Concept of Hegemonic Masculinity: A Critique." *Theory and Society* 30 (3): 337–61.

D'Emilio, John. 1983. *Sexual Politics, Sexual Communities: The Making of a Homosexual Minority in the United States, 1940–1970.* Chicago: University of Chicago Press.

———. 1989. "The Homosexual Menace: The Politics of Homosexuality in Cold War America." In *Passion and Power: Sexuality in History,* ed. Kathy Peiss and Christina Simmons with Robert Padgug, 226–40. Philadelphia: Temple University Press.

———. 2002. *The World Turned: Essays on Gay History, Politics, and Culture*. Durham: Duke University Press.

D'Emilio, John, and Estelle Freedman. 2012. *Intimate Matters: A History of Sexuality in America*. 3rd ed. Chicago: University of Chicago Press.

Denizet-Lewis, Benoit. 2003. "Double Lives on the Down Low." *New York Times Magazine*. April 3.

Diamond, Lisa M. 2008. *Sexual Fluidity: Understanding Women's Love and Desire*. Cambridge: Harvard University Press.

Diaz, Rafael. 1998. *Latino Gay Men and HIV*. New York: Routledge.

Di Leonardo, Micaela. 1987. "The Female World of Cards and Holidays: Women, Families, and the World of Kinship." *Signs* 12 (Spring): 410–53.

Douglas, Mary. (1966) 1970. *Purity and Danger: An Analysis of Concepts of Pollution and Taboo*. London: Routledge.

Du Bois, W. E. B. 1969. *The Negro American Family*. New York: Negro Universities Press.

DuCille, Anne. 1989. "Blues Notes on Black Sexuality: Sex and the Texts of Jessie Fauset and Nella Larsen." In *American Sexual Politics*, ed. John C. Fout and Maura Shaw Tantillo, 193–219. Chicago: University of Chicago Press.

Duggan, Lisa. 2000. *Sapphic Slashers: Sex, Violence, and American Modernity*. Durham: Duke University Press.

———. 2003. *The Twilight of Equality: Neoliberalism, Cultural Politics, and the Attack on Democracy*. Boston: Beacon.

Duggan, Lisa, and Nan D. Hunter. 2006. *Sex Wars: Sexual Dissent and Political Culture*. New York: Routledge.

Durell, Megan, Catherine Chiong, and Juan Battle. 2007. "Race, Gender Expectations, and Homophobia: A Quantitative Exploration." *Race, Class & Gender* 14 (1–2): 299–317.

Durkheim, Émile. (1915) 1995. "Contribution to an Enquiry on the Work of H. Tame." *Durkheimian Studies* 1.

Dworkin, Andrea. 1987. *Intercourse*. New York: Free Press.

Dworkin, Andrea, and Catharine MacKinnon. 1988. *Pornography and Civil Rights*. Minneapolis: University of Minnesota Press.

Dyer, Richard. 1997. *White*. New York: Routledge.

Egan, Patrick, and Kenneth Sherrill. 2009. "California's Proposition 8: What Happened and What Does the Future Hold?" Unpublished paper commissioned by the Evelyn and Walter Haas, Jr. Fund in San Francisco. National Gay and Lesbian Task Force.

Ehrenreich, Barbara. 1983. *The Hearts of Men: American Dreams and the Flight from Commitment*. New York: Anchor Press/Doubleday.

———. 1995. "The Decline of Patriarchy." In *Constructing Masculinity*, ed. Maurice Berger, Brian Wallis, and Simon Watson, 284–90. New York: Routledge.

Eitzen, D. Stanley, Maxine Baca Zinn, and Kelly Smith. 2012. *In Conflict and Order: Understanding Society*. Boston: Pearson Education.

English, Deirdre, Amber Hollibaugh, and Gayle Rubin. 1981. "Talking Sex: A Conversation on Sexuality and Feminism." *Socialist Review* 11 (4): 43–62.

Epstein, Debbie, and Richard Johnson. 1998. *Schooling Sexualities*. Buckingham, UK: Open University Press.

Epstein, Steven. 1996. "Queer Encounter: Sociology and the Study of Sexuality." In *Queer Theory/ Sociology*, ed. Steven Seidman, 145–76. Oxford, UK: Wiley.

———. 1999. "Gay and Lesbian Movements in the United States: Dilemmas of Identity, Diversity, and Political Strategy." In *The Global Emergence of Gay and Lesbian Politics: National Imprints of a Worldwide Movement*, ed. Barry D. Adam, Jan Willem Duyvendak, and André Krouwel, 30–90. Philadelphia: Temple University Press.

Eskridge, William. 1999. *Gaylaw: Challenging the Apartheid of the Closet*. Cambridge: Harvard University Press.

Espiritu, Yen Le. 1992. *Asian American Panethnicity: Bridging Institutions and Identities*. Philadelphia: Temple University Press.

Faderman, Lillian. 1981. *Surpassing the Love of Men: Romantic Friendships and Love between Women from the Renaissance to the Present*. New York: Morrow.

———. 1991. *Odd Girls and Twilight Lovers: A History of Lesbian Life in Twentieth-Century America*. New York: Penguin.

Faludi, Susan. 1999. *Stiffed: The Betrayal of the American Man*. New York: HarperCollins.

Felmlee, Diane. 1994. "Who's on Top? Power in Romantic Relationships." *Sex Roles* 10: 106–35.

———. 1999. "Social Norms in Same- and Cross-Gender Friendships." *Social Science Quarterly* 62 (1): 53–67.

Ferguson, Roderick. 2004. *Aberrations in Black: Toward a Queer of Color Critique*. Minneapolis: University of Minnesota Press.

Ferree, Myra Marx, Judith Lorber, and Beth Hess, eds. 1999. *Revisioning Gender*. Thousand Oaks, CA: Sage.

Finlay, Barbara and Carol Walther. 2003. "The Relation of Religious Affiliation, Service Attendance, and Other Factors to Homophobic Attitudes among University Students." *Review of Religious Research* 44: 370–93.

Fisher, Randy, Donna Derison, Chester Polley, Jennifer Cadman, and Dana Johnston. 1994. "Religiousness, Religious Orientation, and Attitudes towards Gays and Lesbians." *Journal of Applied Social Psychology* 24: 614–30.

Flocker, Michael. 2003. *The Metrosexual Guide to Style: A Handbook for the Modern Man*. Cambridge, MA: Da Capo.

Foucault, Michel. 1978. *The History of Sexuality*. Vol. 1, *An Introduction*. New York: Vintage.

Frank, Katherine. 2008. "'Not Gay, but Not Homophobic': Male Sexuality and Homophobia in the 'Lifestyle.'" *Sexualities* 11 (4): 435–54.

Frankenberg, Ruth. 1993. *White Women, Race Matters: The Social Construction of Whiteness*. Minneapolis: University of Minnesota Press.

Frazier, E. Franklin. 1948. *The Negro Family in the United States*. New York: Dryden.

Freud, Sigmund. (1922) 1949. *Group Psychology and the Analysis of the Ego*. Trans. James Strachey. London: Hogarth.

———. 1962. *Three Essays on the Theory of Sexuality*. New York: Basic Books.

Frey, William. 1998. "The Diversity Myth." *American Demographics*, June, http:/www. demographics.com/publications/ad/98_ad/980626.htm.

Friedan, Betty. 1963. *The Feminine Mystique*. New York: Norton.

Froyum, Carissa. 2007. "'At Least I'm Not Gay': Heterosexual Identity Making among Poor Black Teens." *Sexualities* 10 (5): 603–22.

Fuss, Diana, ed. 1991. *Inside/Out: Lesbian Theories, Gay Theories*. New York: Routledge.

Gallup. 1977–2013. "Gay and Lesbian Rights." Retrieved January 1, 2013. http://www. gallup.com/poll/1651/Gay-Lesbian-Rights.aspx.

Gallup, George, and Lindsay D. McDonald. 1999. *Surveying the Religious Landscape: Trends in U.S. Beliefs*. Harrisburg: Morehouse.

Gallup, Gordon. 1995. "Have Attitudes toward Homosexuals Been Shaped by Natural Selection?" *Ethology and Sociobiology* 16 (1): 53–70.

Gamson, Joshua. 1998. *Freaks Talk Back: Tabloid Talk Shows and Sexual Nonconformity*. Chicago: University of Chicago Press.

———. 2002. "Sweating in the Spotlight: Lesbian, Gay and Queer Encounters with Media and Popular Culture." In *Handbook of Lesbian and Gay Studies*, ed. Diane Richardson and Steven Seidman, 339–54. Thousand Oaks, CA: Sage.

———. 2005. "The Intersection of Gay Street and Straight Street: Shopping, Social Class, and the New Gay Visibility." *Social Thought and Research* 26 (1–2): 3–18.

Gans, Herbert. 1999. "The Possibility of a New Racial Hierarchy in the Twenty-First-Century United States." In *The Cultural Territories of Race: Black and White Boundaries*, ed. Michele Lamont, 371–90. Chicago and New York: University of Chicago and Russell Sage Foundation.

Garber, Eric. 1989. "A Spectacle in Color: The Lesbian and Gay Subculture of Jazz Age Harlem." In *Hidden from History*, ed. Martin Duberman, Martha Vicinus, and George Chauncey, 318–31. New York: Meridian.

Garfinkel, Harold. 1967. *Studies in Ethnomethodology*. Englewood Cliffs: Prentice-Hall.

Gates, Gary, Brad Sears, and Holing Lau. 2006. "Asians and Pacific Islanders in Same-Sex Couples in the United States: Data from Census 2000." *Amerasia Journal* 32 (1): 15–32.

Gentry, Cynthia. 1987. "Social Distance regarding Male and Female Homosexuals." *Journal of Social Psychology* 127: 199–208.

Gerson, Kathleen. 2010. *The Unfinished Revolution: Coming of Age in a New Era of Gender, Work, and Family*. New York: Cambridge University Press.

Ghaziani, Amin. 2008. *The Dividends of Dissent: How Conflict and Culture Work in Lesbian and Gay Marches on Washington*. Chicago: University of Chicago Press.

———. 2010. "The Reinvention of Heterosexuality." *Gay and Lesbian Review* 17 (3): 27–29.

———. 2011. "Post-Gay Collective Identity Construction." *Social Problems* 58 (1): 99–125.

Gilligan, Carol. (1982) 1993. *In a Different Voice: Psychological Theory and Women's Development*. Cambridge: Harvard University Press.

Glaser, Barney G., and Anselm L. Strauss. 1967. *The Discovery of Grounded Theory: Strategies for Qualitative Research*. New York: Aldine de Gruyter.

Glazer, Nathan. 1983. *Ethnic Pluralism and Public Policy: Achieving Equality in the United States and Britain*. Lexington, MA: Lexington Books.

Glick, Peter, and Susan Fiske. 1999. "Gender, Power Dynamics, and Social Interaction." In *Revisioning Gender*, ed. Myra Marx Ferree, Judith Lorber, and Beth Hess, 365–98. Walnut Creek, CA: Altamira.

Goffman, Erving. 1959. *The Presentation of Self in Everyday Life*. New York: Anchor.

———. 1963. *Stigma*. New York: Simon and Schuster.

Golden, Carla. 1996. "What's in a Name? Sexual Self-Identification among Women." In *The Lives of Lesbians, Gays, and Bisexuals: Children to Adults*, ed. Ritch Savin-Williams and K. M. Cohen, 229–49. Fort Worth: Harcourt Brace.

Gray, Mary. 2009. *Out in the Country: Youth, Media and the Politics of Visibility in Rural America*. New York: New York University Press.

Grazian, David. 2007. "The Girl Hunt: Urban Nightlife and the Performance of Masculinity as Collective Activity." *Symbolic Interaction* 30 (2): 221–43.

Green, Adam. 2010. "Remembering Foucault: Queer Theory and Disciplinary Power." *Sexualities* 13 (3): 316–37.

Griffin, Horace. 2006. *Their Own Receive Them Not: African American Lesbians and Gays in Black Churches*. Cleveland: Pilgrim Press.

Gross, Larry. 2001. *Up from Invisibility: Lesbians, Gay Men, and the Media in America*. New York: Columbia University Press.

Hacker, Andrew. 2003. *Mismatch: The Growing Gulf between Women and Men*. New York: Scribner.

Halberstam, Judith. 1998. *Female Masculinity*. Durham: Duke University Press.

———. 2005. *In a Queer Time and Place: Transgender Bodies, Subcultural Lives*. New York: New York University Press.

Hall, Stuart. 1996. "Introduction: Who Needs 'Identity'?" In *Questions of Cultural Identity*, ed. Stuart Hall and Paul du Gay, 1–17. Thousand Oaks: Sage.

Halperin, David. 2012. *How to Be Gay*. Cambridge: Harvard University Press.

Hamilton, Laura. 2007. "Trading on Heterosexuality: College Women's Gender Strategies and Homophobia." *Gender & Society* 21: 145–72.

Harper, Shaun R. 2004. "The Measure of a Man: Conceptualizations of Masculinity among High-Achieving African American Male College Students." *Berkeley Journal of Sociology* 48 (1): 89–107.

Harvey, David. 1990. *The Condition of Postmodernity*. Cambridge, MA: Blackwell.

Hawkeswood, William. 1996. *One of the Children: Gay Black Men in Harlem*. Berkeley: University of California Press.

Hays, Sharon. 1996. *The Cultural Contradictions of Mothering*. New Haven: Yale University Press.

Heap, Chad. 2009. *Slumming: Sexual and Racial Encounters in American Nightlife*. Chicago: University of Chicago Press.

Heasley, Robert. 2005. "Queer Masculinities of Straight Men." *Men and Masculinity* 7 (3): 310–30.

Hennen, Peter. 2005. "Bear Bodies, Bear Masculinity: Recuperation, Resistance, or Retreat?" *Gender & Society* 19 (1): 25–43.

———. 2008. *Fairies, Bears, and Leathermen: Men in Community Queering the Masculine.* Chicago: University of Chicago Press.

Henslin, James, ed. 1971. *Studies in the Sociology of Sex.* New York: Apple Century Crofts.

Herdt, Gilbert. 1981. *Guardians of the Flutes: Idioms of Masculinity.* New York: McGraw-Hill.

Herek, Gregory. 1986. "On Heterosexual Masculinity: Some Psychical Consequences of the Social Construction of Gender and Sexuality." *American Behavioral Scientist* 29: 563–77.

———. 1988. "Heterosexuals' Attitudes toward Lesbians and Gay Men: Correlates and Gender Differences." *Journal of Sex Research* 25 (4): 451–77.

Herek, Gregory, and John Capitanio. 1995. "Black Heterosexuals' Attitudes toward Lesbians and Gay Men in the United States." *Journal of Sex Research* 32 (2): 95–105.

Hess, Beth, and Myra Marx Ferree, eds. 1987. *Analyzing Gender.* Thousand Oaks, CA: Sage.

Hicks, Gary, and Tien-tsung Lee. 2006. "Public Attitudes toward Gays and Lesbians: Trends and Predictors." *Journal of Homosexuality* 51 (2): 57–77.

Higginbotham, Evelyn Brooks. 1993. *Righteous Discontent: The Women's Movement in the Black Baptist Church, 1880–1920.* Cambridge: Harvard University Press.

Hine, Darlene Clark. 1989. "Rape and the Inner Lives of Black Women in the Middle West: Preliminary Thoughts on the Culture of Dissemblance." *Signs* 14 (4): 915–20.

Hochschild, Arlie Russell. 2003. *The Commercialization of Intimate Life: Notes from Home and Work.* Berkeley: University of California Press.

———. 2012. *The Outsourced Self: Intimate Life in Market Times.* New York: Metropolitan Books.

Hochschild, Arlie Russell, with Anne Machung. (1989) 2012. *The Second Shift: Working Families and the Revolution at Home.* Rev. ed. New York: Penguin.

hooks, bell. 2004. *We Real Cool: Black Men and Masculinity.* New York: Routledge.

Hughey, Matthew. 2012. "Stigma Allure and White Antiracist Identity Management." *Social Psychological Quarterly* 75 (3): 219–41.

Hunter, Marcus Anthony. 2010. "All the Gays Are White and All the Blacks Are Straight: Black Gay Males, Identity and Community." *Journal of Sexuality Research and Social Policy* 7: 81–92

Hunter, Margaret. 2011. "Shake It, Baby, Shake It: Consumption and the New Gender Relation in Hip-Hop." *Sociological Perspectives* 54 (1): 15–36.

Hurston, Zora Neale. (1937) 1969. *Their Eyes Were Watching God.* Greenwich, CT: Fawcett.

Ingraham, Chrys. 1996. "The Heterosexual Imaginary: Feminist Sociology and Theories of Gender." In *Queer Theory/Sociology*, ed. Steven Seidman, 168–93. New York: Blackwell.

———. 1999. *White Weddings: Romancing Heterosexuality in Popular Culture*. New York: Routledge.

———. 2005. *Thinking Straight: The Power, the Promise, and the Paradox of Homosexuality*. New York: Routledge.

Jackson, Stevi. 1999. *Heterosexuality in Question*. London: Sage.

———. 2006. "Gender, Sexuality, and Heterosexuality: The Complexity (and Limits) of Heteronormativity." *Feminist Theory* 7 (1): 105–21.

Jones, Nikki. 2010. *Between Good and Ghetto: African American Girls and Inner-City Violence*. New Brunswick: Rutgers University Press.

Kaplan, Anne. 1983. "Is the Gaze Male?" In *Powers of Desire: The Politics of Sexuality*, ed. Ann Snitow, Christine Stansell, and Sharon Thompson, 309–27. New York: Monthly Review Press.

Katz, Jonathan Ned. 1983. *Gay and Lesbian Almanac*. New York: Harper and Row.

———. 1996. *The Invention of Heterosexuality*. New York: Plume.

Kaye, Jeremy. 2009. "Twenty-First-Century Victorian Dandy: What Metrosexuality and the Heterosexual Matrix Reveal about Victorian Men." *Journal of Popular Culture* 24 (1): 103–25.

Kazyak, Emily. 2012. "Midwest or Lesbian? Gender, Rurality, and Sexuality." *Gender & Society* 26 (2): 825–28.

Kennedy, Elizabeth Lapovsky. 1996. "'But We Would Never Talk about It': The Structures of Lesbian Discretion in South Dakota, 1928–1933." In *Inventing Lesbian Cultures in America*, ed. Ellen Lewin, 15–39. Boston: Beacon.

Kennedy, Elizabeth, and Madeline Davis. 1993. *Boots of Leather, Slippers of Gold: The History of a Lesbian Community*. New York: Routledge.

Kennedy, Philip. 2011. *Christianity: An Introduction*. New York: Palgrave Macmillan.

Kimmel, Michael. 2003. "Adolescent Masculinity, Homophobia, and Violence: Random School Shootings, 1982–2001." *American Behavioral Scientist* 46 (10): 1439–58.

———. 2004. *The Gendered Society*. 2nd ed. New York: Oxford University Press.

———. 2005. *The Gender of Desire*. Albany: State University of New York Press.

———. 2008. *Guyland: The Perilous World Where Boys Become Men*. New York: HarperCollins.

———. 2012. *Manhood in America: A Cultural History*. 2nd ed. New York: Free Press.

Kimmel, Michael, and Michael Messner, eds. 2010. *Men's Lives*. 8th ed. Needham Heights, MA: Allyn and Bacon.

King, J. L. 2004. *On the Down Low: A Journey into the Lives of "Straight" Black Men Who Sleep with Men*. New York: Random House.

Kinsey, Alfred, Wardell Pomeroy, and Clyde Martin. 1948. *Sexual Behavior in the Human Male*. Philadelphia: Saunders.

Kinsey, Alfred, Wardell Pomeroy, Clyde Martin, and Paul Gebhard. 1953. *Sexual Behavior in the Human Female*. Philadelphia: Saunders.

Knox, David, Tiffany Beaver, and Vaiva Kriskute. 2011. "'I Kissed a Girl': Heterosexual Women Who Report Same-Sex Kissing (and More)." *Journal of GLBT Family Studies* 7 (3): 217–25.

Kondo, Dorinne. 1996. *About Face: Performing Race in Fashion and Theater*. New York: Routledge.

Kunzel, Regina. 1994. "White Neurosis, Black Pathology: Constructing Out-of-Wedlock Pregnancy in the Wartime and Postwar United States." In *Not June Cleaver: Women and Gender in Postwar America, 1945–1960*, ed. Joanne Meyerowitz, 304–31. Philadelphia: Temple University Press.

Kymlicka, Will. 1995. *Multicultural Citizenship: A Liberal Theory of Minority Rights*. New York: Oxford University Press.

———. 1997. "Ethnicity in the USA." In *The Ethnicity Reader: Nationalism, Multiculturalism, and Migration*, ed. Montserrat Guibernau and John Rex, 29–47. Cambridge, UK: Blackwell.

LaMar, Lisa, and Mary Kite. 1998. "Sex Differences in Attitudes toward Gay Men and Lesbians: A Multi-Dimensional Perspective." *Journal of Sex Research* 35: 189–96.

Lamont, Michele. 2000. *The Dignity of Working Men: Morality and the Boundaries of Race, Class and Immigration*. Cambridge: Harvard University Press.

Larna, Enrique, Hank Johnston, and Joseph R. Gusfield, eds. 1994. *New Social Movements: From Ideology to Identity*. Philadelphia: Temple University Press.

Laumann, Edward, John Gagnon, Robert Michael, and Stuart Michaels. 1994. *The Social Organization of Sexuality: Sexual Practices in the United States*. Chicago: University of Chicago Press.

Lemelle, Anthony, and Juan Battle. 2004. "Black Masculinity Matters in Attitudes towards Gay Males." *Journal of Homosexuality* 47 (1): 39–51.

Leong, Russell, ed. 2011. *Asian American Sexualities: Dimensions of the Gay and Lesbian Experience*. New York: Routledge.

Levine, Martin. 1979. "Gay Ghetto." *Journal of Homosexuality* 4 (4): 363–77.

———. 1998. *Gay Macho: The Life and Death of the Homosexual Clone*. New York: New York University Press.

Lewin, Ellen. 1993. *Lesbian Mothers: Accounts of Gender in American Culture*. Ithaca: Cornell University Press.

———. 2009. *Gay Fatherhood: Narratives of Family and Citizenship in America*. Chicago: University of Chicago Press.

Lewis, Carolyn Herbst. 2010. *Prescriptions for Heterosexuality: Sexual Citizenship in the Cold War Era*. Chapel Hill: University of North Carolina Press.

Lewis, Gregory. 2003. "Black and White Differences in Attitudes towards Homosexuality and Gay Rights." *Public Opinion Quarterly* 67: 59–78.

Linneman, Thomas. 2008. "How Do You Solve a Problem Like Will Truman? The Feminization of Gay Masculinities on *Will & Grace*." *Men and Masculinities* 10 (5): 583–606.

Liptak, Adam. 2008. "U.S. Imprisons One in 100 Adults, Report Finds." *New York Times*, February 29.

Lofland, John, and Lyn H. Lofland. 1995. *Analyzing Social Settings: A Guide to Qualitative Observation and Analysis*. Belmont, CA: Wadsworth.

Loftus, Jeni. 2001. "America's Liberalization in Attitudes toward Homosexuality, 1973 to 1998." *American Sociological Review* 66 (5): 762–82.

Logan, John, Richard Alba, Tom McNulty, and Brian Fisher. 1996. "Making a Place in the Metropolis: Locational Attainment in Cities and Suburbs." *Demographics* 33 (4): 443–53.

Lorber, Judith. 1999. "Embattled Terrain: Gender and Sexuality." In *Revisioning Gender*, ed. Myra Marx Ferree, Judith Lorber, and Beth Hess. Thousand Oaks, CA: Sage.

Lorber, Judith, and Lisa Jean Moore. 1993. *Gender and the Social Construction of Illness*. Oxford, UK: Rowman and Littlefield.

Lubiano, Wahneema. 1992. "Black Ladies, Welfare Queens, and State Minstrels: Ideological War by Narrative Means." In *Race-ing Justice, En-gendering Power*, ed. Toni Morrison, 323–63. New York: Pantheon.

Luciano, Lynne. 2001. *Looking Good: Male Body Image in Modern America*. New York: Macmillan.

Lystra, Karen. 1989. *Searching the Heart: Women, Men and Romantic Love in Nineteenth-Century America*. New York: Oxford University Press.

Mac an Ghaill, Mairtin. 1994. *The Making of Men: Masculinities, Sexualities and Schooling*. Buckingham: Open University Press.

MacKinnon, Catharine. 1987. *Feminism Unmodified: Discourses on Life and Law*. Cambridge: Harvard University Press.

———. 1989. *Toward a Feminist Theory of the State*. Cambridge: Harvard University Press.

Majors, Richard. 2001. "Cool Pose: Black Masculinity and Sports." In *The Masculinities Reader*, ed. Stephen Whitehead and Frank Barrett, 208–17. Cambridge: Polity Press.

Majors, Richard, and Janet Billson. 1992. *Cool Pose: The Dilemmas of Black Manhood in America*. New York: Lexington Books.

Marable, Manning. 1995. "The Black Male: Searching beyond Stereotypes." In *Men's Lives*, ed. Michael Kimmel and Michael Messner, 3rd ed., 26–32. Needham Heights, MA: Allyn and Bacon.

Martin, Karin. 1996. *Puberty, Sexuality, and the Self: Girls and Boys at Adolescence*. New York: Routledge.

———. 2009. "Normalizing Heterosexuality: Mothers' Assumptions, Talk, and Strategies with Young Children." *American Sociological Review* 74 (April): 190–207.

Massey, Douglas, and Nancy Denton. 1993. *American Apartheid: Segregation and the Making of the Underclass*. Cambridge: Harvard University Press.

McCall, Leslie. 1992. "Does Gender Fit? Bourdieu, Feminism, and Conceptions of Social Order." *Theory & Society* 21 (6): 837–67.

McCormack, Mark. 2010. "The Declining Significance of Homohysteria for Male Students in Three Sixth Forms in the South of England." *British Educational Research Journal*, iFirst 1–17.

———. 2011. "Hierarchy without Hegemony: Locating Boys in an Inclusive School Setting." *Sociological Perspectives* 54 (1): 83–101.

——. 2012. *The Declining Significance of Homophobia: How Teenage Boys Are Redefining Masculinity and Heterosexuality*. New York: Oxford University Press.

McCormack, Mark, and Eric Anderson. 2010. "'It's Just Not Acceptable Any More': The Erosion of Homophobia and the Softening of Masculinity at an English Sixth Form." *Sociology* 44 (5): 843–59.

McGovern, James. 1968. "The American Woman's Pre–World War I Freedom in Manners and Morals." *Journal of American History* 55 (2): 315–33.

McGruder, Kevin. 2010. "Pathologizing Black Sexuality: The U.S. Experience." In *Black Sexualities: Probing Powers, Passions, Practices, and Policies*, ed. Juan Battle and Sandra Barnes, 101–18. New Brunswick: Rutgers University Press.

Meeks, Chet. 2002. "Civil Society and the Sexual Politics of Difference." *Sociological Theory* 19 (3): 325–43.

Merriam-Webster. 2008. *Merriam-Webster's Collegiate Dictionary*. 11th ed.

Messner, Michael. 1997. *The Politics of Masculinities: Men in Movements*. Thousand Oaks, CA: Sage.

——. 2002. *Taking the Field: Women, Men, and Sports*. Minneapolis: University of Minnesota Press.

Meyerowitz, Joanne. 1988. *Women Adrift: Independent Wage Earners in Chicago, 1880–1930*. Chicago: University of Chicago Press.

——. 1990. "Sexual Geography and Gender Economy: The Furnished Room Districts of Chicago, 1890–1930." *Gender and History* 2 (3): 274–96.

——. 1994a. "Beyond the Feminine Mystique: A Reassessment of Postwar Mass Culture, 1946–1955." In *Not June Cleaver: Women and Gender in Postwar America, 1945–1960*, ed. Joanne Meyerowitz, 229–62. Philadelphia: Temple University Press.

——, ed. 1994b. *Not June Cleaver: Women and Gender in Postwar America 1945–1960*. Philadelphia: Temple University Press.

——. 1996. "Women, Cheesecake, and Borderline Material: Responses to Girlie Pictures in the Mid-Twentieth Century US." *Journal of Women's History* 8 (3): 9–35.

——. 2010. "'How Common Culture Shapes the Separate Lives': Sexuality, Race, and Mid-Twentieth Century Social Constructionist Thought." *Journal of American History* 96 (4): 1057–84.

Michael, Robert, John Gagnon, Edward Laumann, and Gina Kolata. 1994. *Sex in America: A Definitive Survey*. Boston: Warner.

Miles, Matthew B., and A. Michael Huberman. 1984. *Qualitative Data Analysis: A Sourcebook of New Methods*. Beverly Hills, CA: Sage.

Miller, Toby. 2005. "A Metrosexual Eye on Queer Guy." *GLQ: A Journal of Lesbian and Gay Studies* 11 (1): 112–17.

Mishkind, Marc, Judith Rodin, Lisa R. Silberstein, and Ruth H. Striegel-Moore. 1986. "The Embodiment of Masculinity." *American Behavioral Scientist* 29 (5): 545–62.

Mitchell, Michele. 1999. "Silence Broken, Silence Kept: Gender and Sexuality in African-American History." *Gender & History* 11 (3): 433–44.

——. 2004. *Righteous Propagation: African Americans and the Politics of Racial Destiny after Reconstruction*. Chapel Hill: University of North Carolina Press.

Mock, Roberta. 2003. "Heteroqueer Ladies: Some Performative Transactions between Gay Men and Heterosexual Women." *Feminist Review* 75 (1): 20–37.

Moffatt, Michael. 1989. *Coming of Age in New Jersey: College and American Culture.* New Brunswick: Rutgers University Press.

Moon, Dawne. 1995. "Insult and Inclusion: The Term Fag Hag and Gay Male 'Community.'" *Social Forces* 74 (2): 487–510.

———. 2004. *God, Sex, and Politics: Homosexuality and Everyday Theologies.* Chicago: University of Chicago Press.

Moore, Mignon. 2010a. "Articulating a Politics of (Multiple) Identities: LGBT Sexuality and the Inclusion in Black Community Life." *Du Bois Review* 7 (2): 315–34.

———. 2010b. "Black and Gay in LA: The Relationships Black Lesbians and Gay Men Have to Their Racial and Religious Communities." In *Black Los Angeles: American Dreams and Racial Realities,* ed. Darnell Hunt and Ana-Christina Ramón, 182–214. New York: New York University Press.

———. 2011. *Invisible Families: Gay Identities, Relationships, and Motherhood among Black Women.* Berkeley: University of California Press.

Morrison, Toni, ed. 1992. *Race-ing Justice, En-gendering Power: Essays on Anita Hill, Clarence Thomas, and the Construction of Social Reality.* New York: Pantheon.

Moynihan, Daniel P. 1965. *The Negro Family: The Case for National Action.* Washington, DC: Government Printing Office.

Muñoz, Carlos, Jr. 1989. *Youth, Identity, Power: The Chicano Movement.* New York: Verso.

Muraco, Anna. 2006. "Intentional Families: Fictive Kin Ties between Cross-Gender, Different Sexual Orientation Friends." *Journal of Marriage and Family* 68 (5): 1313–25.

———. 2012. *Odd Couples: Friendships at the Intersection of Gender and Sexual Orientation.* Durham: Duke University Press.

Nardi, Peter. 1999. *Gay Men's Friendships: Invincible Communities.* Chicago: University of Chicago Press.

———, ed. 2000. *Gay Masculinities.* Thousand Oaks, CA: Sage.

Nardi, Peter, and Beth Schneider, eds. 1998. "Kinsey: A 50th Anniversary Symposium." *Sexualities* 1 (1): 83–106.

Nayak, Anoop, and Mary Jane Kehily. 1997. "Masculinities and Schooling: Why Are Young Men So Homophobic?" In *Border Patrols: Policing the Boundaries of Heterosexuality,* ed. Debbie Epstein and Richard Johnson, 138–61. London: Cassell.

Nero, Charles. 1999. "Signifying on the Black Church." In *Black Men on Race, Gender, and Sexuality: A Critical Reader,* ed. Devon Carbado, 276–82. New York: New York University Press.

Newton, Esther. 1993. "The Mythic Mannish Lesbian: Radclyffe Hall and the New Woman." In *Hidden from History,* ed. Martin Duberman, Martha Vicinus, and George Chauncey, 281–93. New York: Meridian.

Nicholson, Linda. 1986. *Gender and History: The Limits of Social Theory in the Age of the Family.* New York: Columbia University Press.

——. 2008. *Identity before Identity Politics*. New York: Cambridge University Press.

Oliver, Melvin, and Thomas Shapiro. 2006. *Black Wealth/White Wealth: A New Perspective on Racial Inequality*. 2nd ed. New York: Routledge.

Olson, Laura, Wendy Cadge, and James Harrison. 2006. "Religion and Public Opinion about Same-Sex Marriage." *Social Science Quarterly* 87: 340–60.

Omi, Michael, and Howard Winant. 1994. *Racial Formation in the United States*. 2nd ed. New York: Routledge.

Oppenheimer, Valerie Kincade. 1997. "Women's Employment and the Gain to Marriage: The Specialization and Trading Model." *Annual Review of Sociology* 23: 431–53.

Parreñas, Rhacel. 2011. *Illicit Flirtations: Labor, Migration, and Sex Trafficking in Tokyo*. Palo Alto: Stanford University Press.

Parsons, Talcott. 1954. *Essays in Sociological Theory*. New York: Free Press.

Pascoe, C. J. 2007. *Dude, You're a Fag: Masculinity and Sexuality in High School*. Berkeley: University of California Press.

Peiss, Kathy. 1983. "Charity Girls and Other Pleasures: Historical Notes on Working-Class Sexuality, 1880–1920." In *Powers of Desire: The Politics of Sexuality*, ed. Ann Snitow, Christine Stansell, and Sharon Thompson, 74–87. New York: Monthly Review Press.

——. 1986. *Cheap Amusements: Working Women and Leisure in Turn-of-the-Century New York*. Philadelphia: Temple University Press.

Perry, Pamela. 2002. *Shades of White: White Kids and Racial Identities in High School*. Durham: Duke University Press.

Peterson, John. 1992. "Black Men and Their Same-Sex Desires and Behaviors." In *Gay Culture in America: Essays from the Field*, ed. Gilbert Herdt, 147–64. Boston: Beacon.

Pew Forum on Religion and Public Life. 2008. *US Religious Landscape Survey*. Washington, DC: Pew Research Center.

Pharr, Suzanne. 1988. *Homophobia: A Weapon of Sexism*. Inverness: Chardon.

Pheterson, Gail, ed. 1989. *A Vindication of the Rights of Whores*. Seattle: Seal.

Phillips, Layli. 2005. "Deconstructing 'Down Low' Discourse: The Politics of Sexuality, Gender, Race, AIDS, and Anxiety." *Journal of African American Studies* 9 (2).

Pitt, Richard. 2010. "'Killing the Messenger': Religious Black Gay Men's Neutralization of Anti-Gay Religious Messages." *Journal for the Scientific Study of Religion* 49: 56–72.

Pitzulo, Carrie. 2011. *Bachelors and Bunnies: The Sexual Politics of Playboy*. Chicago: University of Chicago Press.

Plummer, David. 2001. "The Quest for Modern Manhood: Masculine Stereotypes, Peer Culture, and the Social Significance of Homophobia." *Journal of Adolescence* 24 (1): 15–23.

Plummer, Kenneth, ed. 1992. *Modern Homosexualities*. London, UK: Routledge.

Radicalesbians. (1970) 1997. "The Woman-Identified Woman." In *The Second Wave: A Reader in Feminist Theory*, ed. Linda Nicholson, 153–57. New York: Routledge.

Raeburn, Nicole. 2004. *Changing Corporate America from Inside Out: Lesbian and Gay Workplace Rights*. Minneapolis: University of Minnesota Press.

Rahman, Momin. 2004. "Is Straight the New Queer? David Beckham and the Dialectics of Celebrity." *Media/Culture* 7 (5): 1–5.

Rasmussen, Birgit Brander, Irene Nexica, Eric Klinenberg, and Matt Wray, eds. 2001. *The Making and Unmaking of Whiteness*. Durham: Duke University Press.

Reiss, Ira. 1967. *The Social Context of Premarital Sexual Permissiveness*. New York: Holt, Rinehart and Winston.

Rich, Adrienne. (1980) 1993. "Compulsory Heterosexuality and Lesbian Existence." In *The Lesbian and Gay Studies Reader*, ed. Henry Abelove, Michèle Aina Barale, and David Halperin, 227–54. New York: Routledge.

Richardson, Diane, ed. 1996. *Theorising Heterosexuality*. Buckingham: Open University Press.

———. 2000. *Rethinking Sexuality*. London: Sage.

Ridgeway, Cecilia. 2011. *Framed by Gender: How Gender Inequality Persists in the Modern World*. New York: Cambridge University Press.

Riggs, Marlon T. 1991. "Black Macho Revisited: Reflections of a Snap! Queen." *Black American Literature Forum* 25: 389–94.

Roberts, Dorothy E. 1997. *Killing the Black Body: Race, Reproduction, and the Meaning of Liberty*. New York: Pantheon.

Roediger, David. 2005. *Working toward Whiteness: How America's Immigrants Became White*. New York: Basic Books.

Rose, Tricia. 2003. *Longing to Tell: Black Women Talk about Sexuality and Intimacy*. New York: Farrar, Straus and Giroux.

Rubin, Gayle. 1975. "The Traffic in Women." In *Toward an Anthropology of Women*, ed. R. Reiter, 157–210. New York: Monthly Review Press.

———. 1984. "Thinking Sex." In *Pleasure and Danger: Exploring Female Sexuality*, ed. Carole Vance, 267–319. Boston: Routledge and Kegan Paul.

Rupp, Leila J. 1989a. "Feminism and the Sexual Revolution in the Early Twentieth Century: The Case of Doris Stevens." *Feminist Studies* 15 (2): 289–309.

———. 1989b. "'Imagine My Surprise': Women's Relationships in Mid-Twentieth-Century America." In *Hidden from History*, ed. Martin Duberman, Martha Vicinus, and George Chauncey, 395–410. New York: Meridian.

———. 2001. "Romantic Friendship." In *Modern American Queer History*, ed. Allida M. Black, 13–23. Philadelphia: Temple University Press.

———. 2009. *Sapphistries: A Global History of Love between Women*. New York: New York University Press.

Rupp, Leila J., and Verta Taylor. 2010. "Straight Girls Kissing." *Contexts* 9 (3): 28–32.

Russo, Vito. 1987. *The Celluloid Closet: Homosexuality in the Movies*. 2nd ed. New York: Harper and Row.

Rust, Paula. 2000. *Bisexuality in the United States: A Social Science Reader*. New York: Columbia University Press.

Ryan, Mary P. 1983. *Womanhood in America: From Colonial Times to the Present*. 3rd ed. New York: Watts.

———. 2006. *Mysteries of Sex: Tracing Women and Men through American History*. Chapel Hill: University of North Carolina Press.

Salzman, Marian, Ira Matathia, and Ann O'Reilly. 2005. *The Future of Men*. New York: Palgrave Macmillan.

Sanday, Peggy. 1990. *Fraternity Gang Rape: Sex, Brotherhood, and Privilege on Campus*. New York: New York University Press.

Schilt, Kristin, and Laurel Westbrook. 2009. "Doing Gender, Doing Heteronormativity: 'Gender Normals,' Transgender People, and the Social Maintenance of Heterosexuality." *Gender & Society* 23 (4): 440–64.

Schippers, Mimi. 2000. "The Social Organization of Sexuality and Gender in Alternative Hard Rock: An Analysis of Intersectionality." *Gender & Society* 14 (6): 747–64.

———. 2007. "Recovering the Feminine Other: Masculinity, Femininity, and Gender Hegemony." *Theory and Society* 36: 85–102.

Schrock, Douglas, and Michael Schwalbe. 2009. "Men, Masculinity, and Manhood Acts." *Annual Review of Sociology* 35: 277–95.

Schulte, Lisa, and Juan Battle. 2004. "The Relative Importance of Ethnicity and Religion in Predicting Attitudes towards Gays and Lesbians." *Journal of Homosexuality* 47: 127–42.

Sedgwick, Eve. 1990. *Epistemology of the Closet*. Berkeley: University of California Press.

———. 1992. *Tendencies*. Durham: Duke University Press.

Segal, Lynne. 1990. *Slow Motion: Changing Masculinities, Changing Men*. London: Virago.

———. 1994. *Straight Sex: Rethinking the Politics of Pleasure*. Berkeley: University of California Press.

———, ed. 1997. *New Sexual Agendas*. New York: New York University Press.

Seidman, Steven. 1991. *Romantic Longings*. New York: Routledge.

———. (1993) 2009. *The Social Construction of Sexuality*. New York: Norton.

———, ed. 1996. *Queer Theory/Sociology*. Malden, MA: Blackwell.

———. 1997. *Difference Troubles: Queering Social Theory and Sexual Politics*. Cambridge: Cambridge University Press.

———. 2002. *Beyond the Closet: The Transformation of Gay and Lesbian Life*. New York: Routledge.

———. 2009. "Critique of Compulsory Heterosexuality." *Sexuality Research & Social Policy* 6 (1): 18-28.

Sheff, Elisabeth. 2006. "Poly-Hegemonic Masculinities." *Sexualities* 9 (5): 625–47.

Singleton, Royce A. Jr., Bruce C. Straits, and Margaret Miller Straits. 1993. *Approaches to Social Research*. New York: Oxford University Press.

Smith, Barbara. 1982. *All the Women Are White, All the Blacks Are Men, but Some of Us Are Brave: Black Women's Studies*. Old Westbury: Feminist Press.

Smith-Rosenberg, Carroll. 1975. "The Female World of Love and Ritual: Relations between Women in Nineteenth Century America." *Signs* 1 (1): 1–29.

———. 1989. "Discourses of Sexuality and Subjectivity: The New Woman, 1870–1936." In *Hidden from History*, ed. Martin Duberman, Martha Vicinus, and George Chauncey, 264–80. New York: Meridian.

———. 1993. "Subject Female: Authorizing American Identity." *American Literary History* 5 (3): 481–511.

Snitow, Ann, Christine Stansell, and Sharon Thompson, eds. 1983. *Powers of Desire: The Politics of Sexuality*. New York: Monthly Review Press.

Somerville, Siobhan. 2000. *Queering the Color Line: Race and the Invention of Homosexuality in American Culture*. Durham: Duke University Press.

Stacey, Judith. 1996. *In the Name of the Family: Rethinking Family Values in the Postmodern Age*. Boston: Beacon.

———. 1998. *Brave New Families: Stories of Domestic Upheaval in Late Twentieth-Century America*. Berkeley: University of California Press.

Stacey, Judith, and Timothy Biblarz. 2001. "(How) Does the Sexual Orientation of Parents Matter?" *American Sociological Review* 66: 159–83.

Stein, Arlene. 1992. "Sisters and Queers: The Decentering of Lesbian Feminism." *Socialist Review* 22 (1): 33–55.

———. 1997. *Sex and Sensibility: Stories of a Lesbian Generation*. Berkeley: University of California Press.

———. 2005. "Make Room for Daddy: Anxious Masculinity and Emergent Homophobias in Neopatriarchal Politics." *Gender & Society* 19: 601–20.

———. 2010. "The Incredible Shrinking Lesbian World and Other Queer Conundra." *Sexualities* 13 (1): 21–32.

Stoltenberg, John. 1990. *Refusing to Be a Man: Essays on Sex and Justice*. New York: Meridian.

Stryker, Susan, and Jim Van Buskirk. 1996. *Gay by the Bay: A History of Queer Culture in the San Francisco Bay Area*. San Francisco: Chronicle Books.

Summers, Martin. 2004. *Manliness and Its Discontents: The Black Middle Class and the Transformation of Masculinity, 1900–1930*. Chapel Hill: University of North Carolina Press.

Swidler, Ann. 1986. "Culture in Action: Symbols and Strategies." *American Sociological Review* 52 (2): 273–86.

Takagi, Dana. 1996. "Maiden Voyage: Excursion into Sexuality and Identity Politics in Asian America." In *Queer Theory/Sociology*, ed. Steven Seidman, 243–58. Malden, MA: Blackwell.

Taylor, Verta, and Nancy Whittier. 1992. "Collective Identity in Social Movement Communities: Lesbian Feminist Mobilization." In *Frontiers in Social Movement Theory*, ed. Aldon Morris and Carol Mueller, 104–29. New Haven: Yale University Press.

Teachman, Jay, L. Tedrow, and Kyle Crowder. 2000. "The Changing Demography of America's Families." *Journal of Marriage and the Family* 62: 1234–46.

Terry, Jennifer. 1999. *An American Obsession: Science, Medicine, and Homosexuality in Modern Society*. Chicago: University of Chicago Press.

Thorpe, Rochella. 1996. "'A House Where Queers Go': African-American Lesbian Nightlife in Detroit, 1940–1975." In *Inventing Lesbian Cultures in America*, ed. E. Lewin, 40–61. Boston: Beacon.

Turner, C., H. Miller, and S. Rogers. 1997. "Survey Measurement of Sexual Behavior: Problems and Progress." In *Researching Sexual Behavior: Methodological Issues*, ed. J. Brancroft, 37–60. Bloomington: Indiana University Press.

Twine, France Winddance. 2010. *A White Side of Black Britain: Interracial Intimacy and Racial Literacy*. Durham: Duke University Press.

Twine, France Winddance, and Charles Gallagher. 2008. "The Future of Whiteness: A Map of the 'Third Wave.'" *Ethnic and Racial Studies* 31 (1): 4–24.

US Census Bureau. 2000, 2005, and 2010. "American Community Survey." Washington, DC : US Government Printing Office. Retrieved February 1, 2013. http://factfinder2.census.gov/faces/nav/jsf/pages/searchresults.xhtml?refresh=t.

Vance, Carole, ed. 1984. *Pleasure and Danger: Exploring Female Sexuality*. Boston: Routledge and Kegan Paul.

Veblen, Thorstein. 1899. *The Theory of the Leisure Class: An Economic Study of Institutions*. New York: Macmillan.

Vrangalova, Zhana, and Ritch C. Savin-Williams. "Correlates of Same-Sex Sexuality in Heterosexually Identified Young Adults." *Journal of Sex Research* 47 (1): 92–102.

Waite, Linda. 1995. "Does Marriage Matter?" *Demography* 32: 483–508.

Walters, Andrew 2002. "Attention All Shoppers, Queer Customers in Aisle Two: Investigating Lesbian and Gay Discrimination in the Marketplace." *Consumption, Markets & Culture* 5 (4): 285–303.

Walters, Suzanna Danuta. 2001. *All the Rage: The Story of Gay Visibility in America*. Chicago: University of Chicago Press.

Ward, Jane. 2008a. "Dude-Sex: White Masculinities and 'Authentic' Heterosexuality among Dudes Who Have Sex with Dudes." *Sexualities* 11 (4): 414–34.

———. 2008b. *Respectably Queer: Diversity Culture in LGBT Activist Organizations*. Nashville: Vanderbilt University Press.

———. 2008c. "White Normativity: The Cultural Dimensions of Whiteness in a Racially Diverse LGBT Organization." *Sociological Perspectives* 51 (3): 563–86.

———. 2010. "Gender Labor: Transmen, Femmes, and Collective Work of Transgression." *Sexualities* 13 (2): 236–54.

Warner, Michael. 1993. Introduction to *Fear of a Queer Planet: Queer Politics and Social Theory*, ed. Michael Warner. Minneapolis: University of Minnesota Press.

———. 1999. *The Trouble with Normal: Sex, Politics, and the Ethics of Queer Life*. New York: Free Press.

Warren, Jonathan, and France Winddance Twine. 1997. "White Americans: The New Minority? Non-Blacks and the Ever-Expanding Category Boundaries of Whiteness." *Journal of Black Studies* 28 (2): 200–218.

Waters, Mary. 2002. "The Social Construction of Race and Ethnicity: Some Examples from Demography." In *American Diversity: A Demographic Challenge for the Twenty-First Century*, ed. Stewart Tolnay and Nancy Denton, 25–50. Albany: State University of New York Press.

Weber, Max. 1946. "Class, Status, Party." In *From Max Weber: Essays in Sociology*, ed. Hans Gerth and C. Wright Mills, 159–94. New York: Oxford University Press.

Weeks, Jeffrey. 1977. *Coming Out: Homosexual Politics in Britain: From the Nineteenth Century to the Present*. London: Quartet Books.

———.2007. *The World We Have Won: The Remaking of Erotic and Intimate Life*. New York: Routledge.

Weiss, Robert S. 1994. *Learning from Strangers: The Art and Method of Qualitative Interview Studies*. New York: Free Press.

West, Candace, and Don Zimmerman. 1987. "Doing Gender." *Gender & Society* 1 (2): 125–51.

West, Cornel. 1993. *Race Matters*. New York: Vintage.

White, Kevin. 1993. *The First Sexual Revolution: The Emergence of Male Heterosexuality in Modern America*. New York: New York University Press.

Whitehead, Stephen, and Frank Barrett. 2001. "The Sociology of Masculinity." In *The Masculinities Reader*, ed. Stephen Whitehead and Frank Barrett, 1–26. Malden, MA: Blackwell.

Williams, Christine, Patti Giuffre, and Kirsten Dellinger. 2009. "The Gay-Friendly Closet." *Sexual Research and Social Policy* 6 (1): 29–45.

Williams, Chyvette, Mary Mackesy-Amiti, David McKirnan, and Lawrence Ouellet. 2009. "Differences in Sexual Identity, Risk Practices, and Sex Partners between Bisexual Men and Other Men among a Low-Income Drug-Using Sample." *Journal of Urban Health* 86: 93–106.

Willis, Ellen. 1983. "Feminism, Moralism, and Pornography." In *Powers of Desire: The Politics of Sexuality*, ed. Ann Snitow, Christine Stansell, and Sharon Thompson, 460–67. New York: Monthly Review Press.

Winkler, Kevin. 2000. "'Your Mother Is Working Up Here!' Bette Midler, the Continental Baths, and the Mainstreaming of Gay Male Sensibility." In *Performing Processes: Creating Live Performances*, ed. Roberta Mock, 83–93. Portland: Intellect Books.

Wittig, Monique. (1980) 1992. *The Straight Mind and Other Essays*. Boston: Beacon.

Wolcott, Victoria. 2001. *Remaking Respectability: African American Women in Interwar Detroit*. Chapel Hill: University of North Carolina Press.

Yang, Alan. 1997. "The Polls—Trends: Attitudes towards Homosexuality." *Public Opinion Quarterly* 61: 477–507.

———. 1999. "From Wrongs to Rights, 1973 to 1999: Public Opinion on Gay and Lesbian Americans Moves toward Equality." New York: National Gay and Lesbian Task Force Policy Institute.

Yoshino, Kenji. 2006. *Covering: The Hidden Assault on Our Civil Rights*. New York: Random House.

Young, Iris Marion. 1990. *Justice and the Politics of Difference.* Princeton: Princeton University Press.

Zaretsky, Eli. 2004. *Secrets of the Soul: A Social and Cultural History of Psychoanalysis.* New York: Knopf.

ABOUT THE AUTHOR

James Joseph Dean is Associate Professor of Sociology at Sonoma State University. His research focuses on the sociology of sexualities, particularly the sociology of heterosexualities. Recent publications have appeared in the journals *Sexualities*, the *Sociological Quarterly*, and *Sociology Compass*, and in several edited book volumes.

198003

5486003